THOMAS NELSON
OF YORKTOWN

Revolutionary Virginian

Williamsburg in America Series

X

*The tenth in a series of popular histories
focusing on the roles of Williamsburg and Virginia
in the eighteenth century*

THOMAS NELSON
OF YORKTOWN

Revolutionary Virginian

By

Emory G. Evans

The Colonial Williamsburg Foundation
Williamsburg, Virginia

Distributed by
The University Press of Virginia
Charlottesville, Virginia

© 1975 by The Colonial Williamsburg Foundation
All rights reserved

Library of Congress Cataloging in Publication Data
Evans, Emory G
  Thomas Nelson of Yorktown.
  (Williamsburg in America series; 10)
  Bibliography: p.
  Includes index.
  1. Nelson, Thomas, 1738-1789. I. Title.
  II. Series.
F234.W7W7 vol. 10 [F229]   975.5′03′0924 [B]   74-83323
ISBN 0-87935-024-5
ISBN 0-8139-0515-X (UPVa)

Printed in the United States of America

TO THE MEMORY OF MY
MOTHER AND FATHER

Table of Contents

List of Illustrations

Thomas Nelson at the age of sixteen. By Mason Chamberlin
(facing page 22)

William Nelson and his wife. By Robert Feke [?]
(facing page 23)

Yorktown from Gloucester Point in 1754.
(facing page 54)

The Nelson House in Yorktown.
(facing page 55)

The Nelson-Galt House in Williamsburg.
(facing page 86)

Statue of Thomas Nelson in Richmond.
(facing page 87)

MAP
Military operations in Virginia, 1780-81.
(facing page 118)

Acknowledgments

My interest in Thomas Nelson began with a study of his family in the eighteenth century. This resulted in a dissertation, completed in 1957. The late Samuel M. Bemiss of Richmond, Virginia, suggested the need for a study of the Nelsons, and Professor Thomas Perkins Abernethy directed my work. I am grateful for their help. Later, James Morton Smith recommended that I do a biography of Thomas Nelson and I will always be in his debt for subsequent editorial aid and encouragement. In the latter stages of this study William W. Abbot's help was equally important.

Others who, at one stage or another, have read the entire manuscript and made valuable suggestions are John Selby, William Stanton, Thad Tate, and my colleague Alfred Young. Benjamin Keen, another colleague, helped me with chapters III and IV. I am also grateful for the aid of Edward M. Riley, who made four summers of work in the collections of the Research Department of the Colonial Williamsburg Foundation both pleasant and profitable. Subsequently, he too read the manuscript and made useful comments. I would be derelict if I also did not mention the help of librarians at the University of Virginia, the Virginia Historical Society, the Virginia State Library, and the College of William and Mary.

The initial research on the Nelsons was made possible by grants-in-aid from the Society of the Cincinnati of the State of Virginia and the Patriotic Service Committee of District 9, the National Society of the Colonial Dames of America. The revision of the manuscript was aided by a sabbatical leave from Northern Illinois University during the academic year 1969–70.

Darla Woodward, Alice Powell, and Sue Reynolds typed the entire manuscript, and for their skill and good humor I am most appreciative.

Finally, the patience, understanding, and cheerfulness of Winifred Burton Evans made it all much easier.

Prologue

Thomas Nelson's career offers interesting insight into an important segment of colonial Virginia society. Born the day after Christmas in 1738, the scion of a family that had arrived and made a fortune in half a century, he carried a distinguished name.*

After an expensive education in England he returned in 1761 to a position in his father's mercantile business, marriage with the beautiful daughter of one of Virginia's leading families, and a seat in the House of Burgesses—as well as lands, slaves, and a noble mansion in which he lived "like a prince." [1]

Nor did heavy responsibility rest upon him immediately. For a decade he benefited from the advice and protection of his father, William Nelson, a truly exceptional man and one of Virginia's most powerful public figures. He felt no immediate pressure to prove himself in politics, and his introduction to business was gradual.

In such circumstances the young Virginian might easily have developed the indolent ways of some of the colony's gentry. But Nelson did not succumb to a life of idleness. True, he never became a successful businessman, but it can be argued that the Revolution prevented him from having a fair chance. In politics

---

* In all fairness, the reader deserves forewarning that the Nelson family subscribed to a very confusing practice: successive generations used the same given name over and over again. No less than three Thomas Nelsons figure prominently in this account (and there were others in both collateral and direct lines of descent). The first Thomas Nelson (1677–1745), the merchant, established the family in Virginia; he was the grandfather of our subject. The second-generation bearer of the name, often designated as Thomas Nelson the Secretary (1715–1787), was the uncle of our man, who in turn is sometimes known as Thomas Nelson the Signer (1738–1789). Probably on his return from England in 1761, he adopted the style Thomas Nelson, Jr. That tactic may have clarified identities at the time, but—because his father's name was William—has not always helped in years since.

1

his achievements were important, a fact that has been generally overlooked.

Nelson came to manhood just as the colonies began to protest the new direction in the mother country's policy. In Virginia this protest followed ten years of disagreement with English authorities—beginning in 1752 with the Pistole Fee controversy and the royal repeal of ten of sixty-seven acts passed by the previous legislature, and continuing through the Two-Penny Act controversy of the late fifties and early sixties. Thomas Nelson was in England for most of this time, but his father had been involved in it all and had become convinced that the Virginia legislature had the final authority for the internal affairs of the colony. William passed these views on to his son, who in 1761 began a long career in the elective branch of the General Assembly (House of Burgesses to 1776, House of Delegates from 1776 until 1789, with time out to serve as delegate to the Continental Congress and as governor of the state).[2]

Thomas Nelson did not begin to take on an active role in the House of Burgesses until after the Stamp Act crisis and the Robinson affair in 1766. The latter involved the misuse of over £100,000 of the colony's funds by the late speaker-treasurer, John Robinson. These episodes provided the opportunity for a group of younger Virginians to assert themselves. Nelson was among this group, which began to influence the colony to make increasingly strong responses to British actions, and by the early seventies he had risen to the first rank of leadership in Virginia. He is not commonly thought of as an important political leader, but his role in the associations for nonimportation of British goods in 1769 and 1774, his memberships on important committees in the House of Burgesses, his near election to the Continental Congress in 1774 and subsequent election in 1775 all confirm this judgment.

Gradually his views became more extreme. By 1774 the royal governor was characterizing him as "too violent," and in the fall of that year, as chairman of the York County committee to enforce the nonimportation regulations, he personally threw two half-chests of tea from a vessel belonging to his English merchant friend, John Norton, into the York River. By the fall of 1775, as Nelson took his seat in the Continental Congress in Philadelphia, it seemed to him that independence was the only course, and he returned home in the spring of 1776 determined to get the Virginia Convention, at Williamsburg, to take such a position. There Nelson played a key part in bringing about the vote that directed Virginia's delegates to Congress to propose a declaration of independence. In mid-May he returned to Philadelphia bearing the Virginia resolves. Subsequently he was, of course, a signer of the Declaration of Independence.

Nelson was to remain in Congress until the spring of 1777 (he served again briefly in 1779). Thus he took no part in drafting the Virginia constitution of 1776, nor did he play an important role in framing any of the new state's "reform" legislation. But in Congress and in the Virginia legislature, to which he was continuously elected, he made major contributions in finance and military affairs—obviously crucial matters in the carrying out of a revolution. It was onerous but important work, and it almost brought about his election as governor in 1779. Nelson was also the commander of the Virginia militia in 1777, 1779, and 1780–81, a role that enhanced his political image, and in June 1781 he finally succeeded Thomas Jefferson as governor.

Nelson remained in office only until shortly after the surrender of Cornwallis at Yorktown in October. The ill-health that had hampered his career since 1777 forced him to resign as governor. Thereafter until his death in 1789 his public service was limited.

Thomas Nelson's contributions to Virginia and to American independence were outstanding. As this biography attempts to demonstrate, he was one of the most important of Virginia's revolutionary leaders; he has to be considered in the same category as Thomas Jefferson, Patrick Henry, George Mason, George Wythe, Richard Henry Lee, Benjamin Harrison, and Edmund Pendleton.

Historians have been perplexed by the fact that the great majority of Virginia's social and political leaders vigorously supported the Revolution. Nelson's career helps us approach an understanding of this eighteenth-century paradox. Certainly the rise in power of the representative assemblies in America and the development of the belief that they had final authority in the internal affairs of their respective provinces were major factors in

Nelson's point of view. Related to this, and serving as a constant irritant, were various restrictions on trade that resulted from changes and adjustments in the Acts of Trade and Navigation. Implicit in the response to both sorts of encroachment was a faith in what Nelson called Virginia's rights "confirmed to us by Charter"[3] and the Whig view of natural rights.

Indebtedness to British merchants was not a factor in Nelson's motivation. He had heavy debts but he opposed nonpayment as a tactic to force British authorities to revoke objectionable measures. Similarly during the Revolution he opposed that portion of Virginia's Sequestration Act that allowed the payment of British debts into the state treasury. Then, once the war was over, Nelson made arrangements for paying all the money he owed to British creditors. In general, economic forces do not seem to have had much influence on Nelson's politics. He seemed to be resigned to the possibility of losing his own fortune, and as early as 1774 he warned his constituents that they would have to give up all hope of making fortunes. And finally, there is nothing in Nelson's career to suggest that tensions among social classes significantly influenced the coming of the Revolution in Virginia. The repeated electoral successes that the wealthy Nelson enjoyed may betoken the remarkable support for the Revolution from all free classes in Virginia.

One must conclude, if Thomas Nelson's life is any guide, that by and large the Revolution in Virginia emerged from the political relationships of the colony to the mother country and found its strength in the political philosophy of Virginia's citizens.

Chapter I

The Youth and His Family in Virginia Society

Yorktown, Virginia, in the 1730s was a "delicat village" that stood elevated on a "Sandy Hill like Blackheath or Richmond Hill" in England. It overlooked a "fine river broader than the Thames at those places" and had the "prospect of a noble Bay." The town bustled with activity. Already it was one of Virginia's most important ports. Warehouses and wharves clustered along its shoreline. Above, on the bluff, stood some thirty to forty residences, several of them impressive brick structures surrounded by beautiful gardens.[1]

One of these brick houses, which "you can perceive . . . at first view," was that of the eminent merchant, Thomas Nelson, grandfather of the future signer of the Declaration of Independence, who had settled in Yorktown in 1705. Nelson's career had been unusual because in only thirty years he had become a rich man who would soon see all of his children married into the oldest and most elite families of Virginia. The son of a cloth merchant from Penrith in Cumberland, England, he had gone to Whitehaven on the Irish Sea when just eighteen, and from there had visited Virginia on three occasions before settling in Yorktown. One account suggests that he made these trips as a boatswain on a merchant vessel. At any rate, he had accumulated some capital and this, along with the modest inheritance he received a few years after his arrival, enabled him to establish a mercantile concern.[2]

5

Yorktown, which Lord Adam Gordon called "the pleasantest situation . . . I ever saw," was ideally placed for mercantile operations. Located close to the Chesapeake Bay on the broad and deep York River it was central to the tobacco country. Grandfather Nelson's business operations are only sketchily known, but that he prospered is clear. Within six years of his arrival he had been appointed a member of the County Court, a sure sign of his acceptance by the local elite. By 1714 he was able, with Governor Spotswood and several other leading men, to invest substantially in the Virginia Indian Company, a venture newly formed to recapture the trade with the red man that had been lost to Carolina merchants.[3]

The size of Nelson's investment, evidently £500, coupled with the fact that three members of the Council of State, William Locke, Mann Page, and Nathaniel Harrison, were also in the scheme, suggests not only rising fortunes but also recognition by the upper echelons of Virginia society—two circumstances not unconnected in eighteenth-century Virginia. Land was not the prime object of Nelson's efforts, but it was essential to and a mark of standing, and he acquired it in significant amounts. In addition to 215 acres he had previously acquired in York County, in 1719 he added by headright 3,270 acres in New Kent; by the time of the birth of his grandson his total holdings were well over 6,500 acres, including fourteen choice town lots in Yorktown and Williamsburg.[4]

Success as a merchant made such investment and land acquisition possible. Tobacco was central to his operations. Either buying it on the local market, or receiving it in payment for store goods, he shipped the cured tobacco to England, obtaining credit for the purchase of products saleable in Virginia. The Nelson store evidently did a considerable volume of business, for between 1730 and 1738 Colonel Thomas Jones, a Hanover County planter, ran up bills of over £6,600. Unable to pay a good portion of this debt, Jones had to deed Nelson a 3,375-acre plantation. Supplementing the tobacco business was the provision trade with the West Indies, and as early as 1720 Nelson owned one-third interest in the sloop *Martha,* which was carrying Virginia pork and corn to Barbados.[5]

The sale of slaves, largely on consignment from English firms, was also a Nelson venture. Perhaps the slave trade made him decide to settle in Yorktown in the first place. At the time he arrived in Virginia the trade in Africans was steadily increasing, and it centered on the York River. Between March 1718 and March 1727 over eleven thousand Negroes were brought to Virginia by Bristol, London, and Liverpool traders. Coming from Calabar, Gold Coast, Sierre Leone, Angola, and Guinea, eighty-five hundred of them were brought into the York River. There is good reason to believe that Nelson was extensively involved in this traffic.[6]

In 1728 Thomas Nelson secured permission from the Council of State to enlarge his wharf and warehouse facilities on the York River. By this time he had acquired a half interest in the Swan Tavern in Yorktown, owned a mill, and operated the ferry between Yorktown and Tindal's Point. Shortly he was also to invest £500 in an iron mine near Fredericksburg, in partnership with Governor William Gooch and three other gentlemen. The grandfather of young Thomas was a hard working, imaginative, and tough-minded businessman, and he prospered.[7]

But business success was not the only ingredient necessary for movement into the upper strata of Virginia society. A good marriage was also important, and of this fact Thomas Nelson was well aware. Nelson married Margaret Reade, daughter of John Reade of Yorktown, in 1711. John Reade was a gentleman justice, but the family had seen better days, for his bride's grandfather, after his arrival in Virginia in the 1630s, had served in the House of Burgesses and had been a member of the Council for fourteen years. The marriage represented a highly acceptable if not brilliant union. When Margaret Nelson died, leaving two sons and a daughter, the Yorktown merchant made an equally acceptable match in 1723 with Frances Tucker, the forty-one-year-old widow of Robert Tucker of Norfolk. Only one child, a daughter, resulted from this marriage.[8]

Nelson provided well for his four children. Both sons, William, born in 1711 and Thomas, the uncle-to-be, who was born in 1715, were sent to England for their education. This was the exception rather than the rule for Virginia families of quality at the time because of the heavy expenses, the prolonged stay (often ten years or more) and because of the danger of the unexposed colonial catching smallpox. But Nelson wanted the very best for his sons and though an English education was not viewed as essential, it was highly respected in Virginia. William was trained, where it is not clear, to take over his father's business, while Thomas studied law, eventually completing his work at the Inner Temple. On their return, William, who was described to Sir Hans Sloan as "a young Gentleman of merit and fortune," immediately entered the mercantile concern, and Uncle Thomas received a large plantation and began a long and fruitful career of public service.[9]

But perhaps as important as the education for his sons, at least with respect to the status and influence of the family, was the fact that Nelson saw all of his children allied through marriage with Virginia's "best" families. The eldest daughter, Mary, married Edmund Berkeley of Barn Elms in Middlesex County in 1728. The Berkeleys were an old and respected family, and Edmund's father had served as a member of the Council. His mother was Lucy Burwell of the politically powerful Burwell clan that had given Governor Alexander Spotswood so much trouble. Spotswood had written in 1714 that "not less than seven [of the Council were] so near related that they will go off the Bench whenever the cause of the Burwells come to be tryed."[10]

In February 1738 William, the father of the future signer of the Declaration of Independence, wed Elizabeth Burwell the daughter of Lucy Burwell's brother Nathaniel, who had married Elizabeth Carter the eldest daughter of Robert "King" Carter. Ten months later on December 26, Elizabeth Burwell gave birth to a son Thomas. Elizabeth had been described as "a very genteel accomplish'd Young Lady, of great merit and considerable fortune," and when she married William Nelson an old Virginia family was joined to a relatively new one. The English Burwells had been early investors in the Virginia Company and the first Lewis Burwell had come to Virginia in the late 1640s. The Nelsons, by contrast, had been in the colony only thirty-three years. The marriage suggested that the Nelsons were becoming one of Virginia's most important families.[11]

The trend was continued by the marriage in 1742 of Sarah Nelson, Thomas Nelson's only child by Frances Tucker, to Robert Burwell of Isle of Wight County. Robert was the brother of William's wife Elizabeth. Finally, in 1745, Thomas, the youngest son, married Lucy Armistead. The Armisteads were not as powerful a family as the Burwells, but they had arrived in Virginia in the mid-1630s, they had had one member on the Council of State, and they were connected to the Burwells by the marriage of Lucy's father, Henry, to Martha Burwell, sister of Lucy Burwell Berkeley.[12]

These marriages suggest how closely the Virginia aristocracy of the eighteenth century was connected. Composed of no more than one hundred families, they knew each other intimately, frequently intermarried, and to some degree were almost all related. Their wealth made it possible for them to devote time to public service which, on the model of the English gentry, they viewed as an obligation. They composed the Council of State and dominated the House of Burgesses, the county courts and the parish vestries. While public office was not automatically theirs, for those who demonstrated ability and industry some position of power would almost inevitably be open. Some of them also exercised economic influence by buying their lesser neighbors' tobacco and selling them manufactured goods.[13]

Consequently the self-conscious influence of the Virginia plutocracy was felt at every level of society. They were, as one observer put it, the "pattern of all behavior" in Virginia. And this position of power and influence caused them, in Governor William Gooch's opinion, to be "both too dear and too Proud. . . ." The hard qualities of great pride, independence, and strong attachment to their interests, somewhat softened by their universally acclaimed hospitality, characterized the Virginia elite. Indolence as well as luxurious and ostentatious living were more evident later in the century.[14]

By the time of the first Thomas Nelson's death in 1745 the family was firmly established as a member of this aristocracy. No doubt his six-year-old namesake thought nothing of the fact that he was a member of a select group. But the accomplishment of his grandfather was not typical. Despite the fact that young Tom and his relations moved among Virginia's first families as if they were charter members, their progenitor had shortened the normal process of social rise in Virginia by at least one, perhaps two generations. In his will the old man left cash bequests of more than £10,000 sterling, and this says nothing of what his eldest son William, who inherited the bulk of the estate, received. But the position of his family, which had been attained in such a brief period of time, resulted not only from his economic success, based on hard work, intelligence, and a modicum of ruthlessness, but also from his shrewd grasp of the rules for social success in Virginia society and his meticulous observance of them.[15]

The second generation improved upon their predecessor's efforts, most dramatically in the political realm. The first Thomas Nelson had served on the York County Court for thirty-three years but he had not held any other office. William Nelson became a member of the County Court soon after his return from England in 1732. After ten years of "seasoning" at the county level he was elected to the House of Burgesses from York and immediately became one of the most important members of this powerful legislative body.[16]

At a time when leadership in the House was limited to a relatively few men, Nelson in his first session was among the ten or twelve who dominated its affairs. When the legislature convened again in 1744 he was among the more powerful of this select group. But already he was being considered for a post of even higher preferment. As early as 1741 Governor Gooch had mentioned him to the Board of Trade as one of those qualified for appointment to His Majesty's Council of State. Then, in 1743, Nelson was recommended to fill the vacancy created by the death of William Byrd II, a recommendation that the king, as a result of the Board of Trade's endorsement, agreed to in 1745.[17]

Meanwhile his brother, having completed his training at the Inner Temple and having been admitted to the English bar, was appointed in 1743 to the powerful and lucrative post of deputy secretary of the colony. Not only did this official appoint all the clerks of the county courts, but he also issued and collected fees on everything from land patents to marriage licenses, which returned an estimated annual income of £1,000 sterling. That same year Governor Gooch also tried to have the new secretary appointed attorney general of the colony. The attempt failed, but it indicates the high favor in which the Nelson family was held.

The Secretary, as Uncle Thomas Nelson was called hereafter, entered the House of Burgesses, where he served four years with a distinction equal to his brother's. Finally, in 1749, he joined William on the Council.[18]

Young Thomas must have become acquainted with the great figures of Virginia, for through the middle decades of the eighteenth century his father and uncle represented perhaps the strongest single family influence in Virginia's governmental affairs. These were crucial years for Virginia—years of war, economic maladjustment, increased assertion of royal authority and resistance to it. The Council in Virginia, unlike many of its counterparts in other colonies, remained a powerful body until the mid-sixties, and the Nelsons were its most important members.

John Blair of Williamsburg was the senior member of the Council of State during most of these years, but the judgment of the two brothers from Yorktown, especially William, was crucial. They framed the appeal to the king in 1752 after he had disallowed ten of some sixty-seven acts passed by the previous Assembly. Many of these acts were part of the revision of the laws that the Nelsons had supported in 1748–49; and over the strong opposition of other legislative leaders they pushed through a vigorous protest to the crown.[19]

The Nelsons also arranged the appointment of George Washington as adjutant of the Northern Neck in 1753. Both brothers served on the important Committee of Correspondence, William as chairman, which the Assembly created in 1759 to present its point of view more effectively to the home government, especially with respect to the emission of paper currency and difficulties with the clergy. As early as 1756 William was described as being, with the exception of the governor, "the greatest man in this Country."[20]

There is evidence to suggest that William Nelson's influence in the Council was powerful, and that Blair did little without consulting the Nelsons. When George Washington, as commander of Virginia's military forces, asked permission to come to Williamsburg, Blair waited until he could confer with the brothers before granting the request. Later, in writing Washington about a vacancy in his command, Blair observed that he had several requests "but I need not mention them after Mr. Nelson's [on behalf of Lieutenant Baker] whom I would fair oblige. . . ." [21]

Over the years William Nelson, as clearly the most powerful member of the Council, undoubtedly resented the fact that John Blair, who had preceded him on the Council by only two years, received the rewards that Nelson must have felt should have been his. After Governor Robert Dinwiddie's departure in 1757, and again after the death of Governor Francis Fauquier in 1768, Blair, as president of the Council, served as acting governor. By this time he was over eighty years of age, and it may have seemed to Nelson that he would go on forever.

When again, at Lord Botetourt's death in 1770, Blair was about to succeed for a third time Nelson evidently moved for a change. Soon the Council announced that Blair was retiring from his presidency because of his age, his concern that "his majesty's Interest and welfare may not . . . be at the least hazard of sustaining any detriment," and the fact that he was also deputy auditor. There is some reason to believe that gentle pressure was applied to Blair. The Council did provide that Nelson would pay Blair £200 a month until a new governor was appointed, and £100 thereafter until the appointee arrived. One critic remarked that "Old Billy has all the rest and that power he has so long panted for. . . ." [22]

Despite modest protestation on Nelson's part that he brought to office no capacity except what "a Heart disposed to do right . . . could furnish him with," he was clearly delighted with the position. Later, when the new appointee, Lord Dunmore, asked to keep his old post as governor of New York, William hoped with all his heart the request would be allowed, for he would have "the longer Run in a pretty Good Pasture by it." Dunmore finally did accept the appointment to Virginia, but Nelson had served as acting governor for eleven months. In his case ambition was fortunately linked with ability. He served efficiently and well, climaxing a long career of public service. [23]

The position of the Nelsons sprang from a combination of wealth, ability, and power. Secretary Nelson contributed the latter through his extensive rights of appointment. Lord Dunmore observed that he possessed "the best power of any man" on the Council, "which is that of a number of offices to dispose of." But it was William who possessed the greater ability and it was he who more effectively used the power his brother brought to the combination. After William's death the secretary was fairly ineffectual.[24]

Of course, the underpinning to this political potency had been and continued to be strong economic position, and it was William Nelson, one of the wealthiest men in Virginia, who continued to make this position possible. Taking over the mercantile concern from his father, William kept it going in the same train, except that he seems to have been less involved in the slave trade. His operations as a merchant are much clearer to history than those of his father, and what emerges is a picture of a Virginia-born merchant with ample capital and wide contacts, whose relations with English merchants were those of an equal. The mention of Nelson's name was enough to open doors for planters seeking credit in England. Merchant Charles Goore told Edmund Berkeley that it was not usual to send goods in advance of payment, "yet your naming of Mr. Nelson is sufficient for me to send anything you [sent?] for." [25]

William regularly did business with eight or ten English firms located in London, Bristol, Liverpool, and Whitehaven. These places provided Yorktown's "principal Merchant" with goods for an extensive wholesale and retail trade. He sold goods wholesale at a markup of 100 percent and retail at 110 percent. This trade in Virginia was not limited to the York River and its headwaters, but extended throughout the colony. Indeed, his business contacts ranged as far as Philadelphia and New York.[26] At one time Nelson owned a half interest in one, and possibly two, merchant vessels, and in the absence of banks he also carried on an extensive banking business, lending considerable sums of money. It is difficult to determine the volume of business that he did before 1765, but in June and July of 1761 over £2,000 in bills of exchange were credited to him. After 1765, his annual volume of business ranged at a minimum, between £5,000 and £10,000.[27]

Nelson was also a planter, with holdings of almost thirty thousand acres. In good years these lands produced more than three hundred hogsheads of tobacco, frequently described as the best in Virginia. In Hanover County his property was so extensive that in addition to overseers he had to retain William Dabney and his son as farm managers. Plantation and mercantile concerns alike he managed with careful attention. Whether it was planting clover to restore the fertility of his lands or collecting an unpaid debt, he let no detail escape him. And in Virginia, which was noted for the heavy indebtedness of its citizens, William Nelson was able to keep himself free from this burden. When he found himself owing the firm of Edward Hunt & Son £1,000 in 1767 he remarked that "to remain in debt I could never bear but with the greatest pain," and he refrained from ordering any goods from the firm until the debt was paid. Among Virginians of Nelson's class this was an exceptional action, which gives some insight into his character and success.[28]

Such was the family and society into which Thomas, William's eldest son, was born. And young Tom grew up with all possible advantages. His father lived "in all respects, allowing for the different circumstances of the Place, in as grand a manner" as the English nobility. Soon after Tom's birth he moved his family into a large brick H-shaped house that stood in the center of town. There was a white housekeeper, nurses for the children, and a bevy of Negro servants.[29]

Tom must have grown up feeling a certain sense of importance. His father was Yorktown's leading merchant, the most important member of the York County Court, and the dominant figure on His Majesty's Council of State. After his father and uncle purchased a house in Williamsburg, near the Capitol, Tom undoubtedly stayed there sometimes when William was attending meetings of the Council. To his father's house in Yorktown came many of Virginia's leading men. William Byrd II, among others, was a frequent partaker of William Nelson's hospitality.[30]

Just the physical presence of so many Nelsons in their fine houses in Yorktown must have made the boy feel as if much of the world revolved around their activity. Across the street stood his grandfather's house, next door was the store, and down the "Great Valley," which ran next to the store, were his father's warehouses and wharf. Several blocks to the east his uncle built his elegant dwelling.[31]

It was a small world in which Tom spent his early years, but not an unimportant or uninteresting one, especially for a young boy. To Yorktown's harbor came merchant vessels from Britain, continental Europe, Africa, the West Indies, and the mainland colonies, bringing with them the excitement of strange and distant places. Many of these vessels were owned by merchants who did business with William Nelson. Tom, who frequently ran errands for his father, saw these vessels first hand—their crews and cargoes. The county court was in Yorktown, and the court's monthly meeting brought a flood of people to town to sue and be sued, to do business, and to visit. The courthouse was in sight of William's house, as was Yorkhampton Parish Church. Nelson was a very religious man, and on Sundays would frequently spread a hearty table for those who came from a distance.[32]

Yorktown and the Nelson household, thus, saw a constant bustle of activity. If all of this was not enough to occupy a growing boy, the sparkling York River provided fishing and swimming, and the steep ravines leading from the bluff to the river provided exciting places for Tom, his brothers (there were ultimately four other boys in the family), cousins, and other children of the town to play[33]

For Tom, Yorktown was a pleasant place in which to grow up. But a boy must also acquire the discipline and learning that formal education provides. William Nelson had a respect for and a love of learning. Throughout his life he read widely, with an emphasis on history. He probably hired a tutor for his son during Tom's early years. Then in 1751 he sent Tom across the river to Gloucester County where William Yates, minister of Abingdon Parish, instructed twelve scholars in the well-known Peaseley School. Among young Nelson's classmates were two Gloucester residents, John Page of Rosewell and Francis Willis, who were to be his lifelong friends. Other students were Severn Eyre from the Eastern Shore, Christopher Robinson from Middlesex, Edward Carter from Albemarle, and cousin Robert Tucker from Norfolk. The Reverend Mr. Yates, a man of "passionate disposition," stressed the study of Latin grammar no doubt to the agony of some of his pupils.[34]

William Nelson kept Tom at the Peaseley School until the summer of 1753 when he packed him off to England for the completion of his education. According to one account his father sent him to England earlier than had been planned because he was concerned about his playing with black children, and perhaps he felt, as did William Byrd I, that his children could learn nothing among a "great family of Negroes." More likely he simply thought his son ready, for William Nelson himself had gone to England when only eleven and Tom was now fourteen. A portrait of young Tom painted about this time shows a stocky boy, with a round face, light-colored hair, a full but firm mouth, and piercing blue eyes. From all accounts he was a spirited, perhaps willful youth, and Nelson may have come to the conclusion that it was time his son settled down to serious pursuits.[35]

So the young Virginian went on the long voyage to the mother country, there to be placed in the care of William's merchant friend, Edward Hunt of London. For his companion on the voyage Tom had Gawin Corbin, son of Richard Corbin, receiver general for His Majesty in Virginia. Young Corbin's stay in England was to be the same length as Tom's, but he was to return home a Tory in his sentiments. In fact Nelson was to say later that of the nine or ten young Virginians who were in England with him for their education, he was the only one not to return a Tory.[36]

On the boy's arrival in England, Hunt placed him in a prominent private school conducted by a Mr. Newcome at Hackney, a village a few miles to the northeast of London. Hackney was noted for its boarding schools (the daughters of William Byrd I attended school there), and earlier in the century it served as a suburban retreat for the London aristocracy and gentry. By the 1750s the aristocracy had moved to the western suburbs and their places had been taken by London merchants, who caused it to excel "all other villages of the Kingdom . . . in the Riches and Opulency of its inhabitants." Probably Edward Hunt himself had a home in Hackney. No doubt Hunt's presence there, or at least in London, as well as the reputation the public schools were acquiring as hotbeds of vice and brutality, influenced William Nelson's decision to send his son to Hackney rather than elsewhere.[37]

Students at the small private school were not restricted to a fixed curriculum, and Tom, whose formal schooling had been brief, could receive the attention he needed in those subjects in which he was ill prepared. Almost certainly his course of study included such subjects as English, the classics, modern languages, penmanship, arithmetic, merchants' accounts, mathematics, modern geography, experimental philosophy, and astronomy. And Mr. Newcome, who had received the degree of Doctor of Laws from Cambridge in 1751, was unquestionably a well-qualified master.[38] Soon Nelson was anxiously inquiring of Hunt if Tom showed "a disposition to idleness and pleasure," since he feared the "spirited character" of his son would lead him astray. Evidently Hunt kept a close rein on the boy during his four years at Hackney, and Tom seems to have survived his stay relatively unblemished.[39]

On May 15, 1758, Thomas entered Christ College, Cambridge, as a pensioner, to study under the Reverend Beilby Porteus. Again his father had chosen a mentor he could trust to keep a close and friendly eye on Tom. Although Porteus had been born in England, both of his parents, Robert and Elizabeth Jenings Porteus, were native Virginians who had lived until about 1720 at New Bottle across the York River in Gloucester County. The Porteuses had kept close ties with Virginia, and their son Beilby was an able and learned man. An excellent mathematician, he had received his B.A. from Christ College in 1752 and that same year was elected a fellow. In 1757 he was ordained deacon and priest. Porteus also wrote poetry, some of it rather bad, but the year after Nelson entered Cambridge he won the Seatonian Prize for a poem titled "Death." Much later he was to be made bishop of London. Nelson was in good hands as he journeyed the fifty-two miles from London to Cambridge to begin his college career.[40]

Tom took two rooms at Christ College for which he paid £1 15s. a quarter. No doubt Gawin Corbin welcomed his arrival; his companion on the trip to England had entered in 1756. Also present was Philip Thomas Lee from Charles County in Maryland. And at Trinity College Robert Beverley, grandson of the historian, had been in residence since 1757. In 1759 Thomas Smith from Middlesex County joined them. Certainly Nelson could not have felt alone as he began his studies.[41]

Thomas's precise course of study is not known, but since Porteus's strongest subjects were mathematics and literature (Latin and Greek), he must have spent a good deal of time with both. Added to these were probably logic, rhetoric, and modern history—certainly the latter because of his father's strong interest.

Nelson continued to be concerned about the development of his son's character. To steer him clear of temptations during vacation time, "especially such as are [to be found] far away from friends," he requested that Porteus place the young man with some eminent scientific agriculturist to better prepare him to cultivate the soil of America.[42]

But with all of William's planning to keep Tom usefully occupied, the young man found time for other concerns. He became quite a trencherman (a Nelson weakness), acquired a taste for liquor, possibly at the Brazen George across St. Andrews Street from the college, and began to smoke. Perhaps he also took the opportunity to go up to Norfolk with his friend John Frere to do some hunting.[43]

Thomas completed his residence at Cambridge on March 25, 1761, but did not take a degree. His ever-watchful father ordered him to delay his departure because he did not wish him to travel with two young Virginians of bad reputation. Perhaps the pair were Gawin Corbin and Robert Beverley, both of whom returned to Virginia several months before Nelson. In any case, Tom did not embark until August. His traveling companion was Samuel Athawes, son of London merchant Edward Athawes. Athawes had long been involved in the Virginia trade and his son was coming over to acquaint himself with Virginia in preparation for taking over the business. Unable to book passage for Virginia, the young men had to settle for a vessel bound for New York. It was wartime, the voyage took eleven weeks, and Tom's parents were much relieved to hear of his safe arrival in late October or early November. By the middle of November Thomas Nelson was back in Yorktown after an absence of eight years.[44]

Despite all his care William was disappointed in the results of his son's English experience and resolved not to send his other sons abroad: "The Temptations to Expense and Dissipation of Money and Time are too great for our Estates" and the "improvements . . . are seldom answerable to such great Expenses as they often incurr." In fact, many Virginians were beginning to question the value of an English education. Some of its products were returning "inconceivably illiterate . . . corrupted and vicious." Thomas certainly did not fit this description, but he was "inclined to Juvenile Diversions." There had to be a period of settling down.[45]

Chapter II

Planter and Businessman

Thomas Nelson returned in 1761 to a Virginia little changed during his eight-year absence. Yorktown was still the same busy place, and his father remained its leading citizen. The population of the colony had increased, but there had been no radical rearrangement in Virginia society. Men such as his father and uncle still controlled political life; they remained responsive to the electorate, however, since the franchise was broad and the voter independent. Nelson no doubt noticed an increase in the number of Scottish merchants in Virginia. Since their low freight rates and chain stores were a constant topic of conversation, he could have hardly ignored this development. But it was the only real change on the economic scene and it had been emerging since the 1740s.[1]

The young Virginian may have noticed some change among the gentry, the class in which he and his family loomed so large. Many of the Virginia elite were spending themselves deeply into debt. His father, who was no spendthrift, voiced displeasure at the situation. There are two related explanations for this development. A gradual rise in tobacco prices over the thirty years before the Revolution had given the planters a chance to make more money. Increased incomes and an easy credit system, coupled with social maturation and stability, conspired to induce not only the elite, but other members of society as well, to live beyond their means. Virginians desired to live more elegant lives, and they rapidly began to acquire the refinements associated with such an existence.[2]

That this desire to acquire more of life's amenities outran their incomes few commentators failed to mention. Merchant John Wayles pictured the circumstances graphically when he explained

19

that in 1740 a debt of £1,000 seemed tremendous, yet in 1766, when he was writing, ten times that amount "is now spoke of with Indifference." Estates had grown "more than ten fold," property values had gone up, and hand in hand with this had come "Luxury and expensive living." "In 1740 I don't remember to have seen such a thing as a turkey carpet in the Country except a small thing in a bed-chamber. Now nothing are so common as Turkey or Wilton Carpets, the whole furniture, Roomes, Elegant and every appearance of opulence." [3] This extravagant living was accompanied by a loss of vigor and drive among many of the elite who were reaching maturity during the middle years of the century. [4]

Thomas represented the third generation of Nelsons in Virginia—a bad omen perhaps—but social decline was far from his thoughts as he returned home. The heir apparent to a large fortune and the recipient of a "liberal and expensive education," the hopes and expectations of both himself and his family could not help but be high. William Nelson expected his son to take on an active political role immediately. In the fall of 1761, almost certainly before he returned home, the young man was elected to the House of Burgesses from York County. He was also appointed justice of the peace and was soon to be made colonel of the county militia. Thomas Nelson, only twenty-two and long absent from Virginia, could not have received such recognition on the basis of his reputation. William Nelson was still arranging his eldest son's life, and the election and appointments are not only a measure of the hopes he had for his son's future but also of his power and influence. [5]

Politics, despite his father's plans, were not to occupy much of Thomas Nelson's time for the next few years. Soon after his return home he fell in love with Lucy Grymes, the "greatest Belle" in Virginia. The daughter of Philip Grymes of Brandon in Middlesex County, Lucy was not only beautiful but talented. Just eighteen, she was well educated for the time, having been instructed by William Yates at the Peaseley School where Thomas had gone earlier. She had become proficient in arithmetic and acquired a fondness for reading. Her father, a colleague of William Nelson's on the Council, lived in Williamsburg when the Assembly and the General Court were in session. Lucy took harpsichord lessons in Williamsburg from "the modern Orpheus —the inimitable [Peter] Pelham," organist at Bruton Parish Church. She became an "elegant dancer," perhaps under the tutelage of Chevalier Peyronney, the dashing young Frenchman who served so gallantly with Washington at Fort Necessity and was killed with Braddock on the banks of the Monogahela. Lucy loved dancing, which most Virginia women were "immoderately" fond of; but in every other respect she differed from the generality, who, lacking in education, were described as "seldom accomplished" and "unequal to any interesting conversation." [6]

Perhaps the young people had met when children. But it was in Williamsburg in the fall of 1761, probably while Thomas was attending his first session of the House of Burgesses, that he was captivated by the charming Lucy. William Nelson certainly approved of and encouraged the courtship. The Grymes's pedigree was impeccable. The first Grymes had come to Virginia in the 1640s. The family had done well. Philip Grymes's mother was a Ludwell and he himself had married Mary Randolph, daughter of Sir John Randolph. In addition, Grymes's membership on the Council and the fact that the family, like the Nelsons, were "remarkably religious" people, made the match eminently acceptable.[7]

Thomas and Lucy were married in Williamsburg on July 29, 1762. Their old teacher William Yates, now rector of Bruton Parish Church and president of William and Mary College, performed the ceremony. The union was a happy one and might easily have served as proof of the observation of a British military officer who visited the colony about this time. Virginia women, he said, make "excellent wives" and "great Breeders," and it is "much the fashion to marry young and what is remarkable in a stay . . . of near a month in the province I have not heard of one unhappy couple." [8]

Lucy and Thomas lived with William Nelson during the first five years of their married life. It must have been a busy household for Thomas's four younger brothers were at home, and the young couple began to produce children with rythmic regularity —thirteen eventually, eleven of whom lived to maturity. Five boys, William, Thomas, Philip, Francis, and Hugh were born between August 1763 and September 1768. The birth of so many

boys caused Thomas and his father to envisage the fame and fortune of the Nelsons extending into future generations. There "is
no great fear of the name being extinct" the young father proudly
proclaimed. And the grandfather boasted that "We are the
proper sort of people to fill a young Country." [9]

In 1766 Frances Nelson died at the age of eighty-three, and
the following year Thomas Nelson moved his family into his
grandfather's house. This large and handsome home with its wide
halls and extensive grounds provided an excellent place in which
to raise a large family. Thomas was going to need all this room
because two daughters, Elizabeth and Mary, were born in 1770
and 1774, and Lucy Nelson's three sisters joined the household
sometime after the death of Philip Grymes in 1762. The two
eldest boys remained across the street to keep their maternal
grandmother company, but despite this the Nelson house must
have seen few dull moments. At the same time, family life was
not chaotic, for Lucy was a strict disciplinarian and before long
Thomas hired a tutor to provide for his children's education. Just
before the Revolution, the tutor was Jacob Hall, Jr., a Pennsyl-
vanian, who was paid £50 a year, furnished with room, board,
and a servant, and enjoyed the use of Nelson's fine library.[10]

Thomas's move into his grandfather's house not only provided
more room for his burgeoning family, it also evidenced his rising
status. During the first ten years of married life he began to acquaint himself with his father's estates and business. In addition,
William Nelson had given his son property in Yorktown, including the Swan Tavern, and at least two plantations, in York and
Albemarle counties, on which he was producing food for his
family and tobacco for export. Thomas was also becoming more
and more active on the County Court and in the House of Burgesses. Soon he would be appointed to the vestry of Yorkhampton Parish—a position of importance. Later his public interests
included an agricultural company that Philip Mazzei, an Italian
immigrant organized for the purpose of "raising and making
Wine, Oil . . . and Silk" in the hope that this would be a start
towards the diversification of Virginia agriculture. The venture,
in which Thomas purchased one share for £50, was to show
promise only to fall a casualty to war.[11]

Unlike William Nelson, Thomas does not seem to have been

Thomas Nelson at the age of sixteen (1754) by Mason Chamberlin. The only known portrait of Nelson painted from life, it was done in London while he was a student there. Reproduced by permission of the Virginia Museum of Fine Arts, Richmond.

William Nelson and his wife, Elizabeth Burwell Nelson, attributed to Robert Feke. When and where these portraits were painted cannot now be ascertained. Reproduced by permission of the owner, Mrs. Douglas Crocker, Fitchburg, Massachusetts.

driven to excel in business or, initially anyway, in politics. And although at later date he was to show some talent in business, he readily admitted that it was not something he enjoyed. Thomas was an easygoing, good-natured, generous, and benevolent man, fairly quick tempered but easily mollified. Fat and fond of the good life, he liked his glass of wine and his evening pipe. At the same time he was physically active and loved the outdoors, especially fox hunting. Like many of his contemporaries he was very interested in horses and from time to time he imported them from England in an attempt to improve the Virginia breed.[12]

Happiest when he was with his family, he could not understand those who denied themselves the pleasures of family life. Something of Nelson's character can be seen in a letter to his London friend, Samuel Athawes, who, he complained, was inconsistent and too often had the "Hyppo"—a condition he ascribed to Athawes's single state. Nelson advised Athawes to mount his "little Chesnut Mare and gallop away to some acquaintances House where there are a parcel of pretty Girls and Chat with them an Hower or two. You old Bachelors are strange beings, why don't you get a Wife? The many solitary Howers you must pass. I should detest the thought of going to bed alone so often as you do. Prithee look out for some pretty lady . . . that [will] make you pass the waves of this troublesome World with satisfaction." [13]

Thomas had another characteristic common to his class—not being able to live within his income. He had expensive tastes. A visitor to his home in 1768 reported that "Colonel Nelson" lived like a prince. By 1770 he owed £852 to London merchant John Norton, a debt that exceeded £1,000 in 1773. It is highly probable that this was not his only debt. But indebtedness did not really bother him until his father's death.[14]

William Nelson died on November 19, 1772, of an intestinal disorder. His passing left a large gap in Virginia society, for as Robert Carter Nicholas put it, "No man amongst us better understood and no one was more strenuous in promoting the true Interest of his Country, whether viewed in a political or commercial light." The loss his family felt can easily be imagined, for he was a warm and affectionate parent as well. The responsibility suddenly thrust upon Thomas must have seemed overwhelming.[15]

William Nelson provided handsomely for Thomas. He left him well over twenty thousand acres of Virginia land, the bulk of it in Hanover County, and a small estate in Cumberland County, England. The Main Street and waterside stores in York- town were given to Thomas and his brother Hugh as tenants in common. The mercantile concern was relatively unencumbered with debt—in fact some £33,500 sterling was owed the busi- ness. After approximately £19,000 in cash bequests had been paid out of this book indebtedness the remainder was to go to Thomas. Precisely how much more Thomas received from his father's estate is not clear. The will specified exactly what Eliza- beth Nelson and her younger sons were to receive and then pro- vided that "All the rest and residue of my estate of what nature of quality soever, whether real or personal in Virginia or else- where, I give . . . to my son Thomas Nelson. . . ."[16]

After his father's death Thomas and his brother Hugh took over the operation of the mercantile concern. Thomas, who was the guiding force in the business, hoped that it would "furnish an employment for us and I hope some little profit." His hopes were justified, for William Nelson had left the business in good shape. With most of the English merchants with whom he dealt, there was a balance in his favor. Only in his account with the London firm of Thomas and Rowland Hunt was there a consider- able amount on the debit side, totaling almost £1,600. Despite this large debt the brothers ordered from the Hunts their goods for the coming year. The Nelson firm had dealt with the Hunts for many years, and Thomas and Hugh Nelson did not perceive, nor did most people, that this was a bad time to become heavily indebted.[17]

Unfortunately, overextension of credit, coupled with consider- able speculation, had brought on a crisis in the British mercantile community. News of falling tobacco prices and many failures in England and Scotland were already filtering into Virginia. Many British merchants had extended themselves far beyond what their capital should have allowed, and the Bank of England began to refuse to discount risky bills. As one observer pointed out, "this has been the occasion of many stopages, Bankruptcys and Sui- cides."[18]

The ramifications of this crisis were felt throughout the colonial world. In Virginia the results were a tightening credit, a demand for debt payment, and an increasing scarcity of circulating money. Thus when William's executors began to try to collect the money owed him they found his debtors unable to pay because of the scarcity of money, and it was virtually impossible to turn land or other assets into cash. In the spring of 1775, of the £33,500 owed the firm there was still £27,500 on the books, only half of it secured by bond.[19]

The Nelson firm soon faced serious difficulties. Bills of exchange had been sent to the Hunt firm totaling over £1,000, but their debt had risen to about £2,300 as a result of the large order of goods soon after the death of their father. The Hunts were loath to sell them additional goods with this debt on the books. In fact, they had been hesitant to fill even the first order, but had sent it out of regard for the young Nelsons' father. Merchant John Norton wrote his son in Virginia that the Hunts were "on demur whether to supply the Nelson's Store or not, the fears of Disappointment in Remittances and splitting on the same Rock many others, have done, have caused a general alarm among all our Merchants here."[20]

This hesitancy on the Hunts' part infuriated Thomas and Hugh Nelson. Thomas wrote the London firm that since there seemed to be a "disinclination" to continue the correspondence "between the two Houses that had subsisted for so many Years," they would break off the relationship, at the same "time wishing you better correspondents in our room." Speaking bluntly, if somewhat naïvely, he stated that a merchant who would not advance £3,000 or £4,000 on occasion "is not the man for me." He was sending his order for fall goods to another firm and furthermore the Hunts were to get only forty-two hogsheads of tobacco, less than usual, for which they could thank themselves.[21]

By fall Thomas had cooled off, largely because of conciliatory letters from the Hunts. Things had, after all, not gone too far, and he was willing to "let the Hatchet be buried," but only on certain terms. Since William Nelson had usually given from eighteen to twenty-four months credit, the Nelsons' customers could not be made to pay within a year. Hence the Nelsons could not import goods unless they themselves were given at least twelve months of interest-free credit. Robert Cary and Company had offered them these terms plus a discount for any amount paid within the twelve-months period, and if the Hunts wanted to do business on these terms it would be fine; if not, they were to present their invoice for goods to the Cary firm.[22]

Thomas also had the problem of tobacco production with which to deal. The 1772 tobacco crop had to be shipped. The previous year's crop was always shipped in the following spring and summer, and in the summer of 1773 Thomas Nelson exported 269 hogsheads. It is probable that around 200 hogsheads were of his own crops, and that he had purchased the remainder in the hope of profiting on the difference between prices in Virginia and those in England.[23]

By the end of that summer Thomas had learned more of the difficulties of operating a mercantile concern. He found that though others owed him a large amount of money, collecting it was almost impossible. Getting people to pay their debts in Virginia had always been difficult, but now distressed times made it even more so. Tobacco had fallen in price from twenty or twenty-five shillings a hundred pounds to twelve shillings and sixpence. Nelson wrote to Robert Cary that "our Country is at present in so deplorable a situation that a person who may have thousands due to him can command no more than he who has little, or I may say nothing." Thomas, like his father, did not hesitate to take cases of debt to court, but such cases were usually settled at 50 percent of the debt and therefore at a considerable loss. When some of his bills of exchange were protested as worthless in England, Thomas began to feel as if he and his brother Hugh were not as well acquainted with business as they had thought. They decided to take into partnership Augustine Moore, who had been apprenticed to their father around 1746 and who, after his apprenticeship was completed, had continued to work for Nelson. Moore was characterized as "a Man conversant in business and of the greatest integrity." Henceforth the Yorktown firm was to be known as Thomas Nelson, Jr., and Company.[24]

Thomas had also made plans to sell the estate in Cumberland County, England, which he had inherited from his father. His kinsman, William Cookson, a Penrith grocer, together with his father's friend, Samuel Martin, a Whitehaven merchant, were to handle the sale. At first Thomas had planned to take the money he would get from the sale and buy land in Virginia for one of his younger sons, but by December 1773 he was still so much in debt that the money was earmarked to go to the Hunt firm.[25]

In addition to the large sum of money the Nelson firm owed Thomas and Rowland Hunt, Nelson was also indebted to the Hunts on his private account for an unknown but evidently significant amount. This debt and the sum of over £1,000 that he owed merchant John Norton were annoying, but paying them off does not seem to have been his first concern. In May of 1773 he purchased 120 acres of land in York County from Thomas Archer; in August and November he acquired three more slaves. In the same period he ordered for his mother a "genteel chariot with six Harness to be painted of a grave colour," and with the Nelson coat of arms on the side, costing about £100 sterling. He then purchased for himself a "neet plain post chaise," as his old one was "Broke to pieces." This spending was partly balanced by the sale, for £550, of the lot and buildings located next to the Swan Tavern in Yorktown.[26]

The year 1774 brought a further healing of the breach between the Nelsons and Thomas and Rowland Hunt. The Hunts were evidently willing to continue business arrangements and in May Nelson spoke of the great pleasure he felt over the prospect of "the Harmony that had subsisted so long, between the two families" being "renew'd upon a permanent basis." He felt that terms of business which were acceptable to both parties were now clearly understood and had this been the case at first "the little fracas would never have happened."[27]

But by fall it appeared that the difficulties were not settled. The London firm continued to charge Nelson interest on goods he purchased after six months had elapsed, and he bluntly told them that it would be impossible to do business on those terms. In addition, much was awry in the Hunts' last shipment of goods: they had sent six horn rather than six tin lanterns; the saddles cost too much; there was a bad assortment of teapots and milk pots; the portmanteau trunks were "large and clumsy things"; and the shoes were "so unreasonably large that they will fit none but now and then a Country Girl who have been accustomed to go barefoot from her childhood. . . ."[28]

Nor were these all of his problems. Difficulties now arose in

the sale of the Penrith estate. William Cookson, one of the persons handling the sale, had died, and a new power of attorney
had to be sent; Samuel Martin, the Whitehaven merchant who
was handling the sale with Cookson, was irritated because the
necessary papers had not been sent as soon as he thought they
should; and some of Nelson's relatives were claiming that the
estate was rightfully theirs. All of these things got on Nelson's
nerves and to merchant Samuel Athawes, who was forever "hem-
ing and Hawing" about how much tobacco Thomas should send
him, he wrote requesting that he be permitted in the future to
send as much as he wanted and if, he added, Athawes himself
did not feel like handling it, then let him give the shipment to
someone else.[29]

To add to Nelson's troubles the excessively hot weather in the
summer of 1774, made him feel little inclination, he said, "to
do any kind of business which I am not fond of at anytime." But
he was not idle. During the summer he shipped 307 hogsheads of
tobacco, a considerable shipment for any year, and in this case he
seems to have erred in judgment, for only 122 hogsheads of the
total were his own crop, the remainder having been purchased.
Why he had bought so much tobacco is difficult to explain, for it
was still bringing an extremely low price in England and Nelson
had lost money on his tobacco purchase the previous year.[30]

To the Hunts, who received one hundred of these purchased
hogsheads, he explained that he had done a lot of buying because he did not want the firm's ship to go home only partially
loaded. Thomas probably felt obligated to the Hunts because
he was so much in debt to them. Furthermore, he hoped that the
Hunts would stop the heavy load of interest on the money he
owed them since he had made such large purchases for their
benefit. Whatever the case, Nelson would have been better off
had he not ventured so much, for his losses were to be great.[31]

By 1775 Thomas confessed that his business affairs were in an
unhappy state. It was almost impossible to collect the money
owed him and he was still heavily indebted to Thomas and Rowland Hunt. He admitted that he could not wipe the debt off at
this time, adding, nevertheless, that he had done everything in
his power to achieve that purpose. Furthermore, his tobacco
shipment for that summer was small, totaling only seventy-nine

hogsheads. He had had a bad crop, and was not able to buy any tobacco, for in his own words "I have burnt my fingers so much by purchasing that I have given that over and my debtors choose rather to let other people have what little they made than myself." [32]

Nelson took over the business at a difficult time. The deteriorating economic situation in Great Britain after 1772 had an adverse effect on Virginia. And Thomas, who was not so skilled a businessman as his father, found himself almost immediately in financial difficulty—a circumstance that was not helped by his apparent inability to live within his income. If it had not been for the Revolution his fortune would probably have been gradually dissipated. As things turned out, the fight for independence brought on a steeper decline in his economic position while, at the same time, catapulting him into a public prominence he would hardly have otherwise achieved.

Chapter III

A Whig Planter Revolts

Thomas Nelson entered the House of Burgesses in the fall of 1761, elected no doubt while still on the voyage home. Having grown to manhood in England he had no public experience at any level. William Nelson, proud of and ambitious for his eldest son, certainly used his influence to get him elected. The son did not live up to his father's expectations for a number of years. The General Assembly of which he became a member in 1761 was not dissolved until 1765. During this period it met eight times, and apart from the sessions of May 1763 and January 1764 Nelson's attendance seems to have been reasonably good. Yet in these four years he did nothing to merit attention. Beginning in the fall of 1762 he served on the standing committee of Propositions and Grievances, but this was his only assignment and he was not one of its important members.[1]

Thomas, in fact, played no vigorous political role until the end of the decade. But this is not to say that the events of the 1760s had no impact on him. The House of Burgesses was becoming the most important influence in the government of Virginia. Earlier controversies over the Pistole Fee and the Two-Penny Act had served to confirm the burgesses in their belief that final authority over the internal affairs of the colony belonged to them. Thus their response to the Sugar Act of 1764 and the Stamp Act of 1765 was predictable. The elected representatives of the people were the only ones who could levy taxes. Economic pressure in the form of the nonimportation of manufactured goods and, in Virginia, the closure of the courts, which prevented suits for debts, helped bring about repeal of the Stamp Act in 1766. But Parliament continued to assert that it had the right to tax.

This position, in addition to a stricter enforcement of the Acts of Trade and Navigation and an economic slump in Virginia, assured the continuance of ill-feeling towards the mother country. That feeling was strengthened by the increasing influence in the House of Burgesses of a younger group of politicians led by Patrick Henry and including Thomas Nelson. Governor Francis Fauquier called these legislators "hotheaded" and "inexperienced." In fact they were not politically radical; moderate whig is the best way to classify them. But they were younger than the men who had dominated Virginia politics and were inclined towards a more militant response to British actions.[2]

Thomas fitted well into this group. He was a stout but vigorous man who possessed a quick although short-lived temper. There was no pretense about him; he was forthright and honest almost to a fault. Unlike many Virginians educated with him in England he did not hold English society in awe, nor did he long to return to the mother country. Virginia was home—it was his country. His political views were strongly influenced by his father.[3]

William Nelson, although a member of the Council who had not served in the House of Burgesses for twenty-five years, held views on British actions not far removed from those of the more militant leaders in that body. Despite the repeal of the Stamp Act he was still restive under the Navigation Acts which, he said, placed "cruel Impositions and clogs on our trade." English politics were corrupt, and he thought it a farce for the English people to pride themselves on being "the freest people on Earth. . . ." They were not governed by representatives of their own choosing because "half the members [of Parliament] are imposed upon them by some Great Lord or rich commoner and are bought and sold a whole borough at once, as we have purchased a cargo of slaves." In contrast America was a land of hope where "many brave men" came during the "Usurpation of the Last Century" and "here in the Wilderness Enjoyed Liberty and Ease and laid the Foundation of what may in the future ages become a mighty Empire." Thomas subscribed to these views as did most of Virginia's leadership.[4]

The Townshend Acts, passed in June 1767, brought forth a further affirmation of this position. William Nelson said the acts raised the question of whether or not Americans were *"to be slaves or Freemen."* Freemen had the natural constitutional right to dispose of their property, while slaves did not. By placing import duties on glass, lead, paint, paper, and tea, Parliament was taking part of the Americans' property away from them without their consent and as a result was trying to enslave them. It affected, he wrote, all that he held near and dear, his fortune, his children, "and their children to the latest Posterity." [5]

In close agreement with his father, Thomas became increasingly active in politics. In 1769 he accepted additional assignments in the House of Burgesses. In addition to the Committee of Propositions and Grievances he now served on the Committee of Religion and the powerful Committee of Privileges and Elections, an appointment that suggests his growing influence and prestige. In May 1769, when the new governor, Norborne Berkeley, Baron de Botetourt, dissolved the Assembly because of its resolutions against the Townshend duties, Nelson joined with eighty-eight other members of the House of Burgesses in an association for the nonimportation of British products. The purpose was to force the British mercantile community to bring about repeal of the hated duties. [6]

The following year, after the repeal of all the Townshend duties save the tax on tea, Nelson participated in a revised association designed to be more effective in getting Virginians not to import British goods. Duties still remained for revenue alone, and Virginia's leadership was determined to keep up the pressure until all such taxes were repealed. Thomas and his father exerted great efforts to make nonimportation work. Both wore suits made from cloth of their own manufacture. Their shirts were of Virginia linen and their shoes, hose, buckles, wigs, and hats were all made in Virginia. Even more impressive, William Nelson decreased his imports by about 50 percent in 1770. [7]

Initially the nonimportation measures gained wide support— so much so that a Norfolk merchant, James Parker, later in the loyalist camp, suggested a connection between the large debts of Virginians and their hostility to British measures. He charged that only seven of the original signers of the Association of 1769 could obtain "credit for One Shilling . . . in England," an assertion that was false as it applied to Thomas Nelson and most of the other signers. Parker went on to assert that those who were "most in debit and have no credit at all are the warmer patriots."

According to this view Virginians were moving towards independence from England in the hope of gaining debt repudiation. The facts do not support Parker's theory. Virginians were striving in 1769–70 for legislative independence in the field of internal taxation, not for separation from England.[8]

But despite the early enthusiasm, the Virginia Association was not generally effective. The defection of the northern colonies, led by New York, where William Nelson said "the Dutch Blood, thirsting for present Gain seems to still flow in their Veins . . . ," had its effect on Virginia. Merchant John Norton wrote in the spring of 1770 that the invoices of Virginians were increasing rather than decreasing, which caused the elder Nelson to say that he wished "such People were of any other Country than mine." Both Thomas and his father continued to adhere to the rules, but by 1770 William found the "spirit of association to be cooling every day" and was convinced that it would "soon die away and come to noght." He wrote this when he became the temporary head of the Virginia government after the death of Lord Botetourt in the fall of 1770. The prediction proved true. On July 18, 1771, a brief notice in the *Virginia Gazette* announced the demise of the Association.[9]

The next two years, although relatively quiet for Virginia, were unsettling for Thomas. The death of his father in November 1772 brought to him, as the eldest son, heavy responsibility for many family and business problems. It also raised the possibility of his filling his father's seat on the Council of State. Nelson was continuing to play a prominent role in the House of Burgesses but there was apparently no question in his mind but that he should continue in his father's footsteps on the Council. Nor was there any inconsistency between his desire to be appointed to the Council and his commitment to the patriot cause. The Council, contrary to stereotypes, was not a Tory body; it contained many staunch Whigs.[10]

Appointment to the Council, however, did require the cooperation of Virginia's new governor, John Murray, earl of Dunmore. Dunmore was to prove himself an arrogant and thoroughly unpleasant man, but Nelson was not aware of this as he began to seek the position in the fall of 1772. He asked many of the merchants with whom his father had done business to use their influence. The earl of Stamford, the duke of Beaufort, and Edward Montague, agent of the colony, added their weight in Nelson's favor, but to no avail. The governor favored John Page, Jr., and as John Norton wrote, "Ld. Dunmore's Recommendation exceeds any Interest that can be made. . . ." Dunmore professed to have no objection to Nelson, but "as he is the Elder Son of our late worthy President and Just deceased, I apprehend it contrary to the policy of government to let the Son Succeed immediately to the father in those appointments." [11]

Page received the appointment in the spring of 1773. Many evidently thought that the best man had been passed over, for as Robert Carter Nicholas remarked, "his [Nelson's] pretensions are superior, all things consider'd, to those of any other." In fact, Nicholas continued, "I believe he has as good a Heart as any Man living; his morals are sound, his Conduct steady, uniform and Exemplary; and in point of Fortune, which necessarily gives a Man an Independency of Spirit, he is inferior to very few." [12]

Lord Dunmore's position on Thomas Nelson's candidacy for the Council appointment did not appear unreasonable to most people. In fact the governor had given the citizenry no real reason for concern, and they were pleased by his avowed intention to make a home in Virginia. But in the spring of 1773 things began to turn sour. In March he called the Assembly into special session to deal with the problem of counterfeit currency. After legislation on that matter had been passed Dunmore prorogued the Assembly, announcing that the business for which it had been called was finished. [13]

More probably the prorogation stemmed from the governor's extreme irritation at the burgesses. The legislators had criticized him for having the counterfeiters tried outside the county in which they were apprehended, and had established a Committee of Correspondence to keep in touch with other colonies about any attempts by the mother country to deprive them of their "ancient, legal, and constitutional right." More than a year passed before the governor again called the legislature together. [14]

When the Virginia Assembly finally did meet on May 5, 1774, the ties that bound Britain and the colonies together had again been subjected to great stress. By this time the Boston Tea Party had occurred. Parliament had responded by closing the Port of

Boston; limiting town meetings; and altering the government of Massachusetts by making General Gage, already commander in chief of the British army in America, also governor of that colony with authority to use troops to compel obedience.

The Virginia Assembly had been in session nearly two weeks when news of Parliament's action reached it. Several days later Robert Carter Nicholas rose in the House of Burgesses and stated that the House was "deeply impressed with apprehension of the great dangers, to be derived to british *America* from the hostile Invasion of the City of *Boston*. . . ." Since Boston harbor was to be closed to all commerce on June 1, he moved that this date be set aside by the members of the House as "a day of Fasting, Humiliation, and Prayer. . . ." Two days after the House adopted the resolution, Dunmore called the burgesses to the Council chamber and stated that the resolve of the House reflected "highly upon his Majesty and the Parliament of Great Britain; which makes it necessary for me to dissolve you. . . ." [15]

On May 27, 1774, some of the burgesses, not to be squelched by the governor, convened at the Raleigh Tavern as they had in 1769. There, in the Apollo Room, Thomas Nelson and eighty-eight colleagues signed another association protesting the Boston Port Bill and calling on the Committees of Correspondence in the various colonies to consider appointing delegates to a Continental Congress. The other signers included Peyton Randolph, Robert Carter Nicholas, Thomas Jefferson, Patrick Henry, George Washington, Archibald Cary, and Benjamin Harrison. [16]

Several days later Peyton Randolph met with Nelson and other burgesses to consider dispatches the local Committee of Correspondence had received, nearly all of which recommended that exportation to and importation from Great Britain be stopped. Of the twenty-five members who attended the meeting, most favored nonimportation and some nonexportation as well; but they concluded that they were too few to speak for the whole colony. Instead they requested the members of the dissolved House of Burgesses to convene in Williamsburg on August 1 to chart Virginia's course. On May 31 they sent a circular letter to all members asking their attendance and urging them to sample opinion of the counties they represented. [17]

Nelson evidently did not remain in Williamsburg for the

prayer service at Bruton Parish Church. But he certainly attended such a service in Yorkhampton Parish, and perhaps he heard his rector, as churchgoers in Richmond County heard theirs, "pathetically exhort the people . . . to support their liberties. . . ."[18]

Like other burgesses, Nelson and Dudley Digges called the freeholders of York County together to formulate a course of action against British oppression. At the Yorktown meeting on Monday, July 18, Nelson was chosen moderator and opened with a heated address, the only one for these years of which a record has survived. The British Parliament, he said, had attacked "what is dearer to Americans than their Lives, their Liberties"; what had taken place in New England was only a prelude "to the designs of Parliament upon every other Part of this wide-extended continent."[19]

"You all know what it is to be *Freemen;* you know the blessed Privilege of doing what you will with your own, and you can guess at the misery of those who are deprived of this Right," he argued. "Which of these will be your case depends upon your present Conduct." Since "Petitions and Remonstrances" had no effect on Parliament, it was time to try "other Expedients," which would make the British "feel the Effects of their mistaken . . . and arbitrary Policy." Nelson felt that it was absolutely necessary that all imports from England be stopped. As for exports, he was doubtful if it was consistent "with Justice, as a People in Debt," to stop them. Stopping of imports would of course mean great inconvenience, but what was inconvenience when opposed to a loss of freedom? Nelson admitted that they must "resign the Hope of Making Fortunes," but, after all, why should fortunes be made "when they may be taken from us at the Pleasure of others?"[20]

Obviously aroused by this address, the York freeholders agreed to send Nelson and Digges to the convention in Williamsburg, instructing them "to exert their utmost Abilities to put a Stop to that growing System of ministerial Despotism which has so long threatened the Destruction of America." They were directed specifically, in instructions very likely drafted by Nelson himself, to elect representatives of Virginia to meet in a "general congress of America" to draw up a "Declaration of American Rights."[21]

The "Sentiments of the People of this County" were that the colonies should remain "in due Subjection to the Crown" but should at the same time have all the rights of the people of England. Taxation without consent was illegal. The king should "restrain the different states of his extensive dominions" from enacting laws which "destroy the Freedom and prejudice Interests of one another." And though the king "in his Parliament" had the right to regulate trade, "all the British Colonies" should "enjoy free Trade with each other and no . . . Tax, Duty, or Imposition whatsoever" could be rightfully "laid by the British Parliament on any Article which the American Colonies are obliged to import from Great Britain only." The tax on tea was of course illegal, the Boston Port Bill "oppressive and unconstitutional," and the "murdering Bill," which allowed Americans to be sent to England for trial, "shocking to human nature." [22]

The York freeholders recommended nonimportation as the best means of bringing this invasion of American rights to an end. "Industry and Frugality" were urged "in their largest extent," and "Horse racing and every other form of expensive Amusement" must "be laid aside as unsuitable to the Situation of the Country, and unbecoming Men who feel for its Distresses." Finally, they agreed to a subscription for the relief of the inhabitants of Boston. [23]

Meetings such as Yorktown's were held throughout Virginia. Merchants' representative William Carr predicted early in June that when the dissolved burgesses had returned to their localities they would find the attitudes of their constituents to be far ahead of the "mild and modest" resolves of late May. Though sentiment in Williamsburg was "pacific," he argued, it was not so in the "adjoining and Frontier Counties," whose representatives were sure to return to the capital on August 1 in a "more violent" mood. [24]

Carr's prediction was right, for Virginians were more aroused than they had been at any time since the Stamp Act. He reported that two-thirds of the public favored strong measures; and though it was charged that "honest 6 hogshead planters Downward know little or nothing of this accursed dispute," all the evidence points to great unanimity. Feelings ran high in May and June, and every subsequent month seemed to bring a stronger, more unified, position. James Parker, who was critical of the protest movement, confessed that "the whole colony" was "against taxes without consent." And merchants' representative Harry Piper, who was a more impartial observer, warned that "if things are carried to an extreme [it] probably may end in the Ruin of both Great-Britain and the Colonys for I believe that the Americans will undergo many hardships before they will part with their liberty. . . ." [25]

In seeking a solution to their problems, Virginians looked back to the Stamp Act crisis and the methods effective then in gaining repeal. Would not the same methods work again? Long before any common action had been agreed upon, counties and individuals were applying time-proven pressures. For example, Dunmore's dissolution of the Assembly in May had prevented a renewal of the law fixing court fees, and colonists used this as an excuse to stop the proceedings of the courts in civil cases. In 1765 the closure of the courts had proved an effective weapon in getting British creditors to press Parliament for the repeal of the Stamp Act, and in 1774 it was aimed at these same people again. In June and July, before the meeting in Williamsburg, many county courts were refusing to do business. Nonimportation was also a tried and true method and many planters were independently applying it before August 1. Even a conservative like John Tayloe of Mount Airy in Richmond County ordered one of his correspondents to send no goods until the "Boston Port Act be repealed and all duty or tax Bills be wholly laid aside for altho I do not sign Associations I heartily concur in such measures as I think conducive to the preservation of my Country in Liberty. . . ." [26]

There was some difference of opinion among Virginians during this summer of 1774 as to how far they should go. According to James Parker, who seemed to know everything, George Mason, Patrick Henry, Richard Henry Lee, and Robert Carter Nicholas were in favor of closing the courts, nonpayment of debts, and "no exportation or importation," while Thomas Nelson, Paul Carrington, Carter Braxton, Edmund Pendleton, and Peyton Randolph would not go so far as to stop debt payment and exports. The debates on the issue were "violent." In his speech to the York freeholders, Thomas Nelson expressed doubt, as noted above, that it was consistent with justice for a "People in Debt" to stop exports. George Washington felt the same way and urged that nonpayment of debts be resorted to only in the "last extremity," for while accusing others of "injustice, we should be just ourselves." [27]

The assumption underlying such a position was that Virginia's quarrel was not with the British mercantile community. Virginians on a "variety of occasions" had made "many plausible Promises of immediate and future Consignments" of tobacco to British merchants "in order to procure the Use of Their Money," and British merchants had often responded with a generous extension of credit. As a result they were heavily involved in Virginia, and sudden application of a nonexportation policy, even though only temporary, might ruin them. [28]

Those who favored nonexportation replied that the seriousness of the crisis required every available pressure. Landon Carter, a vigorous exponent of this position, argued that in not protesting the "Arbitrary proceedings of their Parliament" the people of Great Britain, including the merchants, "had consented to a Manifest Violation of our whole Constitution." For that reason Virginians were justified in having "as little commerce with them as Possible; and farther to refuse to do them the service to determine their suits for their debts. . . ." He reminded his Richmond County neighbors that their fellow subjects in Boston were suffering, and he charged that those who would not resort to nonexportation, because they wanted to pay their debts, were but "half patriots." Such a position was "treachery, and Hypocrisy to America. . . ." The men on both sides of the issue were all patriots, and the question was not debt repudiation but whether or not temporary nonpayment was a proper device to use in bringing Britain into line. [29]

The question was resolved when the delegates from Virginia's counties met. The Virginia Convention began its deliberations on August 1 in Williamsburg with a fuller attendance than George Washington had ever seen at a session of the House of Burgesses. The oppressive August heat did not deter the aroused delegates, who completed the business of the convention in six days. They formed an association to bar the importation of "Goods, Wares, or Merchandise" from England after November

1 and forbid the purchase of imported slaves after that date. On the touchy question of nonexportation, they reached a compromise. If American grievances were not redressed by August 10, 1775, they would allow no further exports to England; thus those who wished to pay their debts had a year to do so.[30]

The convention also elected Virginia's delegates to the Continental Congress to be held in Philadelphia in September, choosing Peyton Randolph, speaker of the House and moderator of the Convention, as its first selection. The distinguished delegation also included Richard Henry Lee, George Washington, Patrick Henry, Richard Bland, Benjamin Harrison and Edmund Pendleton. Nelson and Jefferson missed being elected by twelve votes, each with fifty-one votes to Pendleton's sixty-two. Lord Dunmore later said that Nelson was not elected because his speech to the York freeholders was "too violent." Even if true, the votes indicate how high he stood among the most able of Virginia's patriot leadership.[31]

On August 7, the day after the convention adjourned, Nelson, still full of the arguments of the meeting, began to write his mercantile correspondents urging them to use their efforts to gain repeal of the oppressive acts. Americans "are not a conquered People" he told Samuel Athawes. We "cannot, we will not suffer our property to be taken without our consent" for "(setting aside natural rights) we have this right confirmed to us by Charter, which, tho I would not put . . . in competition with the former, Yet is of too sacred a Nature to be broken. . . ."[32]

To merchants Thomas and Rowland Hunt he listed the British acts that he and the majority of the convention members considered most reprehensible. First came the Boston Port Bill, "by which 15,000 People are punished for the Violence of a few"; second, the "Murder Act," which would deprive Americans of trial in the colonies; third, the virtual abrogation of the charter of Massachusetts by the Massachusetts Government Act; and fourth, the Quebec Act, which, among other things, he felt made the Roman Catholic church pre-eminent in Canada. "Was there ever such a thing done by a Protestant Parliament before?" Nelson asked. He did not mention the threat this act posed to Virginia's Ohio Company by extending Quebec's borders into land that Virginia claimed. In any case only the Quebec Act and the

"Murder Act" immediately affected the Old Dominion, and Virginia's concern indicates a real depth of intercolonial feeling and unity.[33]

The efforts of York County to give aid to distressed Boston underscored the feeling of colonial solidarity. Soon after Nelson's return from the Convention the inhabitants of York County subscribed 403 bushels of wheat, 115 bushels of corn, 2 barrels of flour, and £11 5s. to be sent to Boston. Of this amount Nelson personally gave 100 bushels of wheat as well as 20 bushels of corn, and he obtained pledges for an additional 118 bushels of wheat.[34]

Meanwhile Lord Dunmore had issued writs for the election of a new Assembly to meet on August 7. But when he found that the people had re-elected substantially the same burgesses as before, he declined to face a body that would not be led—except in the direction they wanted to go. Consequently he prorogued them before they met, and did not allow the Assembly to meet until June, 1775.[35]

Early in the fall Nelson again sought a seat on the Council. John Page, chosen over Nelson for the previous vacancy, had died of a "bilious complaint" on September 30. A week later Nelson wrote the earl of Stamford and his merchant friends, John Norton and Samuel Athawes, asking their aid. To Athawes he remarked, "If I do not succeed I will give it over and confine myself to my Farm, where I find a vast deal of happiness, perhaps more than I shall in a more exalted Station: however I have a little ambition at this time So you will do what you can for me." [36]

But Nelson's extremist views were already widely known, and the efforts of Thomas and his friends came to naught. One critic of the patriot cause opposed the appointment of "Young Tom Nelson" for "he is as Violent as any [Modern?] Patriot of them all." Lord Dunmore agreed, and in December he struck Nelson from the list of those suitable to fill Council vacancies.[37]

Nelson was too busy to fret over his failure. As an active patriot, public business increasingly demanded his attention. To the northward in Philadelphia the Continental Congress formed an association modeled after Virginia's, providing for immediate nonimportation and nonconsumption of British products—with nonexportation to go into effect the following September. These regulations were to apply to all the colonies (except Georgia, which sent no delegates) and were to be enforced by committees elected in every county, town, and city. In York County, Nelson was elected chairman of the local committee.[38]

Early in November his committee learned that merchant John Norton's ship *Virginia,* which was anchored at Yorktown, had on board two half-chests of tea consigned to Robert Prentis and Company in Williamsburg. Norton should have known better. He had once lived in Virginia, and had even served in the House of Burgesses; his son, John Hatley Norton, had married a Virginia girl and now represented the firm there. The captain of his vessel, Howard Esten, reportedly had begged Norton "to desist from sending the Tea by him. . . ." Norton's action predictably provoked the local patriots, because the Tea Act was viewed "as the detested means" by which the government hoped "to establish a president [*sic*] which would be likely . . . to subjugate the whole Continent." With Thomas Nelson in the chair, the York committee, after discarding a plan to burn the *Virginia,* decided to destroy the tea and send the vessel home without allowing it to take on its expected cargo of tobacco. On November 7 the committee boarded the *Virginia,* and Nelson personally threw the tea, shipped by his friend John Norton, into the York River.[39]

Virginia's other county committees were just as zealous. "The People," wrote William Carr, "are so determined to oppose" the Tea and Coercive acts "that I am persuaded they will go naked rather than have any commerce or connection with Great Britain. . . . I never expected to see such a spirit of opposition as now prevails amongst all sorts of People indeed it appears to me they are ready for Battle. . . ." Writing from Yorktown, William Reynolds stated that the "Common people in this County and I believe all through the Colony are so much inflamed that they publickly declare they will sacrifice their lives, rather than submit to Tyrannical oppression of a Corrupt Minister." In Williamsburg feelings ran so high in November that a bag of feathers was suspended over a tar barrel on Duke of Gloucester Street and objectionable merchants were dragged before it to repudiate their alleged crimes against the people. Militia were reported to be drilling, and Carr wrote London merchant James Russell, "for god sake do not send any kind of goods on any of your ships unless it is Powder, lead or Guns. . . ." These items, he said, "will be winked at."[40]

Despite such ominous warnings there was still hope in the winter of 1774–75 that the differences between Britain and her colonies would be amicably settled. Virginians assumed that the British mercantile community would respond as they had in the past in getting Parliament to repeal the objectionable measures. The merchants understood clearly what was expected of them. James Russell wrote Thomas Jones of Hanover County that when the resolves of the Continental Congress arrived in London he would "endeavor to get a petition presented to the new Parliament praying a redress of the hardships America suffers by the late Acts, I hope to get many of the most eminent Merchts here to join in that Petition it will give me real pleasure to do everything in my power to promote the interest of the colonies." During the winter and spring, London merchant William Lee constantly urged friends in Virginia to stand firm. He warned that it might take two years for things to be settled, for the government was "rotten," the whole administration "are your inveterate enemies," and "nothing but necessity will induce them to change the present iniquitous system in less than 12 mos. after American trade is completely stopd." Lee also worked vigorously to unify British merchants and manufacturers behind the American cause.[41]

The merchants of London met on January 4, but Lee found that though they planned to petition Parliament they were not yet overly concerned and were moving slowly. After the petitions were presented Lee found that they were having little effect because "the Ministry knew well enough" that "the Merchts except for 2 or 3 of us were not at all serious." It was also rumored that the Glasgow merchants had sent a strong petition, but had told Lord North, through their member of Parliament, D. F. Campbell, "that they did not mean any opposition, but that they wanted to gain credit in America and thereby more easily collect their debts."[42]

That stance by the merchants encouraged the British administration to continue its course, as did the advice from some of the royal governors. Dunmore told the secretary of state that the "middling and poorer sort" who "live from hand to mouth" had been "duped by the richer Sort" into supporting the Association. He estimated that the rich could exist satisfactorily for two or three years without exporting or importing, but that the poorer people could not. "What then," he queried, "is to deter" the lower classes "from taking the Shortest mode of Supplying themselves and unrestrained as they are by laws from taking whatever they want from wherever they can find it?" Although Dunmore completely misunderstood the nature of the patriot movement in Virginia and the extent of its popular support, the North ministry based its position on such advice.[43]

Delay by the British ministry did not deter colonial action. The Continental Congress of 1774 resolved that if Parliament had made no effort to redress American grievances by May of 1775, a new congress would be held in Philadelphia. For this reason, another convention was scheduled in Virginia early in 1775, primarily to elect delegates to the congress. It would also consider what was to be done about the worsening relationship between the colonies and the mother country. The meeting was to be held on March 20 in Richmond, safely away from Dunmore and turbulent Williamsburg.[44]

Late in February Thomas Nelson and Dudley Digges were unanimously elected to represent York County, and they, with other restive representatives, assembled on Tuesday, March 21, in St. John's Church, the only building in Richmond large enough to accommodate the crowd. Tuesday and Wednesday were spent reading and agreeing to the proceedings of the first Continental Congress, but on Thursday the fireworks began when the delegates considered a memorial that the General Assembly of Jamaica had sent to the king suggesting that the colonies make a pledge of nonresistance. The delegates were in no mood to support so meek a position. They drafted a polite but noncommital reply to Jamaica that closed with a pious hope for "a speedy return of those halcyon days, when we lived a free and happy people."[45]

Obviously irritated by the mildness of the reply, Patrick Henry quickly gained the floor. In a series of resolves designed to put the colony on record as favoring strong measures against the mother country, he asked that a committee be appointed "to prepare a plan for embodying, arming, and disciplining such a number of men," as might be sufficient to put the colony into a state of defense. Such moderates as Richard Bland, Benjamin Harrison, Edmund Pendleton, and Robert Carter Nicholas opposed precipitate action. But Nelson supported Henry's motion in the warmest terms, arguing "that if any British troops should be landed within the County, of which he was lieutenant, he would await for no orders, and would obey none, which should forbid him to summon his militia and repel the invaders at the waters edge." [46]

Jefferson and others came to Henry's aid, but the resolves were not carried until Henry had delivered a violent and decisive speech. Accounts vary as to what he actually said. James Parker reported that Henry "called the K[ing] a Tyrant, a fool, a puppet and a tool to the ministry," and said "he could not have been more completely scurrilous if he had been possessed of John Wilke's Vocabulary." But whether Henry's address was a harangue or an eloquent oration, ending with "give me liberty, or give me death," it did not have the effect commonly attributed to it. Often ignored is the fact that despite Henry's great powers of persuasion the resolves passed by only the slimmest of margins. Virginians were still divided as to what the extent of their actions against British measures should be.[47]

After Henry's vigorous plea the work of the Convention proceeded more quietly. A committee presented plans for revamping the militia. Nelson, Robert Carter Nicholas, and Thomas Whiting constituted a central committee in charge of supplies. Through them every county was to issue each militiaman his supplies. Each county was also to raise a troop of light horse. The Convention then elected delegates for the Second Continental Congress, to be held in May, returning the previous representatives. This time Nelson and Jefferson were passed over by a large margin, receiving only sixteen and eighteen votes respectively. Before adjourning on March 27, however, the Convention appointed Jefferson to serve in the place of Peyton Randolph in case he was not able to attend.[48]

Although the Virginia Convention authorized the raising of a military force, the moderates prevented a complete takeover of the colony's government. Virginians were preparing for the worst, but they still hoped that they would not be forced to take up arms "against a King and People whom we have been taught from our Infancy to respect." So Virginia presented the strange picture of militia drilling, county courts doing virtually no business, and county committees ferreting out and suppressing Tories, while Lord Dunmore remained in Williamsburg as the recognized head of the government.[49]

Well aware of what was taking place in Virginia, Dunmore did all in his power to frustrate any possible effort at seizure of the government. Between three and four o'clock on the morning of April 21 Captain Collins of the armed British schooner *Magdalene* carried out the governor's order to remove the entire powder supply of the colony from Williamsburg and place it on board his vessel anchored at Burwell's Ferry on the James River. When the burgesses immediately demanded that the powder be returned, Dunmore replied that he had heard there was an insurrection in a "neighboring county"; if the powder was not needed there and should be needed in Williamsburg it could be returned quickly.[50]

But this excuse did not lull the people. News of the seizure spread throughout Virginia and rifle companies began to gather. One thousand men poured into Fredericksburg, six hundred of them "good riflemen" attired in hunting shirts with tomahawks in their belts. Charles Yates was convinced that they "would have marched to Boston if desired." Michael Wallace from neighboring King George County estimated that ten thousand men could have been collected, because "all of the frontier Countys were in motion," even as far west as Hampshire and Fincastle. In Hanover County Patrick Henry was also raising an independent company. Several patriot leaders, including Peyton Randolph and George Washington, prevailed upon the Fredericksburg and Albemarle companies to disperse; but Henry, after haranguing his volunteers at Newcastle on May 2, began a march on Williamsburg.[51]

Lord Dunmore, alarmed by the news, sent his wife and children on board an English-bound schooner in the York River, placed cannon in the Palace yard, armed his servants, and asked for a detachment of marines from the man-of-war *Fowey,* anchored at Yorktown. Soon after this action, the *Fowey's* commander, Captain Montague, warned Secretary Nelson, who was president of the Council, that if either the governor or the detachment sent to protect him were molested, he would bombard Yorktown. In threatening to fire on the town, the Secretary replied, Montague "has testified a spirit of cruelty unprecedented in the Annals of civilized times . . . ," particularly since he (the Secretary) had made and was making every effort to protect the governor.[52]

The outbreak of fighting seemed imminent. But when Richard Corbin, the loyalist-minded receiver-general, learned that a party of Henry's men had broken into his house, he decided on a concession to the colonial forces, sending a rider with an offer to pay Henry for the powder. The volatile leader refused to accept Corbin's offer, but Thomas Nelson arranged a settlement that averted trouble. Accompanied by Robert Carter Nicholas he rode out to meet Henry, intercepting him about fifteen miles from Williamsburg, and persuaded him to accept Nelson's note for the powder. Since the source was untainted, Henry accepted the note of a fellow patriot, and thus placated, promised to send the money to the Virginia delegates in Congress for the purchase of more powder. Once this arrangement was accomplished Corbin reimbursed Nelson.[53]

Things had not gone as smoothly in Massachusetts. On April 19, British soldiers had moved from Boston to Concord to take military supplies stored there, and the first shots of the American Revolution had been fired. News of this action reached Virginia before April 29. Despite a feeling that war was not far off, the governor called for a meeting of the Assembly on June 1, and plans were made to go ahead with it. The legislature convened and heard the governor ask for cooperation with the mother country, particularly since Parliament had agreed to levy only regulatory taxes on any colony that would tax itself to provide for the common defense, the civil government, and the judiciary within its own province. The House of Burgesses listened attentively and then proceeded as they pleased, launching an investigation of Dunmore's administration of the colony's affairs and particularly requesting information on the expense incurred by Dunmore's calling up the militia in 1774 for the expedition against hostile Shawnee Indians. They also stated that they did not intend to re-open the courts until Great Britain made it possible for "all things" to be restored to the happy condition that had existed before 1763.[54]

On June 5 a committee, which included Thomas Nelson, Hugh Mercer, Robert Carter Nicholas, and Thomas Jefferson, was appointed to examine the Public Magazine in Williamsburg and report to the House on the stores there. This was a slap at Dunmore, who had made no effort to return the colony's powder. When the committee asked for the key to the Magazine, Dunmore stalled for time: all the members of the committee were known to the governor, but he sent a note to the House stating that "some Persons, I know not whom," had requested the key, and asking if they were the proper representatives of the burgesses. The House replied in the affirmative, and, like the governor, feigned ignorance; the reason for the inspection of the Magazine, they said, was because they understood it had been broken into. On June 7, after further hedging, Dunmore finally ordered that the key be given to them.[55]

The following day the governor fled to the *Fowey,* which was anchored at Yorktown, condemning "the blind and unmeasurable fury" of the patriots but maintaining that he did not intend to interrupt the Assembly. The Assembly tried to get Dunmore to return, promising his safety, but to no avail. Maintaining that Secretary Nelson, the president of the Council, was legally qualified to carry out the governor's duties in his absence, the Assembly completed its business, adjourning on June 24. Thereafter, the president and the Council continued to run the government until the Convention, which had been called to meet in Richmond in July, made different arrangements. Virginia and the other colonies had by now reached the point of no return unless the home government would make some major concessions, which seemed hardly likely.[56]

When the third Virginia Convention convened on July 17, 1775, it considered the possibility that Virginia might be invaded by Lord Dunmore himself and made preparations for any eventuality. On the nineteenth Thomas Nelson, who again represented York County, was appointed to a committee headed by Richard Bland to bring in an ordinance for raising and equipping an armed force to protect the colony. The legislation established three regiments and on August 5 the Convention chose the regimental officers.[57]

Thomas Nelson, Patrick Henry, Hugh Mercer, and William Woodford were nominated for colonel of the 1st Regiment. Of the four, Mercer was the only one with any real military experience, and Nelson supported him, forswearing any votes for himself. On the first ballot Mercer got forty-one votes to Henry's forty, while Nelson and Woodford brought up the rear with eight and one respectively. Henry was not present, being enroute from the Continental Congress, but he had a solid block of followers and on the second ballot was elected. Virginia now found herself in the odd situation of having a man at the head of her first regiment whose only military experience was that of leading the Hanover militia almost to Williamsburg! On succeeding ballots Nelson was elected to lead the second regiment, and William Woodford the third.[58]

Whatever Nelson's qualifications for this position might have been, he was not to have an opportunity to display them. Less than two weeks after receiving his colonelcy, he was elected a delegate to the Continental Congress and resigned his command. Four of Virginia's seven delegates had to be replaced: Washington (who was now serving as commander-in-chief of the Continental Army), Edmund Pendleton, Patrick Henry, and Richard Bland. In the voting, Nelson stood fifth—behind the four incumbents, Jefferson, Richard Henry Lee, Peyton Randolph, and Benjamin Harrison—quite a creditable showing among distinguished company. The other new faces were George Wythe and Francis Lightfoot Lee. On August 14 the Convention gave Nelson leave of absence to get his business affairs in order before he departed for Philadelphia.[59]

Thomas Nelson and many of his countrymen were already on a course that threatened to lead to a full break with Great Britain. Although essentially a moderate man, Nelson felt so strongly about his country's political rights that he was willing to risk a great deal. A compromise of political rights would certainly lead to the loss of the rights of individuals. Yet the course he chose to follow was not an easy one. He felt close to the mother country for many reasons. He had spent eight years of his life there, and he had many friends and several relatives who still lived in England. Furthermore, the patriot cause by no means had the full support of all Americans—even in Virginia, where loyalism was at low ebb.

As chairman of the county Committee of Safety, Nelson saw more clearly than most people that a civil war was also emerging. A portent of this internal struggle occurred in July 1775, when the York committee seized Bernard Carey, a Williamsburg cloth merchant who had advised various people not to take up arms against the mother country. Carey had sold his business and was fleeing the country when he was seized and his money taken from him. Nelson, informed of what had happened, arranged for Carey's release and the return of his money. The division of opinion came even closer home when Nelson's wife's brother, John Randolph Grymes, left Virginia because of his sympathy for the British position. Both Thomas and Lucy Nelson were related to the Randolphs, and they saw that family torn apart when John Randolph, the attorney general, left Virginia with Dunmore, while his son, Edmund, remained a firm patriot.[60]

It was disturbing for Thomas Nelson, "an easy good natured indolent man" to find himself in the vortex of approaching revolution and civil war. A decade earlier he could hardly have forseen that the son of William Nelson, leading member of the Council, nephew of the secretary of the colony, would have thrown tea into Yorktown harbor or been branded as too violent by Governor Dunmore. Yet, had he looked back, it must also have seemed that he had no other choice. He had the Whig view of history and politics. The loss of natural and constitutional rights meant slavery. He accepted a role of leadership as a matter of course. His personal fortune might suffer. But, as he had told the York County freeholders in 1774, they must "resign the Hope of making Fortunes," for why should fortunes be made "when they may be taken from us at the Pleasure of others?" Thus had the planter become the rebel.[61]

Chapter IV

Member of the Continental Congress

Independence was certainly on Thomas Nelson's mind as he prepared to depart for Philadelphia in late August of 1775. A year before he had told Samuel Athawes that Virginians did "not wish . . . to throw off . . . [their] dependency. . . ."[1] Much had happened since then. He had dumped John Norton's tea into the York River. He had warmly supported Henry's motion to put the colony into a defensible state, and he headed a committee charged with properly equipping Virginia's militia. Most recently he had been one of the authors of an ordinance that provided for the creation of three regiments, and of the second of these he had been elected commander. Lord Dunmore had fled Williamsburg and Parliament had made no move to redress grievances.

As Thomas Nelson, Peyton Randolph, and George Wythe traveled north together to the Quaker city they certainly discussed their feelings concerning the relationship with Great Britain. The three men were of similar mind and, if they had not already decided, they were close to taking a position that independence was the only solution.

The trip of the three delegates and their wives could not have been a light-hearted one and it certainly was not easy. The Randolphs traveled in the Nelsons' carriage, and the Wythes joined them in their own equipage as they followed the rutted road through Bowling Green to Fredericksburg and Alexandria, where they crossed the Potomac. On the Maryland side Nelson's carriage broke down, and he borrowed another vehicle from a local resident. They had not proceeded far when, as the *Virginia*

Gazette phrased it, "through the unskillfulness of the driver . . . [the carriage] run against a tree, and was entirely demolished." [2]

At this point the Randolphs deserted the Nelsons and completed their journey probably with the Wythes. How Thomas and Lucy Nelson finished the trip is not known, but by September 13 they were in Philadelphia and had taken lodgings in the house of Benjamin Randolph on Chestnut Street. Jefferson, Wythe, and Randolph were also lodged there, though, unlike the others, Jefferson did not have his wife with him. Peyton Randolph was not to be with them long, for late in October he died of apoplexy. [3]

One of the first things Nelson did on his arrival in Philadelphia was to have Lucy and the servants who accompanied them inoculated against smallpox. Evidently Nelson had already been inoculated, but his fellow delegates, George Wythe and Francis Lightfoot Lee, had not, and they, their wives, and their servants, also underwent the ordeal. Dr. William Shippen, Jr., who had previously inoculated Jefferson, probably performed this service for the Virginians. [4]

The Philadelphia in which the Nelsons found themselves was the most populous city in America and the fourth largest in the British empire. Sitting close to the Delaware River it was a busy, noisy place, and its population of more than thirty thousand inhabitants was a varied lot, ethnically and religiously. Lucy Nelson, who had never heard a dissenting minister, attended both Presbyterian and Catholic churches with Mrs. Shippen. She remained in Philadelphia through the fall, returning to Virginia some time before Christmas and joining the children at Nelson's Hanover County estate, safe from the danger that would occur if Lord Dunmore attacked Williamsburg or Yorktown. [5]

While Mrs. Nelson was enjoying her first taste of big city life, her husband entered actively into the affairs of the Continental Congress. The day after the credentials of the Virginia delegates were accepted on September 13, Thomas Nelson was being heard on the floor. He made a favorable impression. Even crotchety John Adams, who described him as a fat man, conceded that he was "a speaker, and alert and lively for his weight." Before long Nelson was to become an important and effective member of this the cream of the patriot leadership. This was no mean feat in a body where, as Adams said, "private Friendships and Enmities . . . provincial Views and Prejudices" made it difficult to move anything. Actually Nelson's reputation did not arise from any conspicuous part that he took in the debates of Congress but instead from his diligent committee work and "his sound judgment and liberal sentiments." [6]

Finance was considered Nelson's forte, and soon after his arrival he was appointed to a committee to settle and pay expenses presented to the Congress by various states for the training and equipping of rifle companies. Although an improvement over the previous arrangement, whereby all financial business had been handled by two treasurers who were not members of Congress, the new plan proved inadequate. On September 25 a Committee of Accounts and Claims was appointed, composed of one member from each state, to whom all accounts against the Congress were to be referred. Thomas Nelson represented Virginia so capably on this committee that later in the fall he was appointed to head a committee of three to examine the funds that remained in the treasury and to form an estimate of the public debts that were already incurred and would fall due the next year. Finally, the following February Nelson was appointed to a standing committee of five which was to have general supervision of the treasury and all matters of finance. [7]

For Nelson and his colleagues the business of overseeing government finances was a frustrating experience. The fiscal operations of Congress were of crucial importance to the success of the American cause, but the maintenance of a sound program was virtually impossible because Congress had no authority over the activities of the various states. To meet the expenses of the war, Congress, beginning in June 1775, had resorted to paper money. By December, when Nelson's committee made its report, some $6,000,000 had been emitted. The committee recommended that no more paper money be issued and that necessary funds be borrowed on interest-bearing treasury notes. Although Congress did not act on the committee's proposal, it did ultimately try raising money through the sale of government bonds. But this and other devices proved to be no substitute for paper, and before the end of 1776 $25,000,000 was in circulation. With Congress having

no reliable source of income the inevitable result was depreciation.[8]

Meanwhile Congress hesitated to make the final break with
the mother country. Many Americans still hoped that a satisfactory solution could be worked out, and even when George III
had refused the Olive Branch Petition of the previous summer and
had proclaimed the colonies to be in open rebellion, Congress
continued to hesitate. There was a good deal of opposition to
a break, especially from New York, Pennsylvania, and Maryland. But events were pushing the colonies in the direction of
independence whether all of them liked it or not. In Virginia
the militia commanded by William Woodford defeated a British
force under Dunmore at Great Bridge, forcing the noble lord to
abandon Norfolk; in Canada the combined American forces
under Benedict Arnold and Richard Montgomery were repulsed
before Quebec on December 31. These occurrences, coupled
with a royal proclamation of December 23 closing the colonies to
all commerce as of March 1, 1776, made the breach between
England and the colonies almost irreparable.

An early advocate of independence, Nelson thought that in-
decision by Congress was absurd. "I wish I knew the sentiments
of our people [concerning] independence," he wrote John Page
in January 1776, "for we cannot expect to form a connexion with
any foreign power, as long as we have a womanish hankering
after Great Britain. . . ." In another letter to Page early in February he gave full vent to his feelings:

> Independence, Confederation & foreign alliance are as
> formidable to some of Congress, I fear a majority, as an
> Apparition to a weak enervated Woman. These subjects
> have been but gently touch'd upon. Would you think that
> we had some among us, who still expect honorable pro-
> posals from the administration. By Heavens I am an infidel
> in politicks, for I do not believe were you to bid a thousand
> pounds per scruple for Honor at the Court of Britain that
> you would get as many as would amount to an ounce. If
> Terms should be proposed they will savour so much of
> despotism, that America cannot accept them.
>
> We are now carrying on a War & no War, they seize
> property wherever they find it either by Land or Sea & we
> hesitate to retaliate because we have a few friends in Eng-

Yorktown as seen from Gloucester Point in 1754. This sketch by a British naval officer shows that the Nelson house—two chimneys, directly above the sloop to left of center—was one of the most prominent structures in town. Reproduced by permission of the Mariners Museum, Newport News, Virginia.

The Nelson House in Yorktown in the late nineteenth century.
This picture, from a stereopticon view, was probably made by
the Richmond photographer Huestis Cooke. The National Park
Service is presently (1974) restoring the house to its original
appearance.

land who have ships. Away with such squeamishness say I,
but I cannot do as I would wish.[9]

Nelson's course was set: the American colonies must declare
their independence. By February he had become anxious to return home to test Virginia's political temper. He, of course,
wanted to see his family and give much needed attention to business affairs, but it was crucial that the Old Dominion cast her
vote for a complete break with Great Britain. He wrote Jefferson
rejoicing in the arrival of a ship bearing saltpeter, powder, and
arms, sent him "2 shillings worth of Common Sense," and indicated his intention to leave, after the arrival of Carter Braxton,
for a few weeks. On February 23 Nelson left Philadelphia for
Virginia.[10]

By the time he arrived in Virginia in March there was an air
of expectancy because of the pending Convention, which was to
meet in Williamsburg in early May. Independence was in the
minds of the people, and the *Virginia Gazette* expressed the sentiments of many when, soon after his arrival, it stated that "If we
cannot enjoy the privileges of Englishmen when connected with
them, let us instantly break off those fetters of affection which
have hither to bound us to them. . . ." These were Nelson's sentiments, and despite his membership in Congress, he was chosen
as one of the delegates to represent York County. Realizing that
he would not be able to be present for the entire meeting, the
freeholders of the county elected three delegates rather than two.
Nelson's old compatriot Dudley Digges was one of the representatives and his relative, William Digges, the other.[11]

On May 6, 1776, sleepy little Williamsburg again hummed
with activity. Delegates from the length and breadth of Virginia,
128 of them, poured into the capital city, covered with the red
and gray mud of the Piedmont and the Tidewater, for torrential
rains had hit the colony after a long period of drouth. Many
were accompanied by family and friends, while tradesmen,
farmers, and people who were just curious added to the throngs.
The presence of a detachment of Continental soldiers commanded
by Major General Charles Lee—a most vocal advocate of independence—underscored the seriousness of the times. Probably
few of those present were aware that the oldest representative
body in America was breathing its last on that day. The journal

of the House of Burgesses recorded the fact: "Several members met, but did neither proceed to Business, nor adjourn, as a House of Burgesses." The air was now cleared for the events to follow.[12]

The Convention elected Edmund Pendleton as president, and in the organization of that body Nelson was appointed to the important Committee on Privileges and Elections. It was scarcely necessary for Jefferson to urge his friend Nelson to strive "to bring on as early as you can in the Convention the great questions of the session"; the question in nearly everybody's mind was, What about independence? [13]

Nelson did his utmost to persuade his colleagues that a declaration of independence was imperative. He wrote an unidentified delegate, with whom he had discussed the matter earlier, that "having weighed the arguments on both sides, I am clearly of the opinion that we must, as we value the liberties of America, or even her existence, without a moments delay, declare independence." If his reasons appeared weak "you will excuse them for the disinterestedness of the author, as I may venture to affirm that no man on the continent will sacrifice more than myself by separation." [14]

There was no need, he continued, to first determine the opinions of France and Spain. France would benefit from an American declaration of independence, and the fear that she might be diverted from supporting the colonies by an English offer of additional territory was "chimerical" and contrary to the settled policy of the court of Louis XVI. Furthermore, delay would be ruinous, for the "military in particular, men and officers, are outrageous on the subject" and would abandon the colors if independence were not declared. To cap his argument Nelson assured his correspondent "that the spirit of the people (except a very few in these lower parts, whose little blood has been sucked out by mosquitoes), cry out for this declaration." A "man of your excellent discernment," Nelson added, "need not be told how dangerous it would be in our present circumstances to dally with the spirit or disappoint the expectations of the bulk of the people." [15]

Nelson knew what must be done but Patrick Henry, Virginia's "heaven sent" orator and expected leader of the movement for independence, was strangely hesitant on the subject. Ignorant of

European affairs, he feared the very thing that Nelson said was visionary—that is that England would call on some European ally with the promise of a part of the colonies as a reward for helping to subdue them. Consequently he felt that an American alliance with some foreign power, preferably France or Spain, was first necessary. But Henry was no political novice, and when it became evident that he would lose much of his support unless he led the movement, he took the initiative, allies or no allies. Singling out Nelson, who was squarely behind the independence movement and had been for months, he perfected a plan whereby Nelson would make the motion for independence and Henry would support it. The impetus probably came from Henry, but Nelson certainly needed no encouragement.[16]

On May 14 Nelson presented his resolution "That our delegates in Congress be enjoined in the strongest and most positive manner to exert their ability in procuring an immediate, clear and full Declaration of Independency,"[17] and Henry defended it. Nelson's speech was straightforward and heartfelt; Edmund Randolph describes it well:

> Nelson affected nothing of oratory, except what ardent feelings might inspire, and characteristic of himself, he had no fears of his own which to temporize, and supposing that others ought to have none, he passed over the probabilities of foreign aid, stepped lightly on the difficulties of procuring military stores and the inexperience of officers and soldiers, but pressed a declaration of independence upon what, with him, were incontrovertible grounds; that we were oppressed; had humbly supplicated a redress of grievances, which had been refused with insult; and to return from battle against the sovereign with the cordiality of subjects was absurd.[18]

At least two other motions had been presented to the Convention concerning what course Virginia should take on the matter. One, by Meriwether "Fiddlehead" Smith, made no mention of independence and simply moved that Virginia prepare a declaration of rights and set up a new government. The other, evidently drafted by Edmund Pendleton, recommended that Virginia completely separate herself from England. The final resolutions, unanimously agreed to on May 15, directed that the Virginia delegates to Congress "propose to that respectable body to declare the United Colonies free and independent states, absolved from all allegiance to, or dependence upon, the crown or parliament of Great Britain. . . ." This was, of course, substantially what the Henry-Nelson motion had proposed.[19]

Williamsburg greeted the news of the resolutions jubilantly, and on May 16 troops were reviewed, guns fired, toasts drunk, and refreshments served, the evening concluding "with illuminations, and other demonstrations of joy. . . ." Thomas Nelson probably missed this celebration, for no later than the seventeenth he left for Philadelphia, with the Virginia resolutions in his custody, to resume his seat in Congress. The resolutions were safely delivered, and on June 7, speaking for the Virginia delegation to the Continental Congress, Richard Henry Lee moved that the "United Colonies" declare themselves independent from Great Britain. In accordance with the Nelson-Henry resolves, he also recommended that measures be taken for forming foreign alliances and a plan of confederation.[20]

The Committee of the Whole discussed Virginia's motion the following day and again on Monday, June 10, when it was decided to postpone final consideration until July 1; the middle colonies and South Carolina were not quite ready for the final break, but in three weeks it seemed likely that they would be. To save time, however, a committee, which included Jefferson, Franklin, and John Adams, was appointed to draw up a declaration of independence. Two days later, on June 12, Nelson took his place on another committee, composed of one member from each colony, appointed to prepare a plan of confederation. Here he served with Samuel Adams of Massachusetts, Roger Sherman of Connecticut, Robert Livingston of New York, John Dickinson of Pennsylvania, and Edward Rutledge of South Carolina, among others.[21]

While the recommendations of the Virginia delegation were being acted on in Philadelphia, work began in Virginia on a declaration of rights and a constitution. By June 29 both of these documents, which were to have great influence on the future development of the United States, had been completed and approved. The proposed constitution was brief and to the point. Despite colonial allegiance to the principle of separation of powers, it lodged most of the power in the House of Delegates, the lower elective body of the Assembly, whereas it restricted the influence of the Senate and the governor. All legislation had to originate in the lower house. The governor, who was to be elected annually by a joint ballot of the two houses, could not veto legislation, adjourn or dissolve the Assembly, or appoint judges; and what other powers the Convention saw fit to bestow on him he could exercise only with the advice and consent of a council of eight to be elected by the House and the Senate.[22]

Weak as the executive office was, a surprising amount of interest developed over who was to fill it. Discussion of the matter had begun as early as May 12, and it soon became evident that the tidewater area favored Nelson's uncle, Mr. Secretary Nelson. The secretary had not taken an active part in Virginia's revolt, but no one questioned his loyalty to the cause. And his long governmental experience, his knowledge, and the fact that he had served as president of the Council under the previous government—which made him nominal governor after Dunmore's departure—well fitted him for the place. Furthermore, many leaders thought that Nelson might bring the radical and more conservative elements in the colony together.[23]

Secretary Nelson's opponent in the gubernatorial contest was Virginia's popular demagogue, Patrick Henry, who, while complaining that the governor would be but "a mere phantom," nevertheless thirsted for the honor. This was formidable opposition, and though the venerable secretary had strong support from such important figures as Edmund Pendleton and Richard Henry Lee, Henry's popularity proved too much. When the vote was taken on June 26, Henry won by the margin of sixty to forty-five.[24]

The Convention had also been busy in other ways. After cutting the size of its delegation to the Continental Congress to five members for the coming year, it had elected Thomas Nelson, George Wythe, Richard Henry Lee, Thomas Jefferson, and Francis Lightfoot Lee. Carter Braxton and Benjamin Harrison were passed over. Braxton was already suspected of pro-British leanings, reason enough for his not being reconsidered. No doubt Nelson was disturbed at Braxton's departure, for he had gone security for him for £2,000 and the debt remained unpaid. Although Harrison's loyalty had never been questioned, he was a man with strong prejudices and not overly fond of work—considerations which may have combined to cause his omission, though he was immediately elected to a post on the Council of State.[25]

Braxton's and Harrison's terms did not expire until August 1, and they were in Philadelphia for the great events that took place in late June and July. On July 2, after long and acrimonious debate, Congress finally passed the motion for independence, and two days later approved the Declaration of Independence drafted largely by Thomas Jefferson. There is some debate as to when this historic document was actually signed, but probably those present signed a paper copy on July 4; among them was Nelson. The engrossed parchment copy of the Declaration, which was to be preserved for posterity, was not inscribed until August 2.[26] It bore the signature *Thoˢ Nelson jr.*

By this time the plan of confederation had been completed. On July 12 the committee to draw up the plan presented its proposals to Congress. John Dickinson is credited with having the largest part in framing the Articles of Confederation as they were presented. The role of Nelson and most of the other committee members is unclear. Whatever the case, the plan was laid before Congress in the hope that that factious body would speedily approve it, establishing within a few weeks a form of government under which the rebelling colonies could effectively operate. But that was not to be, largely because the delegates could not agree on three main points. Was voting in the Congress to be in proportion to the size of the states, or was each state to have an equal vote? Were monetary contributions to the central government to be according to the wealth or the population of the various states? And lastly, were state boundaries to be limited to the west, or could they literally stretch to the Mississippi as some of the colonial charters allowed.[27]

The disputes certainly involved a struggle between the large and wealthy states and the small and poor ones. But there was also a parallel dispute between the members of Congress who wanted to create a government strong enough to prosecute the war successfully and those who feared the central power of such a government. The debate dragged on through the hot and humid days of July and August, and as fall approached no decision was in sight. Finally sheer exhaustion with the question, coupled with the British attack on New York, pushed it into the background, and confederation was not to be broached again until spring.[28]

For Thomas Nelson, fat and tired, the summer days and constant attention to the business of Congress were trying. His treasury duties, the debates on the confederation, and requests from constituents and friends at home kept him continuously busy. In mid-September he wrote his good friend John Page that the business of Congress almost had him "overdone" and "if the affair at N. Yorke [the British attack] was favorably determin'd, I should return to Virginia for a little time." [29]

Although the situation of the American army at New York went from bad to worse, Nelson decided to go to Virginia for a short visit anyway. He left Philadelphia around September 21, agreeing to return for duty by November 10. He found that Virginia was even more of an armed camp than when he had left the previous May. All three of his cousins, William, Thomas, and John, sons of Secretary Nelson, were in the army. William and Thomas were serving as major and captain in the 7th Virginia Regiment with Washington in New York, while John was captain of a troop of light horse stationed at Yorktown. Even Thomas Nelson's youngest brother, Billy, was a lieutenant in a company of militia composed of students from the College of William and Mary.[30]

Nelson's visit home proved to be no rest. Despite his service in Congress, the York County electorate returned their favorite son to the Virginia legislature, which met in the fall of 1776. It was the first to meet, as Roger Atkinson put it, "under the happy auspices of the People only." According to Atkinson, the members were "Men not quite so well dressed, nor so politely Educated, nor so highly born, as some Assemblies I have formerly seen," but the change was not dramatic. There were new members, and some, such as French Strother of Culpeper County, subsequently played important roles. But Nelson and most of the old leaders were still present, and this leadership, which had engineered the movement for independence, retained its dominant position.[31]

Atkinson, of course, expressed the hopes of most Virginians

for better government now that they were free of British influence. Only time would tell how well "the People's Men" would perform. Certainly the events of the past year had wrought no metamorphosis in Nelson. He was still the same dedicated public servant, and through the month of October he served in the House of Delegates discharging his duties on the committees of Privileges and Elections, and Propositions and Grievances. He helped in revising the tobacco inspection laws as well as in the drafting of a bill for sending additional Virginia infantry into the Continental service. But as October drew to a close his position in Philadelphia beckoned, and Lucy, who was expecting a baby in January, was left in Yorktown while her husband made his way northward again.[32]

The Congress to which Nelson returned in November was a weak and frustrated body. Its members could not agree on a plan of confederation, yet they were faced with a common war and they had to find common ways and means of waging it. Furthermore, the army they were trying to support was being easily pushed by the British out of New York and across New Jersey. Nelson must have been somewhat disillusioned by the inability of Congress to agree on important points, as well as by the unfavorable turn in military events. Nevertheless, like many others, he stuck to his job, serving on a variety of committees, such as one for considering proper methods for recruiting and training cavalry, and another for better regulating the treasury board. He also acted as chairman of the Committee of the Whole to consider ways and means to raise supplies and support the value of Continental currency for the coming year.[33]

Then in mid-December, with the British army driving through New Jersey closer to Philadelphia, Congress, while protesting that it would not, fled the city and set up business in Baltimore. This was unquestionably the lowest point in the American cause, "the times that try mens souls," as Tom Paine put it. But then, on the day after Christmas, Washington lashed back across the Delaware and caught a garrison of Hessians in Trenton by surprise, taking almost one thousand prisoners. This victory fanned the spark of freedom, giving Americans renewed hope when they needed it most.

Nelson was jubilant. To Jefferson he wrote that "we have at

last turn'd the Tables upon those Scoundrels," though he bemoaned the fact that there was still not a regular army strong enough or a populace sufficiently aroused "to clear the continent of these damn'd Invaders" who played "the very Devil with the Girls and even old Women to satisfy their libidinous appetites." They perpetrated rape, rapine, and murder, leaving scarcely a virgin behind them, he continued, and yet even these things did not seem to rouse the people of New Jersey against them.[34]

General Washington soon cleared the British from western New Jersey. But success in military affairs did not carry over into the sphere of congressional matters. True, Washington's victories raised morale, but they did not answer the question of where the money to further the war effort was to come from. Nelson, who was closely associated with the treasury, wrote his friend Robert Morris that money was so scarce and the treasury in such a bad way that he hated to think about it:

> When I could give satisfactory answers to Congress upon a requisition being made for a sum of Money I took the greatest pleasure in transacting the business of the Treasury Board, but of late we have been so circumstanced that I had almost as live [*sic*] go to jail as go near the Treasury.

Some of the members of Congress put great faith in a lottery as the answer to the problem, but Nelson considered this "but a game." What they really needed, he said, were "able Financiers to supply our Treasury."[35]

As Nelson worried about treasury affairs, the heavy load of Congressional duties began to take its' toll. His health had not been good since the preceding fall and after the move to Baltimore his condition worsened. Finally his physician recommended that he go home for a rest. Many of his colleagues were in the same situation, and most of them ascribed their ills to the unhealthfulness of Maryland's expanding young city. One observer commented that "Congress presents such a scene of yellow death like faces that you would imagine Rhadamanthus had shifted his quarters and was holding court in Baltimore." So, early in February, Nelson headed home.[36]

Thomas's homecoming was a joyful one, for a new daughter, Lucy, born on January 2, 1777, awaited him. He was now back within the fold of his family, from which he had been almost constantly separated for a year and a half; but family joys were dimmed by economic hardships. Conditions had not been good in Virginia before 1776, and the war had seriously disarranged its economy. For merchants almost wholly involved in the consignment of tobacco to Britain, there were few alternatives, and for the Yorktown mercantile concern of Thomas Nelson, Jr. and Company, there was none. On April 11 the *Virginia Gazette* announced the end of the partnership, with a request for payment of money owed to it.[37]

Despite financial difficulties, Nelson felt sufficiently recovered by the middle of April to return to Philadelphia where Congress had reconvened in March. He arrived around the twenty-fifth and again took up his duties with his colleagues Richard Henry Lee, Francis Lightfoot Lee, and Mann Page, Jr. Only eight days after his arrival, Nelson had what contemporaries called an apoplectic stroke on the floor of Congress, and it temporarily affected his memory, making him totally incapable of fulfilling his duties. Thus, within a month of his departure he was back home, taking up residence this time at his simple plantation house, Offley Hoo, located far back in Hanover County, where, separated from the world's problems, he could hope to recover his health in peace and quiet.[38] He was only thirty-eight years of age but, overweight and burdened by private and public responsibilities, his system, that spring of 1777, sustained a shock from which it would never fully recover.

Nelson, it appeared, would be out of public affairs for a while. But the possibility of an enforced absence from political life did not stop him from fretting about the critical situation of his country. On his return to Virginia he immediately wrote George Wythe, speaker of the House of Delegates, urging that a delegate be appointed speedily to fill his place in Congress, as "the Congress are now engag'd in forming the Confederation, in which Virginia is deeply interested." In closing he made this apology: "Nothing but necessity could have induced me to leave Congress at this critical time, and I hope I shall stand excus'd."[39]

Chapter V

General Nelson

When Thomas Nelson returned to Virginia to recover his health, he was convinced that everything possible must be done to bring the war to an early and successful conclusion. During the next four and a half years he exerted himself to the utmost to attain that goal. Despite recurrent illness and great frustration, his efforts never wavered. America's cause was right; it was to everyone's interest to support this cause; and as a person willing to make great sacrifices he was impatient with those who shirked what he considered to be their duty.

He was a sick man that spring and summer of 1777. As late as August he was saying that "such is the Condition of my weak Head, that I have never attempted a letter without experiencing violent Pain in it for Hours after." Later he told George Washington that "the confinement absolutely necessary" for a diligent member of Congress "is totally inconsistent with my Constitution." Surprisingly, this did not seem to cut down significantly on his activity. Before he was back in Virginia the freeholders of York County had elected Nelson and Joseph Prentis as their representatives in the House of Delegates. Soon thereafter he was recommended by the York County Court for the post of county lieutenant and this recommendation was approved by the Council of State.[1]

In late May Nelson, after a brief rest in Hanover, journeyed to Williamsburg to begin his duties in the legislature. Shortly after his arrival he and Prentis prepared a bill requiring the quartermaster to provide tents or barracks for the housing of soldiers in the state instead of quartering them in private dwellings.[2] This was probably a direct result of the destruction of private property in Yorktown by soldiers stationed there. An English visitor, in that same year, described it clearly:

> This is a pleasant town situated upon the York River. . . .
> Close to the town there are several very good Gentlemen's
> houses built of brick and some of their gardens laid out
> with the greatest taste of any I have ever seen in America,
> but now almost ruined by disorderly soldiers, . . . their own
> soldiers. . . . Houses burnt down, others pulled to pieces for
> fuel, everything in disorder and confusion. . . .[3]

But before this question could be resolved another arose that pushed the quartering of soldiers into the background. The temporary council named the previous December was to be replaced by the election of a permanent Council of State. As the balloting began, the voting manifested strict political management. One by one the old members were re-elected, each by large majorities: John Page, Dudley Digges, John Blair, Bartholomew Dandridge, Thomas Walker, Nathaniel Harrison. Then came the vote for Meriwether Smith, a controversial figure who led the field when the ballots were counted but did not have the necessary majority. On the second ballot Thomas Nelson defeated the aspiring candidate from Essex County, seventy to forty-nine. David Jameson, the last of the old members, was elected to the remaining seat.[4]

The bulk of the new Council represented the conservative Tidewater. Since this faction was obviously opposed to Smith, it apparently decided to use the stratagem of pitting a popular figure in the person of Thomas Nelson against him. They must have realized that Nelson would not accept the post; but he certainly gave at least his tacit approval to the plan. On June 27, the last day of the Assembly, Nelson declined the position and Thomas Adams was elected in his place.[5]

After the Assembly adjourned, Nelson spent a quiet July only to have his peace disturbed in August by the arrival in Chesapeake Bay of Sir William Howe with a force of some fifteen thousand British troops. Howe's plan was to continue north to the head of the bay and launch an overland attack on Philadelphia. But Virginians imagined that the attack was to be directed at them, and the Council of State hurriedly began preparations to put the state in a posture of defense.[6]

To command the militia and handle all arrangements for the protection of the Old Dominion, the Council appointed Nelson as brigadier general. He accepted his appointment on August 19, refusing at the same time to receive a salary. The *Virginia Gazette* applauded this appointment in no uncertain terms:

> The appointment of a gentleman so universally beloved and esteemed for his zealous attachment to our sacred cause, cannot fail of giving of the most unfeigned pleasure to every friend to his country, who reflects that, except our noble general in the north, there is not a native of America to whose standard so great a number of warm friends and respectable persons would repair as to that truly noble and worthy gentlemen's.[7]

Like most of his countrymen who had accepted similar positions, Nelson had little or no military experience. To Washington he wrote that the post was "unsolicited, unexpected, and, I wish I could say, it was not unmerited. I confess my want of military Knowledge but . . . I hope to make myself a soldier." His pretensions were modest and he was properly impressed with the difficulty of the task that faced him. "I am sure," he said, "that there never was a People worse prepared for Defense than we are." And he asserted that nothing "but the immediate Danger into which . . . we are likely to fall & a Desire to extricate my Country from it should have induced me to undertake the arduous task." Everyone was uneasy and one Council member, while informing Washington of Nelson's appointment, urged that he "send . . . a General of Experience & Reputation." The reply of the commander in chief to the new general was reassuring. "In our infant State of War, it cannot be expected, we should be perfect in the business of it, [and] . . . I doubt not, that your zeal and assiduity will amply supply any deficiency, your diffidence of yourself leads you suppose, you labour under in that respect."[8]

Zeal and assiduity were certainly not wanting in the person of Thomas Nelson, and with the aid of his newly appointed secretary, the Reverend Robert Andrews, he immediately began preparing the state for the expected attack. The Council had called up approximately four thousand militiamen, most of whom were to rendezvous at Williamsburg. General Nelson reviewed those who had arrived, along with the few regulars present, on August

22. It was a nondescript group that could not have aroused much confidence, but he pronounced them fit and delivered, in the words of the *Virginia Gazette,* "a most animated speech . . . on the present prospects before us."⁹

The following day Nelson sent a circular letter to all of Virginia's county lieutenants warning them of the danger, asking for a complete report on their militia and supplies, and urging that they keep their men in a state of readiness. Within a week, as the reports began to trickle in, he presented to the Council of State a proposal for the organization of Virginia's militia. On Nelson's recommendation, a quartermaster general of the state was appointed. Plans were also made for locating a garrison at Portsmouth and for stationing forces at Yorktown, Hampton, and Williamsburg — an arrangement that Washington cautioned against because of the ease with which stationary forces might be cut off in that area.¹⁰

By early September Nelson began to feel that he was accomplishing something. He was heartened by the conduct of the Princess Anne County militia in capturing fourteen officers and men of the British warship *Solebay.* In general the militiamen had "come in fast" and were behaving "in the most orderly manner. . . ." If Washington could release, for a few months, Captain Thomas Matthews of the 4th Virginia Regiment to serve as his brigade major he felt certain that he would "be able to make the militia of [the] state a very respectable & formidable body of men." But his hopes for building an effective force soon ended when it became clear that Howe had no intention of invading Virginia.¹¹

A struggle then developed between the Council and the militia commander. The state authorities, primarily for financial reasons, began plans to discharge all troops in stages throughout September. Nelson strongly disapproved, because if "the Enemy return in any short time, we shall be nearly in as great confusion as when they made their first appearance." He was convinced that as time wore on militia would play an increasingly important role in the war. For these reasons he wanted to keep some of the militia in "constant training, notwithstanding the expense. . . ."¹²

The Council was not persuaded. They did delay the dismissal of about twelve hundred men for several days in the middle of the month because Nelson had reported the possibility of an attack on Yorktown. But on September 17 these men were sent home, and the remainder were discharged on the thirtieth. That same day Nelson was relieved of his duties while being thanked for his "Activity, Diligence & good Conduct . . . in the Discharge of the Trust resposed in him. . . ."[13]

Nelson was disappointed but not disillusioned, and he continued to pressure the Council to take more positive action in support of the war effort. His brief experience as commander of the militia had been a satisfying one; it seemed logical to keep some portion of the state's military forces in readiness; and he hoped that with the proper exertion of Virginia and other states close to Pennsylvania it might be possible to put "an end . . . to the War this campaign. . . ." With the latter point in mind he now convinced the Council that, because of the "present critical situation of American Affairs," five-thousand men should be sent to join Washington. Orders were given to the quartermaster general to gather tents, camp utensils, horses, and wagons for such a force. But then a letter from Washington to Nelson brought an end to these proceedings. The approaching cold weather and the fact that he could not provide for the militia's clothing and shelter caused the commander in chief to decline the help.[14]

This did not dampen Nelson's ardor, and late in October he wrote General George Weedon, who was serving with Washington, that his feelings for his brave countrymen "who are so nobly enduring the fatigues of war, can be equalled by nothing but my wish to join them with a Body of Men. . . ." In fact, Nelson continued, he was going to "exert every nerve to get a body of men inoculated and train'd" during the winter so that he could join the army in the spring, "for my political system is to put an end to this War as soon as possible. . . ."[15]

To attain this goal Nelson hoped to get the General Assembly to pass legislation that would not only allow him to raise volunteers but would, in general, put Virginia more concretely behind the war for independence. By October 19, after a quick trip to Hanover County, he was back in Williamsburg ready to take his seat in the House of Delegates. He fretted while waiting for the members to assemble, but by the thirtieth a quorum was present. In the organization of the House Nelson was again appointed to his old committees of Privileges and Elections and Propositions and Grievances and given a new assignment on the Committee of Trade.[16]

Nothing beyond organization was accomplished on the first day, for a parade took place in the afternoon to celebrate the defeat of Burgoyne at Saratoga. Promptly at three o'clock as the drums sounded their martial beat, the city militia, along with the regulars stationed in the capital, formed at the east end of town and marched up the Duke of Gloucester Street to the courthouse square. Perhaps the soldiers marched with extra snap (and less precision) as they passed in review before General Nelson and the speakers of both houses of the Assembly, for each militiaman had been given a gill of rum on the order of Governor Henry. After the review, the cannons were fired thirteen times and the infantry fired three volleys, the parade ending with three "huzzas from all present." Bells rang throughout the evening, houses were brightly illuminated, and Williamsburg's populace quaffed many an additional gill of rum—and more gentlemanly drinks—before the night was over.[17]

Next morning the House of Delegates, some members perhaps with aching heads, began the work of the session. Nelson, in line with his earlier intentions, was to play a more central role in this Assembly than in any previous one.

Among the more important questions that the legislature had to resolve was that of raising more money to carry on Virginia's part in the war effort. The previous June a state loan office had been established to borrow money for Virginia, and some funds had begun to trickle into it, largely from private sources. Secretary Nelson had already lent £645; but it soon became evident that this arrangement was far from adequate. As a leading financial expert in the House, General Nelson headed a committee that proposed new taxes on almost everything conceivable, and increases in those already in force. All property, including slaves, was to be taxed at the rate of ten shillings per £100 valuation. Horses, mules, cattle, money, and silver were included in the taxable items as well as all interest-bearing debts, carriages, ordinary and marriage licenses, annuities, liquor, and exported tobacco. On December 13 the House approved all the taxes recommended by Nelson's committee except a tax on dogs.[18]

The second measure designed to raise money was more novel and was largely the work of Thomas Jefferson. It provided that all debts due to British subjects from citizens of Virginia could be paid into the recently established loan office of the state. This office would give the debtor a certificate of payment which would discharge him from future payment to the creditor of the amount he had paid into the loan office. Virginia's citizens, who were indebted to British merchants for between £2 million and £3 million, would thus be allowed to pay their debts in depreciated paper currency. This action benefited not only the debtor, but the state as well by increasing the stability of the paper money and by transforming the liabilities of its citizens into public assets. The responsibility of the state to the creditor, if any, was not mentioned in the bill. Another feature of the bill provided for the sequestration of all real and personal property in Virginia belonging to British subjects, now alien enemies. The owner's title to the property was not disturbed, but all profits that might come from a sequestered estate would go into the state treasury until hostilities had ceased. Jefferson and his colleagues hoped that such measures would help to stabilize the finances of the state and check inflation. They also hoped to nullify the emerging public discontent that resulted from the refusal of merchants and factors, some of them with British connections, to receive paper money in the payment of debts.[19]

Thomas Nelson had as much reason as any Virginian to be in favor of the bill, as he was heavily indebted to British mercantile interests. Nevertheless, he was a man of high personal integrity, and as a merchant himself with a large number of uncollected debts still on his books, he could appreciate the position of the British creditor. When the bill came up for debate, Nelson opposed it on the grounds that it allowed a breach of contract; the debts, he argued, had been incurred and the estates acquired under the sanction of laws and relations known to both parties to the contract, and they were thereafter to be held inviolable. The British government had not sequestered American property, he pointed out, and he viewed the proposed measure as an injustice to innocent people. Finally, Nelson charged that such action showed gross ingratitude to British creditors who in many cases could be regarded as benefactors of Virginians whose capital was small but upon whose honor and integrity the British had relied. And "for these reasons," he concluded, "I hope the bill will be rejected; but whatever its fate, by God, I will pay my debts like an honest man." [20]

In this argument, Nelson was consistent with his position in 1774 on nonexportation. The proposed legislation would affect most severely the British mercantile community, which he did not hold responsible for the present difficulties. But the supporters of the bill enjoyed a strong position—much stronger in fact than the proponents of nonexportation had held. The war had been going on for over two years; the British were now Virginia enemies; and the financial needs of the state were pressing. The bill passed with very little difficulty on January 22, 1778. Although Nelson never took advantage of the act, he seems to have accepted it, and at a later date he worked to improve the provision respecting sequestration. [21]

Along with the need for additional funds, the Assembly faced the vital problem of providing an adequate number of troops for the war. Nelson was, of course, very sensitive to this need. Washington, in at least two letters that fall, urged his friend to use "vigorous and spirited exertions . . . to compleat the Regiments" from Virginia, for unless this were done "I very much fear that all our present labours will be in vain. . . ." [22]

Beginning in November the House of Delegates, well aware of the urgency, applied itself to the task. Nelson was now considered something of a military expert, and on November 21 he served as chairman of the Committee of the Whole when the House discussed the matter generally. And on December 4 he was appointed to a committee with, among others, George Mason, Edmund Pendleton, Benjamin Harrison, and Thomas Jefferson to draft an appropriate bill. [23]

To Nelson's mind the bill should provide a more effective means of drafting men and allow for the raising of a group of short-term volunteers. The legislation of the previous May had left the decision of who was to be drafted to local officials. This had, in his opinion, "been productive of much evil and little good. . . ." Many who had been chosen were "unfit for service," and to his amazement, in some instances, Tories had been picked as a means of punishment. Free "Mulattoes and Negroes" had also been called on "as it was generally thought they could best be spar'd." To a man of his liberal sentiments this was "exceedingly unjust because these poor Wretches after having risk'd their lives & perhaps may have contributed to save America, will not be entitled to the privileges of Freemen." [24]

Another problem was that the existing law allowed any two militiamen who could "procure one able bodied soldier . . . to serve for a term of three years," to be exempted from the draft and militia musters as long as that man remained in the army. That provision resulted in many Virginians offering such a person as much as £100 to serve in their place, and thus had discouraged enlistments in the Continental service "for a bounty of 20 dollars. . . ." Obviously it was not a good arrangement.[25]

The bill, as it began to emerge, addressed itself to most of these problems. Each county was given a quota of men necessary to fill Virginia's line regiments. All single men were eligible, and on a specified day they were to report to the courthouse where slips were to be prepared for all the able bodied. If the quota of the county happened to be thirty, then thirty of the slips would be marked "Service" and the remainder "Clear." All would be put into a hat and every man would draw a slip, those getting "Service" slips being obligated for duty. The term of service would be one year. Substitutes were still allowed, but on a one-to-one basis. The person obtaining the recruit was exempt from the draft for the period of time, after the discharge, that the man had actually served.[26]

These provisions must have pleased General Nelson. But he ran into trouble on his plan to authorize the raising of volunteers for six-months' service. He pressed hard to have this measure included, using in argument Washington's passing comment, after the defeat of Burgoyne, that he wished he had given more serious consideration to Nelson's earlier offer to join him with militia. Nevertheless, as late as December 19, Nelson thought the proposal was lost because many delegates feared "it would interfere with compleating the Regular battalions." [27]

Never one to despair, however, he persevered; and by December 26 authorization to raise volunteers had been approved. In what was certainly Nelson's language, this portion of the bill stated, in part, that since it was "of the greatest importance to the

American cause to open the ensuing campaign as early as possible, and to render its operation more decisive and effectual, that the army under the command of his excellency General Washington should be reinforced by an additional number of troops." No more than fifty-four hundred volunteers could be raised, for six-months duty, they were to remain eligible for the draft until they actually marched to join the Continental army, and they would be exempt from the draft for six months after their discharge. These volunteers were to be commanded by two brigadier generals who along with the field officers, would be appointed by the governor and Council; officers for each company were to be elected. The entire bill became law on January 9. As in the case of the taxation law, Nelson's role had been central. The wisdom of the measure would soon be determined.[28]

Nelson was not present for the final passage of the legislation; the House had excused him on December 31 for the recovery of his health. The almost constant demands of public service during the previous five months had taken their toll. But by January 20, he was again active, participating in the final business of the legislative session and worrying about the inoculation against smallpox of a Virginia regiment that was to join the Continental army. He felt that troops should not be sent unless they were immune to smallpox. If they had not been inoculated the disease might be contracted on their march to, or after they had joined, the main army, and as a result both they and other soldiers could be incapacitated.[29] Nelson had been a member of a committee that had recently drafted legislation to liberalize the state's law respecting smallpox inoculation. The revised law provided that as long as certain safety measures were observed inoculation did not have to be approved by public authorities. Having been inoculated earlier, Nelson could testify to the wisdom of the law and the relative lack of danger involved in the procedure.[30]

Two related matters now concerned him. One was the inadequate provision the state had made to treat the troops; only fifty could be handled at one time, and Nelson thought that this in itself would prevent them marching before "the end of the next campaign." The other was the resistance of both the soldiers and the general citizenry to inoculation. To Washington he wrote that General Howe could accomplish more with a "few Phials of smallpox" in Virginia than with a train of artillery, "yet so perverse are our Countrymen in General, that they would hazard almost American Independence rather than submit to a temporary ill." The General replied that he learned "with pain and grief" of the resistance in Virginia to inoculation, for he had hoped that the "artillery and other Regiments of Infantry" would join him "as soon as the Roads and weather should be a little settled. . . ." The same problem would arise, of course, with the volunteers that Nelson hoped to recruit, and with them he now became preoccupied.[31]

The law that authorized the creation of volunteer forces provided that the militia commanders in each county should immediately call a general muster to recruit men for this service. When, in the judgment of the governor and Council, enough men had volunteered, their commanders would be appointed. But to encourage enlistments it was announced on January 23, that "Thomas Nelson jr & Alexander Spotswood Esquires" would be the ones selected as "Brigadiers General to command the said Troops."[32]

Nelson must have known that such would be the case, for earlier he had written Washington that he hoped to join him for the next campaign. Washington's response may have given him pause. Pointedly remarking that he thought Virginia was trying to do too much "by attempting to raise 5,000 volunteers (which more than probable will not succeed)" and which would impede the "Drafts" for her regiments, he then stated:

> You gave me reason, my dear Sir, to believe, I shall see [you] at the Campaign in the spring. I shall rejoice at it, or to hear of your being in Congress again, as I view with concern the departure of every Gentleman of independent spirit from the grand American Council.[33]

After all, Nelson had left Congress because he was sick; now that he was recovered and performing all types of strenuous duties, it seemed plausible to Washington that he should return to Congress. Washington was influenced by the fact that his own efforts were repeatedly foiled by an incompetent—or at least inefficient —Congress, a Congress from whose ranks the most capable of Virginia's sons, including Thomas Jefferson, George Mason,

George Wythe, Edmund Pendleton, and Thomas Nelson, were absent.

Despite Washington's gentle plea, Nelson did not return to Philadelphia but went ahead with his plan for raising volunteers. This persistence in the face of authoritative advice to the contrary can perhaps be explained by two strong motivations. He had developed a near compulsion to lead troops in the field; and he felt certain that a sizeable addition of troops would enable the Continental army to quickly defeat Howe, which would, in turn, bring an end to the war. In his inexperience, he did not comprehend that it was wiser to add men to Washington's regular forces, where they would serve under seasoned officers and with battle hardened troops, than to bring in a body of untrained soldiers who would be commanded by novices. The general as much as told his friend this and he did say that "unless some vigorous exertions can be used to supply [the army] with provisions, men will avail little, for you can have no conception of our deficiency in this article." Fill up the regular regiments and provide the food to feed them, Washington was urging—then we can talk about separate forces of volunteers. But Nelson was not to be deterred.[34]

Unfortunately the doubts of the commander in chief proved well founded. By the early spring of 1778 the volunteer plan had failed and Nelson was searching for an alternative. He soon found one. Early in March Congress had made an appeal to persons of some means to form troops of light cavalry to serve through the remainder of the year at their own expense, except for provisions for themselves and forage for their horses. In April General Nelson published an address asking for volunteers, and as encouragement to those who could not bear their own expenses he suggested that subscriptions be raised in their respective counties to support them. This suggestion met with some success and Nelson's hopes were raised by the fact that "several of the first gentlemen in the country" had "engaged as privates," including his own brothers Hugh and Robert, and Lewis Burwell of Gloucester County.[35]

More important, when the Assembly met in May it gave state support to the scheme. A bill was passed authorizing a regiment of 350 horses to be raised "for the present campaign," under the command of Nelson. They would receive the same rations and pay as members of the Continental army. Those who could not furnish their own horses and equipment would be supplied at public expense. General Nelson received £4,000 to expend for arms and £4,000 for the purchase of horses. The measure pleased him; and with the *Virginia Gazette* giving it good publicity, he felt sure that the full number of men would volunteer. Nevertheless, though Nelson was "indefatigable in procuring men and horses," one acute observer doubted that the general would be able to "raise half his number." When the troop gathered at Port Royal in Hanover County on June 15, 1778, this prediction proved accurate, there being fewer than one hundred men present.[36]

Nelson had reason to be discouraged and in a letter to Washington he gave vent to his feelings:

> So great is the aversion of the Virginians to engaging in the Army that they are not to [be] induc'd by any method. I cannot say they are in apathy for view them in the mercantile way, and they are as alert as could be wish'd, or rather more so, almost every Man being engag'd in accumulating Money. Public Virtue & Patriotism is sold down to South Quay and there shipd off in Tobacco Hogsheads, nevermore, in my opinion, to return. The number of resignations in the Virginia line is induced by officers, when they have returned, finding that every man, who remains at home is making a fortune, whilst they are spending what they have, in defense of their Country. If a stop be not put to the destructive trade that is at present carried on here, there will not be a spark of Patriotic fire left in Virginia in a few Months.[37]

But his natural optimism, plus reassurance from Washington that he would be happy to see any number that Nelson could bring to his aid, spurred him on. Through June and July, with the temperature hovering around one hundred degrees, the general tried to whip his volunteers into shape at Port Royal. Late in July they headed north to join the army. Washington had advised that the most direct route was through Baltimore, and they followed his advice. Arriving in Baltimore, they were reviewed by Count Casimir Pulaski, newly appointed commander of the Continental cavalry. From Baltimore they moved to Philadelphia, reaching there during the first week in August.[38]

Instead of welcoming the Virginia volunteers, Congress declared that there was now no need for them since the British army had left Pennsylvania for New York. For the unpaid volunteers, many of whom had equipped themselves at their own expense, it was a shocking blow, as it was for Nelson. For over a year he had been striving to get into the fight, and here with the opportunity so close, Congress changed its mind. Congress thanked Nelson and his men "for their brave, generous, and patriotic efforts," and in another resolution, which passed with New York and South Carolina dissenting, advised that in future times of emergency other states should emulate Virginia's action. Nelson politely thanked Congress for its approbation. General Washington expressed disappointment and his appreciation of the effort of Nelson and his cavalry volunteers. He was particularly grateful for the horse that Nelson had given him in a final gesture.[39]

Nelson and his men returned to a water-logged Virginia, their spirits dampened almost as much as the land; for the past nine months the rain had been excessive and there was fear of the loss of the wheat and corn crops. But return to Virginia would have been depressing in any event, for inflation was rampant and the means of making a living slim. Virginia currency had slumped until it took $10 in paper to buy $1 in hard coin, with the upward spiral of prices showing no slackening off; in Richmond, tea sold for £4 per pound, linen for fifty shillings a yard. Nelson's brothers, Robert and Hugh, sold part of their lands in Albemarle and Frederick counties, no doubt for want of other sources of income; his cousin William had to resign his post in the Continental Army to provide for his family.[40]

After his return to Virginia, Nelson resumed his duties in the House of Delegates in October, serving again on his old committees. He busied himself with examining the state of public provisions, trying to get more money for the public printer, and purchasing four of the finest geldings available for Washington as a mark of the state's gratitude for his services. He also worked on legislation to expel from Virginia persons "inimical to the liberties of America," to supply the army with provision, and to train the militia. Much of the session was onerous, but it was brightened somewhat by the birth of his sixth son, Robert, on October 14.[41]

While Nelson wrestled with local legislative questions, he must have occasionally recalled Washington's hint earlier in the year that he should return to Congress. In fact, the commander in chief wrote Benjamin Harrison in December 1778 that he should endeavor to get Virginia's best men back in Congress, to rouse them from their "places of honor or profit" at home, for America was sinking into "irretrievable ruin," while they occupied themselves with local affairs:

> Where is Mason, Wythe, Jefferson, Nicholas, Pendleton, Nelson and another I could name; and why if you are sufficiently impressed with your danger, do you not . . . send an extra number or two for at least a certain limited time till the great business of the Nation is put upon a more respectable and happy establishment.[42]

As if reading Washington's mind, the General Assembly on the day this letter was written unanimously elected Thomas Nelson to fill the place of John Harvie, who had recently resigned from Congress. There is reason to believe that Nelson had agreed to serve for only five months, that he planned to return home in May and again serve in the House of Delegates. Washington would have disapproved of this, and Nelson certainly realized the importance of congressional service. Something that appeared more pressing must have convinced him that his presence in Virginia would be required. In any case, soon after his appointment, the new congressman sold six hundred acres of his York County land for £1,200. Short service or not, one's family had to be provided for, and in those times it was difficult to do, especially from as far away as Philadelphia.[43]

Nelson remained in Virginia throughout January, bitter cold and heavy snow interspersed with violent rains making travel almost impossible. Early in February, the weather turning unseasonably mild, he left home to assume his duties. Peach trees were beginning to blossom and others to bud, while shrubs were in full bloom.[44] But the pleasure of an early spring contrasted starkly with the dismal prospect facing the country. The depleted ranks of the army forced Washington to remain on the defensive.

Neither the necessary men nor supplies were forthcoming from the states. Inflation continued and Congress, unable to find an alternative, persisted in printing paper money. The French alliance of early 1778 had given the country hope that the war would end soon, but the events of the year that followed did nothing to encourage this hope. The best of congresses would have been severely tested, and this one was no more than mediocre. A general feeling prevailed that the members of Congress were more interested in Philadelphia's social life than in the pressing business of the country. Such was the situation into which Nelson stepped.[45]

On February 18, 1779, Nelson presented his credentials to the Congress and immediately entered into the business of government. He was terribly concerned with the critical situation of the country. Never, "since the commencement of the war," he wrote, had America "been in so much danger. . . ." This was due, in his mind, to the "state of our finances, which seem to me to be in strange confusion." Congress, in an attempt to check rampant inflation, had decided to call in the currency emissions of May 1777 and April 1778, with the option "of exchanging bills of these emissions for other bills or subscribing them at the loan office." It hoped that most of the money would be loaned to the government, but such was not the case. In fact, Nelson said, "the present effect is very contrary from what is expected. Our immediate Country is almost thrown into convulsion by it. I fear it has given a deadly stab to the Credit of any Paper money that may hereafter be issued by Congress." His fears proved correct, and within months the government came to the decision not to issue additional paper.[46]

Little else is known of Nelson's feelings about Congress or the problems that faced it. He was regular in his attendance, served on a variety of committees, and took part in the two serious debates during his stay in Philadelphia. The first revolved around the question of what America's demands would be in a peace settlement, and the second concerned the emerging conflict between the South, which desired free navigation of the Mississippi, and New England, which wanted the right to fish off the banks of Nova Scotia. The debates dragged on through March and

April and were not finally settled until long after Nelson had returned to Virginia.[47]

The discouraging thing was that other pressing questions received answers no more quickly. It was enough to make the most optimistic throw up his hands in despair. No doubt feeling that his friend Nelson would need some encouragement, Washington wrote in March to express his pleasure that Nelson had again taken a seat in Congress, for "I think there never was a time when cool dispassionate reasoning; strict attention and application, great integrity, and . . . wisdom were more to be wished for than the present." When the weather got better, Washington concluded, he hoped that Nelson would visit him.[48]

In all probability Nelson never got the opportunity to do so. After April 22 his name ceases to appear in the journals of Congress; and by the first week of May he was back in Virginia, writing the speaker of the Virginia House of Delegates to resign his congressional appointment on account of bad health. Apparently this sickness was similar to the difficulty he had experienced the previous year. Nelson was a man of great energy and bulk, and also of delicate health. Perhaps in this instance illness gave him a good excuse for what he had planned to do in any event. He later told Washington that he left Congress "with reluctance," but it is reasonably clear that he had always intended to resign and run for a seat in the House of Delegates. The puzzling thing about this sickness, as with previous ones that occurred in Philadelphia, was that Nelson returned home to take on tasks as strenuous as those he left behind.[49]

During the second week in May, soon after Nelson's return to Virginia, a British raiding party of two thousand men under the command of Major General Edward Mathew invaded the state. They landed at Portsmouth, seized Norfolk, burned Suffolk, and pillaged much of the lower Virginia countryside. Over two thousand militiamen were called up in response to this invasion, but whether or not Nelson commanded them is uncertain. According to a later report, members of the General Assembly had wanted General Charles Scott, a Virginian and one of Washington's brigade commanders, who was then in the state, to be placed in command of the militia. Evidently there was some embarrassment and much private discussion among the legislators. Some felt that to appoint Scott would be treating Nelson unjustly. The news, of course, got to Nelson who unselfishly announced that he would be honored to serve under General Scott for the duration of the invasion. The governor and the Council were authorized on May 14 to appoint officers to command the militia, but the record does not show whether Scott was actually named. In any case, Nelson, hearing of the British invasion, collected what militia he could in the immediate area and stationed the main force at Yorktown, which he believed would be attacked. There is also reason to believe that he coordinated the operations of other troops located at Williamsburg, Hampton, and on the south side of the James River. Fortunately the British limited themselves to the Norfolk-Portsmouth area and departed on May 26, leaving a shaken but relieved Virginia behind.[50]

Nelson now felt free to turn his attention to the legislature. He had been elected in April, along with James Innes, to represent York County, but his membership in Congress made him ineligible. On his return to Virginia, York County held a second election and Nelson was again chosen. This arrangement had evidently been worked out before Nelson had agreed to serve in Congress.[51]

A new governor was to be elected in this session of the legislature. Patrick Henry had served three one-year terms and was not eligible for re-election. Probably Nelson wanted to succeed Henry and that is why he was anxious to return to Virginia in May. In the pre-election maneuvering Nelson emerged as one of the prime contenders, his chief opponents being John Page, his life-long friend from Gloucester County, and Thomas Jefferson, who was already developing into one of America's premier statesmen. On the first ballot Jefferson, by carrying all of the "back country," held a plurality of fifty-five, while Page and Nelson split the Tidewater with thirty-eight and thirty-two votes respectively. This automatically threw Nelson out of the running, and on the next ballot Jefferson got enough of Nelson's votes to win sixty-seven to sixty-one.[52]

Jefferson's solid support from the western counties and Page's experience as lieutenant governor under Henry were important factors in Nelson's failure. Certainly he was disappointed and he may have been miffed by the fact that Page, who had taken a far smaller part in the Revolution, had killed his chances of election.

Nelson was ambitious and he wanted to serve the American cause to the fullest extent possible. If he had chosen to devote all of his attention either to the military or to politics he probably would have been more successful. To pursue both activities, making the contributions and receiving the rewards that he desired, was virtually impossible.

Nelson was not entirely blind to the problem. Military service agreed with him and he told Washington that he had "often lamented . . . not taking the field with you at the commencement of this War." But now it was too late. What Nelson called a "punctilio" stood in his way, "for to enter in a subordinate rank would not suit my own feelings," and to take a rank higher than those "who had borne the brunt of the war" would indicate "a want of generosity" on his part. Thomas Nelson was—and would remain—a frustrated man. On June 4, perhaps to rest and restore his wounded feelings, he got permission to be absent from the House of Delegates for seven days.[53]

By the following week he was back in his seat, but to little purpose, for, as one observer commented, "they [the General Assembly] go very slowly, and entangle themselves at every step." The delegates spent a great deal of time debating a bill to move the capital to Richmond; it was opposed violently by the Tidewater but the "up country" now held the preponderance in the Assembly. Of more importance were the army's need for men and supplies, and the necessity of dealing with inflation. The legislators had hoped that the Sequestration Act of the previous year would provide needed funds and check inflation, but it had failed to do so. As a result the legislature amended that act to allow the sale of British estates, with the proceeds going to the state. But only time could tell if this device would prove helpful.[54]

In July, after the legislature had adjourned, the freeholders of York County met to discuss ways and means of helping the government restore the value of paper currency. Nelson served on a committee of fourteen that recommended a ceiling on prices. The suggestion, though sensible, seems to have gained no support. To be effective it would have had to be not only statewide, but nationwide, almost an impossibility considering the weakness of the Continental Congress.[55]

At the fall session of the Assembly, Nelson took a substantial part in what was a more productive meeting than the previous one. Apart from an attempt of the "lowland gentlemen" to repeal the law for the removal of the capital, which failed by a vote of forty-five to forty, most of the session dealt with financial matters. The decision of Congress in September to stop issuing paper money placed the main burden of supporting the war on the states. And, of course, the states themselves were in straitened circumstances.[56]

Early in the session the House of Delegates began, in Nelson's words, to "consider . . . measures for complying with the requisitions of Congress as well as to support our own credit." Predictably he was optimistic. Congress could rely on Virginia, he wrote, to raise her quota of money. He did not have the least doubt that this could be done through taxes and loans. Through these two devices, as well as in strengthening earlier legislation, Nelson and his colleagues in the Assembly attempted to solve the problem. They knew that Virginians would react strongly to more taxation, but they saw no alternative save "an humiliating, inglorious and disadvantageous peace." They levied much heavier taxes. They authorized the state to borrow £5 million from its citizens and, to provide for the interest and principal on the loan, they fixed a tax of "thirty pounds of inspected tobacco" per year for the next eleven years on every tithable person, except free white tithables between the ages of sixteen and twenty-one.[57]

Finally, they again amended the Sequestration Act. The law was not producing the money that had been anticipated and it was causing problems for citizens of the state who for legitimate reasons were out of the country. Under its provisions the sale of British estates could easily be tied up in court litigation, while the estates of some absent Virginia citizens were being seized and placed on the auction block. Nelson, Patrick Henry, George Mason, and others were appointed to frame a bill dealing with these problems. On November 3 Nelson presented the committee's work for the consideration of the House and a month later, after debate and revision, both houses of the Assembly agreed to the amendment.[58]

The new law protected the estates of Virginians who had gone abroad for their education or to visit their families. To expedite the sale of British estates, litigation proceedings were streamlined and buyers were given ironclad guarantees respecting the validity of their purchases. Unfortunately, the hopes that this legislation would hasten the flow of money into the treasury proved false. Returns from the sale of British estates and the payment of British debts were meager, and the money that did come in was rendered almost worthless by the continued depreciation of Virginia currency. When the Assembly adjourned on December 24, the outlook for the coming year was dark.[59]

Not only was Virginia saddled with a debt of £26 million, but a British invasion seemed imminent, and the weather was the worst seen in thirty or forty years. The British invasion did not materialize; but while spring brought a break in the weather, no relief appeared for the fiscal situation.[60] In February 1780 the state, as a result of the legislature's authorization, floated a loan of £5 million. But very little money trickled in because people who had funds could get as high as 20 percent interest on private loans, whereas the state paid only 6 percent. Jefferson and the Council, explaining the depleted condition of the treasury, appealed to Virginia's citizens to support the loan drive. The governor also requested certain individuals, who were concerned with the plight of the state, to solicit loans.[61]

Nelson was one of this group. But he, and evidently some of his associates, found so much resistance to their appeal, because of lack of confidence in the ability of the state to repay the loans, that they began to pledge their own security. In this manner Nelson raised £10,974, out of a total of about £60,000, testimony to his belief in the rightness of the American cause and the ultimate success of that cause. But of course the amount, when the needs of the state are considered, was insignificant.[62]

As the state struggled to raise funds, prices continued to rise, with coffee selling for $20 a pound, shoes for $60 a pair, cloth for £200 a yard. As is often the case in wartime, many people pursued their own economic interests with little concern for the war effort. One commentator, distressed with conditions, reported that almost "all ranks are engaged in some sort of traffic or another. But the prevailing and favorite scheme at this time is that of purchasing back lands on the river Ohio." Prudent patriots had the money to purchase land, but at the same time they complained continually about heavy taxation, and when the elections for the legislature rolled around in April they chose, in general, candidates who made promises of relief. In the eyes of a contemporary, "those chosen are men of mean abilities and no rank." [63]

When the newly-elected Assembly convened in 1780, it met at its new home in Richmond. The governor, the Council, and the other administrative offices had moved from Williamsburg in April, and on May 9, the legislature joined them in the little town at the falls of the James. On motion of Thomas Nelson, Benjamin Harrison was elected speaker of the House of Delegates and the session got under way. Congress had asked that the states continue to raise $15 million monthly for the use of the central government; where this was to come from was anybody's guess. The fear of invasion still hung over the state, and to the south, American forces, made up partially of Virginia militia, were meeting with defeat after defeat. Troops were being sent to the Carolinas daily, including Nelson's cousin, Major John Nelson, and his cavalry.[64]

Thomas Nelson served in a variety of important capacities during this session, dealing largely with the pressing subjects of finance and defense. Early in May he headed committees that planned the defense of Virginia and presented proposals for whipping the militia into fighting trim. On the nineteenth he was made chairman of the key Committee of Ways and Means, and the end of the month saw him serving as chairman of the Committee of the Whole when the House considered the plight of the Carolinas and resolved that five thousand troops be raised and sent to their aid.[65]

On May 30, the speaker laid before the House of Delegates a request from Congress for an appropriation of $1,953,200 by June 15. A large French expeditionary and naval force was expected soon to act in conjunction with the American army, and Congress did not have the funds to support any offensive action. The state treasury was in no better shape than that of the central government, but the Assembly took immediate action, resolving on June 1 that money be borrowed from private individuals and that it be supplemented by the sale of 600,000 pounds of state tobacco. Individuals who loaned cash were to be repaid in December, or they could discount the amount from their taxes at the rate of 6 percent interest. If tobacco was advanced, it was to be repaid with good tobacco at 6 percent by April 1, 1781. Nelson,

The Nelson-Galt House in Williamsburg was built before 1718 and is one of the oldest buildings in the colonial capital. Both William Nelson, who bought it before 1749, and his son lived here when in Williamsburg. Colonial Williamsburg photograph.

Statue of Thomas Nelson, one of six surrounding the equestrian figure of George Washington on the state Capitol grounds in Richmond. The sculpture was done by Randolph Rogers in 1867 and must be called a conjectural likeness. Photograph courtesy of the Virginia State Library, Richmond.

Edmund Pendleton, Fielding Lewis, William Armistead, Garland Anderson, Bartlett Anderson, and William Call were authorized to receive the loans, which also could be paid directly into the treasury.[66]

Nelson immediately began vigorous endeavors to secure all money possible, first canvassing his own locality and then traveling south of the James. It was a difficult and thankless task and, as was the case in February, Nelson found that many people were unwilling to lend money on the shaky security of the state. Again Nelson pledged his own security for the payment of these loans in case the state was unable to fulfill its obligations. This time Nelson raised £41,601. When the computing came late in June, Virginia had raised $1,430,239, some $500,000 short of its goal. Governor Jefferson hoped that the remainder would be forthcoming, but it was not. In any event Virginia's contribution, considering the miserable state of her finances, had been a good one, and Thomas Nelson had taken a substantial part in making it possible.[67]

Nelson's contribution, over the past three years, towards American independence had been exceptional. Throughout the entire period from June 1777 to June 1780 he had served in the House of Delegates. His work in the legislature had focused primarily on Virginia's support of the war effort—in providing effective means for the state's defense, raising and equipping troops for the Continental army, and obtaining the money necessary to finance all of these endeavors. He served briefly in Congress. On two occasions he commanded the Virginia militia and he also raised and commanded a troop of cavalry in the summer of 1779. Finally, he played a central role in two state loan drives in the winter and spring of 1780, literally going from door to door to raise money and pledging his own security when he found that many citizens had no faith in the state's ability to repay them.

In his own words, Thomas Nelson had "exerted every nerve," and rarely had he allowed his own personal interests to interfere with those of the country. His fortune, time, energy, and considerable political influence had all been enlisted in the cause. Much had been asked of him and he had given freely. Yet the end was not in sight.

Chapter VI

The General Takes the Field

Thomas Nelson was in Richmond on June 30, 1780, getting 6 percent loan certificates to deliver to the people from whom he had collected money when a courier rode in with the news that a British fleet had appeared in Hampton Roads. Governor Jefferson and the Council immediately met and advised Nelson that if an invasion took place he would be appointed brigadier general to lead the militia in defense of the state. They also directed him to go down the peninsula between the James and the York rivers to alert the county lieutenants as to the number of militiamen he would require and at the same time to try to raise two troops of volunteer cavalry. Nelson immediately turned his attention to his new duties, but within two days the vessels sighted turned out to be only a naval squadron preying on Virginia shipping in the Chesapeake Bay rather than an invasion fleet.[1]

Although Virginia was given another reprieve from British invasion, it was not to last long. In the meantime the populace sweltered through a summer excessively hot and full of troubles. Unrest grew in the back country and Virginia currency further depreciated to the rate of sixty to one. In the Carolinas the war continued to go badly for America's cause, but Virginians in general seem not to have been overly concerned. Patriotism was so lacking that the government could not even get enough saddles to supply Major John Nelson's cavalry because Virginia merchants would accept nothing in payment but hard cash and that was an item conspiciously absent from the treasury.[2]

Early in October Lucy Nelson brought another daughter, Susanna, into the household. The baby probably did not cause much stir, for she was the tenth child—and the third in a little less than four years. In any event Nelson must have savored these days which he spent in close relationship with his family. Well he might, for during the next year he was to be almost constantly away from his loved ones.[3]

On October 20 a British fleet was sighted in Chesapeake Bay. It brought a British force under General Alexander Leslie reported to number five thousand troops. The number later proved to be three thousand, but after several false alarms this seemed to be a real invasion. Immediately the Council called Generals George Weedon and Peter Muhlenburg of the regular army and Edward Stevens and Thomas Nelson of the state militia to command the defenses of the Old Dominion.[4]

Stevens had already gone south with General Gates; of the other three, only Nelson was close enough to be ready for service on short notice. He hurried into the lower tidewater area, south of the James, to organize the militia to repulse the invader but found the region in complete confusion. On the following day when the British landed a detachment of cavalry at Kemp's Landing near Norfolk and proceeded toward Great Bridge, a few miles south, he could offer no resistance. During the next few days the British landed troops on both sides of the James, taking over Hampton and Newport News and establishing their main base at Portsmouth.[5]

In this period General Muhlenburg joined Nelson and assumed command on the south side of the river. Nelson then returned to Williamsburg to organize the militia on the peninsula, but units straggled into the former capital in such small detachments that he found it "impossible to make any proper arrangements." Even when they did come in larger numbers, he lacked enough arms to supply them. Despite these problems, Nelson was able to bring some order out of chaos. State funds not being readily available, he paid out of his own pocket for supplies that were needed immediately. This outlay amounted to about £10,000 in depreciated currency, and was repaid to Nelson in the following year. He also formed one regiment immediately and sent it farther down the peninsula to keep an

eye on the British. When all the British forces moved to the Norfolk area during the first week in November, Nelson was able
to send several detachments to the aid of Muhlenburg.[6]

Leslie's force, curiously, did not act like an invading army.
After some initial depredations at Hampton, the British settled
down at Portsmouth and did little more than seize horses and
supplies. This was probably a good thing for the Virginia militia,
for as Jefferson related, "there is not a single man [among them]
who has ever seen the face of an Enemy." The British had, in
fact, been sent by General Clinton to raid the valley of the
James River and, among other things, prevent supplies and
troops from going to the American army in the Carolinas. But
General Leslie, fearing strong opposition, did not act energeti-
cally and after the defeat of part of Cornwallis's army at King's
Mountain he was ordered to Charleston. Even after the British
troops boarded vessels in Hampton Roads there was some delay, and Nelson wondered "what the devil those fellows can be
waiting for." But on November 22 he reported to Governor
Jefferson that the British fleet "appeared to be standing out for
the Capes." Once again Virginia had escaped extensive damage, but her time was running out.[7]

General Nelson and Virginia's militia were again discharged,
and the whole state relaxed and enjoyed the finest harvest in
many years. Continental troops straggled in from the south,
tattered, sick, and disillusioned, but most Virginians, though
sympathetic, were not impressed with their own danger.[8] Even
when, early in December, Washington reported a large embarka-
tion of British troops from New York "supposed to be destined
Southward," no preparations were made. General von Steuben,
in Virginia as temporary Continental commander recruiting
men and supplies for General Greene's army in the South, recommended construction of various river defenses. Intended to
keep the British from striking into the heart of Virginia on its
numerous waterways, the recommendation was treated lackadai-
sically.[9]

Then, on December 30, 1780, the predictable happened. Late
in the afternoon Commodore James Barron of the Virginia navy
came into Hampton from the bay and reported to Jacob Wray,
a local merchant, that a fleet of twenty-seven sail had been
sighted just below Willoughby Point. Wray immediately sent this

information to Nelson in Yorktown, who in turn relayed it to Governor Jefferson in Richmond. The governor, who received the news early on a Sunday morning, promptly sent Nelson into the "lower country" with blanket authority to call out the militia in the area. But for the next two days Jefferson took no further action. He told a Sunday visitor who found him walking in his garden that it was probably only a foraging party and unless he got further information "he should not disturb the Country by calling out the militia." In fact, still without exact information after fifty hours—largely because the line of post riders had been discontinued for reasons of economy—people in Richmond "totally disbelieved" that this was an enemy fleet. Disbelief quickly vanished on Tuesday morning, however, when Nathaniel Burwell, the lieutenant in James City County, sent information that the enemy had already progressed up the river almost to Jamestown.[10]

It was distressing news, for Virginia was not prepared for actual invasion. Invasion scares and raids of the past several years seem to have made both the public and its leaders less alert than they should have been to the real possibility of full-scale British operations in the state. But the demands on Virginia were tremendous, and understandably Jefferson did not want to take any action that would strain her resources unnecessarily. The state was serving as a troop and supply base for American operations in the Carolinas, and every day was bringing it closer to the end of its financial string. But the reasonable desire for economy seems to have been carried too far when river defenses were neglected and express riders discontinued.[11]

On receiving confirmation that the fleet was British, Jefferson swung into vigorous action, calling out half the militia of the counties surrounding Richmond and a fourth of those farther west. He hoped this would put a total of forty-six hundred men in the field. Nelson, now commissioned brigadier general, received definite power to draw militia from the counties on either side of the James below Richmond, although he was not to have overall command of the state's forces. That responsibility fell on Major General von Steuben—although he was not informed of it until Thursday, when the British were figuratively knocking on Richmond's doors.[12]

Meanwhile, Nelson followed the British vessels up the river.

On Wednesday he was near Jamestown with 175 men. The British contemplated landing there and Brigadier General Benedict Arnold, who commanded the force, sent a letter to Nelson professing surprise at "the Hostil appearance of inhabitants under Arms on the shore" inquiring if they intended "to offer vain opposition to . . . Troops under my Command. . . ." General Nelson "sent his compliments back to Mr. Arnold, *Viva Voce,* appologising that he had not pen and Ink, that he would oppose him, as long as he has a Man to fight." [13]

Fortunately the British changed their minds. The wind and tide favored their going farther up the river, they knew of Nelson's force but not of his scanty numbers, and they were perhaps discouraged by sniping from the shore as their boats took soundings. The militia got some help from George Wythe and several other "old Gentlemen," who in the course of partridge hunting took pot shots at the enemy. In any event, the British moved on and easily forced their way past Hoods, a narrow neck in the river, which Steuben had recommended be fortified strongly but which had been supplied with only four cannon. On Thursday the British landed a force of some twelve hundred men at Westover, the Byrd home, twenty-five miles below Richmond. [14]

It was now generally learned that the traitor Arnold commanded the force, but even this did not arouse the countryside. Nelson, who had hoped to have 350 men by the following day, fell 100 short of his goal. Even in Richmond there were only 100 militiamen under Major Alexander Dick, and these meager forces gave little hope of halting the enemy's advance. On Thursday night, Dick moved slowly toward Nelson on the Chickahominy River. Thus on Friday Arnold marched into Richmond unopposed, proceeded to Westham above the city and burned the ordnance repair shop there, returned to the capital that night, and on Saturday fell back to Westover after burning some of the public buildings and supplies. Within the period of one short week Arnold's army had struck into the very heart of the Old Dominion and hardly a shot had been fired against it. [15]

Steuben, Nelson, and the other military leaders now feared that the enemy would strike at Petersburg, and for this reason Steuben kept the bulk of the militia, who were now streaming in, south of the James. At this point, with about 2,250 men in service, 1,800 of them with Steuben, Virginia's men in arms now outnumbered the British force almost two to one. Unfortunately they had not enough arms and almost no artillery. The shortage was due partially to confusion in the quartermaster department. Muskets and cannon that had been hidden from the British could not be found, other weapons had been handled so roughly in the excitement that they were unserviceable, and it was difficult to get wagons to transport usable arms to the troops who needed them.[16]

Even so, General Nelson hoped that he would be able to deliver a damaging blow as the enemy retreated to Westover. He knew that his own force, totaling only 450 men, could not meet Arnold in open conflict, but he hoped at least to harry the British as they retired toward the Byrd home. But even the elements seemed to conspire against him. "I am pained to the very soul," he wrote Jefferson. "On Saturday night I intended a blow at their Rear, when the Gates of Heaven were opened, and such a Flood of Rain poured down as rendered my plan abortive by almost drowning the Troops, who were in Bush Tents, and by injuring their Arms and Ammunition so much that they were quite unfit for service."[17] The deluge not only ruined any chances Nelson may have had of striking at the British on Saturday night, but also his future opportunities. His ammunition supply had been low anyway, and rain almost completely spoiled what was left. Before any action could be taken this deficiency had to be remedied, and new stores were not to reach him until after Arnold had embarked and headed down the river on January 10.[18]

The British did not appear in any hurry. They moved leisurely down the James plundering at every opportunity on the south side of the river. What they were going to do was anyone's guess, and consequently Nelson followed their movements closely from the shore. Williamsburg and Yorktown looked like possible objectives, but after the British passed Burwell's Ferry, a short distance below Jamestown, an attack on either town seemed less likely. Nelson then moved the bulk of his forces, now numbering about one thousand, to Williamsburg while leaving behind a detachment to observe the enemy's movements. Finally, on

January 19, Arnold gathered his army at Portsmouth and showed every indication of settling down for a while.[19]

General von Steuben, the Virginia commander, now had to decide whether an attempt should be made to dislodge the traitor from his position. On the face of things such a move would have seemed logical, particularly since Virginia's forces now numbered somewhere between three and four thousand men. But Steuben, a fine organizer and trainer of troops, was not noted for brilliant tactical leadership in the field; he was, in fact, overly cautious and his brigade commanders soon appeared to be of similar inclination. On January 20 Steuben crossed the river and went to Williamsburg to confer with Nelson. After some deliberation they came to the conclusion that an attack would be inadvisable. Their exact reasons for this decision are not known, but probably the strong British position at Portsmouth, their own green troops, and an inadequate supply of arms, ammunition, and artillery were important factors.[20]

Steuben decided instead to concentrate on trying to contain Arnold at Portsmouth, keeping him from again raiding the heart of the state. For this task he concluded that he would now need only twenty-seven hundred of the four thousand troops he had originally called for. Consequently he proposed to Jefferson to keep seventeen hundred men south of the James under the command of General Muhlenburg, who had been called in from the west, while the remaining one thousand were to be under Nelson on the peninsula. The governor agreed to this plan.[21]

The problem of keeping even the reduced force in service proved to be a difficult one. Militia enlistments were expiring daily and replacements were hard to find. Nelson was convinced from "disagreeable Experience" that even if the required number of militiamen could be kept, they would not be adequate to defend the state. To Jefferson he explained the situation:

> They [the militia] have been so much harrassed lately that they would give nearly half they possess to raise Regulars, rather than be subject to the Distresses they feel at leaving their Plantations and Families. We have been obliged to call out the whole Militia from several Counties, some of whom I have not been able to discharge for want of men to relieve them. I am order'd by Baron Steuben to keep in

this Neck 1000 or 1200 men, and were I to discharge the Men who were on Duty the last Invasion, which I confess they have a Right to claim, I should not have one third of that Number.[22]

Absence from home and expiring enlistments were not the only things that made militia hard to keep. Food, though plentiful, reached the troops only with difficulty and consisted largely of corn meal. The men were housed badly in brush huts or tents, which in a typically cold, wet, Virginia winter was a circumstance not conducive to the highest morale. Nelson thought that a good supply of whisky might help, but Governor Jefferson, though willing for Nelson to have a supply, reminded him "that [it] would not be allowed as a Part of the Daily ration but only on particular Occasions." [23]

Through late January and early February of 1781 Nelson wrestled with these problems, but despite his efforts his force dropped to eight hundred men. To Steuben he complained that his force was too weak "to defend this Neck," but Steuben nevertheless proceeded to remove two hundred of his men and post them north of the Chickahominy River at Sandy Point. The situation was very discouraging, and Nelson, in low spirits, suggested "with propriety," that General Weedon replace him so that he could look after his family and attend the General Assembly, which was to meet on March 1. There is no extant reply to Nelson's request but obviously it was refused.[24]

At the same time, his gloom was deepened by his part in Captain Beesly Edgar Joel's ill-starred plan to sail a fire ship among the enemy fleet at Portsmouth. Joel's scheme was one of those "chance in a thousand" plans that needed absolute secrecy for any hope of success. Joel intended to acquire "an old Vessel of the most worthless kind" at the state shipyard on the Chickahominy, and take it down the James to Portsmouth for the attack. Nelson, as military commander in the area, was to have general charge of the operation.[25]

Unfortunately, Joel talked too much and the vessel he selected, according to Nelson, was too valuable to risk in such an enterprise. So the general put a stop to the proceedings. To Jefferson he explained that Joel "should have taken some old Hulk that would not have been any loss to the State should the enterprize fail, of which (between friends) there is almost a certainty, it being known to all the lower Country and probably to the British before this day." But, Nelson said, if Jefferson felt that the scheme was too far along to stop, he would return the vessel to Joel.[26]

The governor agreed that Nelson's suspension of the plan was well grounded, as it had become "universally known." Joel was, of course, furious and no doubt conveyed his anger to Nelson, as he did to Jefferson:

> General Nelson was no stranger to my conduct. If he disaproves of it; why not stop it in the Bud? But at the instant when ev'ry thing was prepar'd, and I ensured of success was going to proced [*sic*] on an enterprize, beyond the resolution of everyone, to be thus stop't is surly strange.[27]

If Nelson was disturbed by Joel's anger he was certainly too busy to brood over it long.

Arnold remained a canker in Virginia's side. Governor Jefferson was particularly anxious that the "Parracide Arnold" should be taken, since his raid had caused much public criticism of the government. If he could be captured, it would salve many of the Old Dominion's wounds. A plan was developed for this purpose in which Nelson was to play an important role. Apparently it involved approaching Arnold's headquarters in several small boats, which were to be handled by some paroled men from the lower country. Arnold was to be lured aboard by some pretext. Then if he could be carried clear of the British forces the rest would be easy. By the middle of February this plan was well under way; Nelson had acquired the boats, and final arrangements were being made when an event occurred that seemingly made it all unnecessary.[28]

At three o'clock on the morning of February 15, Nelson was roused by a messenger informing him that a French fleet was in Chesapeake Bay. This was a most pleasant surprise. Virginia had been expecting French aid, but news had arrived several days before that a violent storm had driven their fleet under Admiral Chevalier Destouches back to Rhode Island. The intelligence was correct, but Destouches had detached one sixty-four-gun ship and two frigates under Captain Arnaud Le Gardneur de Tilly to assist Virginia. Nelson was overjoyed. "What you expected has taken place," he wrote Steuben, "I give you joy with all my soul. Now is our time. Not a moment ought to be lost." Here was an opportunity to take Arnold by honest military effort rather than by subterfuge. But, as Nelson indicated, Virginia had to act with expedition so the French would not be discouraged from giving future aid.[29]

With this in mind, he immediately set out for Hampton and on the sixteenth boarded the flagship *Eveille* to talk to de Tilly. In the discussion there was evidently some disillusionment on both sides. The French probably expected an immediate attack to be launched on Arnold while they kept him from escaping by bottling up the English fleet in the Elizabeth River. But Virginia wanted de Tilly to move his ships up into the Elizabeth River and use his guns to make up for the Americans' lack of field artillery. This proved to be impossible, as the river was too shallow for the largest French vessels. Steuben therefore hesitated to call for an attack, since he had only two six-pounders and three hundred bayonets for three thousand men. Why heavier artillery had not been brought to the Portsmouth area is not known; possibly it was not available.[30]

Unfortunately, the French were not prepared to wait until the deficiency could be remedied. On the arrival of the French the British had been able to slip a vessel past them which was reportedly dispatched to New York, and de Tilly, fearing that if he lingered he would be caught by a superior fleet, decided to leave. He calmed Nelson and the other authorities by assuring them that for safety's sake he was going to cruise off the Virginia capes, where he could prey on British supply and dispatch vessels, but that he would come to their assistance, when they were ready for him. This was only a palliative, for de Tilly headed back to join the main French fleet at Newport, Rhode Island, and with him went Virginia's last good opportunity to take Arnold.[31]

Nelson returned to Williamsburg from Hampton on February 18. Steuben had ordered him to take charge of the troops south of the James, relieving General Muhlenburg, who had been ordered back to headquarters. The militia and regular troops in the state were to be separated, and Muhlenburg, as a line officer, was evidently to command the latter. Unfortunately, Nelson developed a severe cold, and though he immediately went to bed, he contracted what was described as "violent pleurisy." Steuben was distressed, but he placed Colonel James Innes in temporary command of Nelson's troops on the peninsula and kept Muhlenburg in command below the James until Nelson recovered.[32]

Innes's task was a thankless one, for Nelson's troops were described as "totally destitute of the necessary cloathing," as well as "lousy dirty and ragged." The force had dropped from eight hundred men to half that number, and some, whose families depended on them for their sustenance, were on the point of mutiny.[33]

As February drew to a close, Nelson began to regain his strength, but a relapse forced him to remain in bed throughout the month of March. Steuben was especially upset, for he had come both to like Nelson and to depend on his advice. Early in March he wrote to Nelson that his indisposition was particularly unfortunate, "as it deprives me of your council and assistance at a time I am in the greatest want of it. You are better acquainted with the Strength and weakness of this state and you have the confidence of the People—judge then how much I regret your absence." The militia and the regular troops were in want of everything and the government did not seem to be able to ease the situation. Militiamen were even refusing to turn out when called. One hundred and four men had recently been called up from New Kent County and only nine had reported for duty. The general wanted Nelson to recover completely, of course, but he needed him desperately and wrote that the "love of your Country and Zeal for the Service invite you to join me as soon as possible to assist me with your Council and your influence."[34] Exactly when Nelson returned to service is not clear; but he was back in command of his brigade by late April.[35]

During Nelson's illness, Virginia's situation had gone from bad to worse. On March 16 a small French fleet, which had been sent to aid the state, was caught off the Virginia capes by the British, and in the ensuing battle was forced to return to Newport, Rhode Island. Ten days later a British force of some twenty-six hundred men, under Major General William Phillips, joined Arnold. Virginia's forces had now dwindled to twelve hundred men. Even if all these troops had been placed before Portsmouth, they could hardly have contained the combined British force. In fact, only seven hundred Virginia troops were south of the James. Although General Lafayette was moving south with an estimated twelve hundred troops and a new group of militia had been called up, it was estimated that the Continental force could not arrive and the militia could not be ready for service before the end of April. Steuben therefore pulled the troops before Portsmouth back toward Petersburg, once again leaving the British free to move as they saw fit.[36]

Phillips and Arnold did not hesitate long. On April 18, twenty-five hundred troops under the direct command of Arnold moved up the James, plundering as they went. They landed at City Point on the twenty fourth and on the following day launched an attack on the supply depot of Petersburg. Generals Steuben and Muhlenburg, commanding about one thousand militiamen, put up a stubborn defense, but by the end of the day British superiority was evident. Steuben ordered a withdrawal, which was carried out in good order, and Arnold then proceeded into Petersburg destroying, among other things, four thousand hogsheads of tobacco. Encouraged by this success, Arnold demolished part of the Virginia navy at Osbornes, a small village on the James some fifteen miles below Richmond, and Phillips proceeded to burn barracks and stores at Chesterfield Court House. Arnold and Phillips then moved toward Manchester, just across the James from Richmond.[37]

General Nelson, making his first appearance since his illness, hastily gathered a handful of militiamen, but things looked bad for the capital city. Fortunately the British did not get to Manchester until the morning of April 30, and on the previous afternoon General Lafayette had marched his nine hundred weary troops into Richmond, after a forced march that had taken them only ten days in miserable weather to cover the 150 miles from Annapolis. Thus, when the British arrived in Manchester, they were confronted across the river by Lafayette's troops located in good position. Though superior in numbers, the British decided not to attack, and after burning some tobacco they dropped down the river, and by May 6, were below Jamestown.[38]

In an effort to put Richmond beyond further attack, Lafayette then moved Nelson and his militia to Williamsburg, his own troops to Bottom's Bridge, between Richmond and the old capital, and had work begun on a redoubt at Hoods. But hardly had his men arrived at their positions before they learned that the British were coming back up the river to meet Lord Cornwallis. After his costly victory over General Greene at Guilford Court House in March, Cornwallis had gone to Wilmington, North Carolina. From there he made plans to march into Virginia and join Phillips at Petersburg. This plan was now being put into effect.[39]

Lafayette, for fear of being cut off on the peninsula, marched back to Richmond. For a week and a half neither he nor the British made any further move. The legislature had planned to meet in Richmond, but clearly that was not going to be a safe place; on May 10 they agreed to convene two weeks later in Charlottesville. In Richmond, meanwhile, Lafayette reorganized his army, which now totaled about nine hundred Continentals plus twelve hundred to fifteen hundred militia, divided into two brigades under Nelson and Muhlenburg. This was considerably less than Phillips had in Petersburg and when Cornwallis arrived on May 20, bringing the British force to around seventy-two hundred, Lafayette commented that he was "not strong enough to get beaten."[40]

As this crisis deepened Nelson became more involved in the difficult and frequently distasteful business of being a military commander in an enemy-invaded area. Disloyal acts became common, and in one case alone, in early May, he was forced to take twelve disaffected persons into custody, including Williamsburg merchant John Greenhow, who had advised a "militia officer to lay aside his Sword because we were already conquered." Horses, which might strengthen an already superior British cavalry, had to be removed from Cornwallis's path. Owners who did not cooperate were to have their animals seized. Nelson also had to oversee the impressment of horses for Lafayette's cavalry. A condition approaching martial law prevailed.[41]

On May 24, Cornwallis marched out of Petersburg, crossed the James, and proceeded toward Richmond to dislodge the Frenchman. Lafayette was not going to risk battle. He wanted to keep his army intact and at the same time prevent Cornwallis from getting between him and General Anthony Wayne who was coming from Pennsylvania with reinforcements. Consequently he retreated rapidly northward toward Fredericksburg with Cornwallis in pursuit. On the march north Nelson took time to go by his Hanover plantation, Offley Hoo, where his family was staying, and send them off to a safer place, probably either his Loudoun County or Prince William County farm. By the twenty-eighth he was back with the army as it crossed the South Anna River. Cornwallis was not far behind, but on the last day of the month, his main force in Hanover, he gave up hope of catching Lafayette and turned his attention to other designs.[42]

Cornwallis's objectives were to destroy a main supply depot at Point of Fork, located some fifty miles above Richmond where the Rivanna River flows into the James, and to capture the Virginia legislature, then in session in Charlottesville—and possibly to take Governor Jefferson. Lieutenant Colonel John Simcoe and five hundred troops accomplished the first objective; Steuben, who was defending the depot with about four hundred militia, retreated in haste. Lieutenant Colonel Banastre Tarleton and 250 cavalry, assigned the second objective, fell upon Charlottesville early on the morning of June 4. Had it not been for the ride of Captain Jack Jouett from Cuckoo Tavern to warn the legislature and the governor, the plan would have been successful. As it was, seven dilatory members of the legislature were captured and the remainder barely had time to flee across the mountains to Staunton.[43]

Jefferson managed to elude the British, but he did not accompany the legislature to Staunton. His term of office had expired on June 2, and he was determined not to run for office again. The gentle Virginian was not a military man, his second term had been a frustrating one, and he was determined to step aside for someone better fitted for the position.[44] A little over a week later, the Assembly meeting in Staunton chose General Thomas Nelson as Jefferson's successor.

Five arduous months of military service, punctuated by a severe illness, were behind Nelson. A much more difficult period lay ahead.

Chapter VII

Governor Nelson

Thomas Nelson was elected governor of Virginia in Staunton on June 12, 1781. No evidence suggests that he had any foreknowledge that he would be nominated, and the events surrounding his election are obscure.[1]

The Assembly was scheduled to vote for governor on June 4 in Charlottesville, but the Tarleton raid put an abrupt halt to that. They reconvened in Staunton on the seventh, and proceeded to delay the election of a chief executive for five days while bitterly debating a motion by George Nicholas to appoint a dictator. Patrick Henry backed Nicholas on the floor, and Richard Henry Lee, though not in Staunton, wrote a series of letters supporting the move. All were strong critics of Jefferson's last term in office, and they pictured the state as completely disorganized and demoralized. Only a dictator, they argued, could stabilize and improve Virginia's critical situation; they suggested both General Washington and General Greene as suitable persons to fill this post. The motion was defeated by a close vote, but only after valuable time had been consumed.[2]

Exactly when Nelson was presented as a candidate is not known. Jefferson stated, some fifteen years later, that "He himself proposed to his friends in the legislature that Genl. Nelson . . . should be appointed Governor, believing that the union of the civil and military power in the same hands, at this time would greatly facilitate military measures." This would suggest that Nelson was under consideration before the exodus from Charlottesville. In any event it is probable that the general was not the only candidate. Jefferson himself was set against running for a third time, but in his absence some of his friends evidently put his name up and he received a few votes.[3]

102

News of his election as governor reached Nelson on June 16. Lafayette was then in the process of following Cornwallis as the British general withdrew down the James past Richmond toward Williamsburg. Nelson, still in command of a brigade of militia under the Frenchman, was encamped with the army at Nathaniel Dandridge's on the South Anna River. His feelings on receiving the news are not known, but later he remarked that to "have declin'd the appointment might have indicated timidity. I, therefore accepted it with a determination to exert every power that I possess'd to give energy to Government and security to the inhabitants of the State." [4]

Nelson left the army immediately and arrived in Staunton on the night of June 18. The following day Sampson Matthews, magistrate for Augusta County, administered the oath of office in the presence of Council members William Fleming, Andrew Lewis, and George Webb. The general now became governor at one of the most crucial periods in Virginia's history. The question of whether or not he was capable of filling this demanding position must have arisen in Nelson's mind, and in the minds of others. Certainly Nelson's long legislative experience and his military service, which had brought him in close contact with the problems that now faced the state, were excellent preparation for his new responsibilities. His election was also a popular one, which gave him a further advantage as he faced the difficult months ahead. The statement of one county official that Nelson's selection "diffused a universal joy and satisfaction" seems to have reflected a generally held opinion. And Washington, in his own direct way, perhaps best summed up the people's feeling: "He is an honest man, active, spirited and decided, and will, I daresay, suit the times as well as any other person." [5]

On the same day that Nelson took the oath of office, the legislature passed a bill giving him extensive powers. The Assembly authorized him, with the consent of the Council, to call out the state militia in such numbers as he saw fit and to send them where their services were required; to impress food and supplies; to seize loyalists and banish them without jury trial; to redistribute the property of persons who opposed laws for calling up militia; to discontinue the state quartermaster department and put it in the hands of Continental officials; and to constitute courts with the same powers as the General Court of the state. Additional legislation provided the death penalty for desertion and empowered the governor and Council to lay an embargo on exports from the state, to declare martial law within a twenty-mile radius of the enemy or American camps, and to strengthen militia regulations so that six months might be added to the service of those who failed to appear when originally summoned. These laws gave Nelson and the Council almost dictatorial powers.[6]

Any comparison of Nelson's administration with that of other war governors, including Jefferson's, must take these extensive powers into consideration. At the same time, it should be remembered that other states did provide their executives with similar emergency powers in crisis situations. Neither the frequent movement of the seat of government (three times in Nelson's case) nor the dispersal of administrative offices resulting from invasion was unique. The difference was that in his brief administration of only five months it soon became evident that unfolding events might bring this long war to a successful conclusion. Thus motivated, Nelson's leadership did take on a vigorous character that was not common.[7]

It is, of course, inevitable that Jefferson's direction of Virginia's affairs during the first five months of 1781 should be compared with his friend Nelson's conduct during the latter part of that eventful year. Some historians have argued that Nelson's election represented a conservative turn in Virginia politics, but in fact at that point the two men held similar political views. Furthermore, Jefferson had definitely been limited in what he could do; the slow pace of the legislative process often precluded quick action, whereas Nelson only had to gain the consent of the Council before acting. In the end, Nelson went beyond the sweeping powers granted him, but even here the situation was different. During the closing months of Jefferson's administration the future appeared bleak indeed and, while he did everything he could within the confines of the law, Jefferson was not prepared to go beyond them. He was no believer in a strong executive, though he eventually came to support greater executive power.[8]

In any event, Jefferson admitted he stepped aside for "talents better fitted than his own to the circumstances. . . ." And Nelson was indeed a different kind of person. A man of direct action, he did not allow his sensitivity to the public's rights and feelings to immobilize him. General Nathanael Greene, in a congratulatory letter, told Nelson that qualities of "both the Citizen and Soldier" were "happily united" in him, and perhaps they were. His administration took the attitude that the legislature had "vested the Executive with extensive powers" which would be freely used because the security of the state depended on it.[9]

When Nelson took office the British army had been able to move about the state almost at will for five months. The morale of the citizenry, already low, was not improved by the absence of a governor for three weeks in June. Public business demanded the executive's attention, particularly his approval of the issuance of funds. And where the funds were going to come from was a question of importance. Virginia faced the heaviest financial demands in its history, yet additional taxes had not been and perhaps could not be levied. A measure of the state's plight can be seen in the lament of one official that the public printer had been seized by the British and without him "we shall be entirely without money." Inflation continued to spiral. (In April the exchange rate had been 150 to 1, when Nelson became governor it was 200 to 1, and by late July it was 350 to 1.) With harvest time drawing near, the state militia began to melt away from Lafayette's army, while to the south General Greene was crying for reinforcements from Virginia. To the north the state's delegates in Congress complained that "unless something is done to furnish us with money to bear our reasonable expenses in this place [Philadelphia] we must sell what little property we possess here or return to Virginia." And, of course, there was the always pressing problem of obtaining and transporting food to the army; in this land of plenty the troops frequently suffered in this respect, because farmers hesitated to sell their produce for devalued currency and transportation was hard to come by. It is not surprising that some persons had called for a dictator.[10]

The new governor, possessing the necessary authority and the appropriate temperament, moved swiftly to deal with these and other needs. Almost immediately he began to use the power of impressment and take steps to deal with the loyalist problem. In the face of an approaching harvest, he made plans to get reinforcements to General Greene and to keep Lafayette's army at its then current strength of three brigades. The French general, though continuing to complain of Virginia's niggardliness, was impressed by the increased exertions.[11]

On June 25 the British army reached Williamsburg. Lafayette and his little force were some ten miles away at Bird's Tavern. Cornwallis, of his own volition, had moved back to Williamsburg in the belief that his march through the state had successfully reduced Virginia's will and ability to engage in any more serious fighting. But Virginians viewed the withdrawal as a retreat and their spirits rose. They fished out many of the arms that the British had thrown in creeks and rivers and, taking stock, found that less damage had been done than they had thought.[12] Governor Nelson decided to move the executive office to Charlottesville, and, if things continued to improve, from there to Richmond. Starting for the village of Charlottesville on June 27, Nelson became ill, and it was July 2 before he was able to do any work.[13]

The governor and Council met only twice in Charlottesville, but Nelson was able to catch up with some of his correspondence before the decision was reached on July 3 to go on to Richmond. Governor Nelson did not arrive in Richmond on the appointed date, Monday, July 9—in fact it was nearly two weeks before he met with the Council. His whereabouts in this period is something of a mystery. He may have gone via Hanover to check on his property, and he probably did visit Lafayette who was then near Williamsburg.[14]

Unfortunately Nelson failed to keep in touch with other governmental departments, including the War Office, much to the consternation of its head, William Davies. On July 12 Davies wrote General von Steuben that "nobody here [in Richmond] knows where the Governor is, nor have we heard the least tittle from him since he left Charlottesville. I hardly know how to account for it." He was fearful that for want of a guard in Richmond the administrative offices would be "swept off one of these days." The capable and hard working Davies was by nature a pessimist and a somewhat contentious one at that, but his concern was warranted. In any event, Nelson was in Richmond on July 16.[15]

For the next month Nelson wrestled with a multitude of problems related to the war effort. Except for a raid by Tarleton through the southern part of the state, the British did not go on the offensive; and so the business that occupied Nelson largely revolved around questions of finance, supply, and keeping the militia in the field. The financial situation remained serious. In the spring the legislature had authorized the emission of up to £35,000,000 in paper money. All Nelson and the Council could do was to decide when the money was to be emitted and how it was to be spent. Warrants for some £15,000,000 were issued while he was in office, virtually all of which was used to provide for the army.[16]

The problem of supply was even more immediate and difficult. Responsibility for coordinating and carrying out the supply function was in the hands of the War Office. All state quartermasters and commissaries, as well as the state clothier and the commercial agent, reported to that office. Fortunately its direction was in the competent hands of William Davies; but no amount of efficiency could compensate for the consequences of rampant inflation, the depredations of the British army, which had been in the state for seven months, and for the fact that for a much longer period Virginia had been serving as a supply base and manpower pool for the army in the Carolinas. The presence in Virginia of a Continental quartermaster who on occasion worked at cross purposes with state authorities did not help matters.[17]

In this situation state officials had little choice but to resort to impressment in order to get the necessary food and equipment. This frequently involved the threat of force, for Virginia farmers were loath to exchange their produce for vouchers which stated the appraised price and were redeemable at a future date. The situation was worsened by a long dry spell culminating in a poor harvest. Even when provisions were acquired a scarcity of wagons made it difficult to get them to the army. Owners often hid their wagons and refused to transport supplies unless they got protection from impressment and assurance that they would be paid for their services. Nevertheless, Nelson continued to operate on the theory that as "disagreeable as impressing is [it is necessary that] everything requisite be taken, wherever . . . [it is] to be found, if not to be procured by other means." [18]

The sort of problem that Nelson had to deal with in supplying the state's armed forces can be seen in the incident involving the seizure of state clothing by General Anthony Wayne and his Pennsylvania troops as they passed through Chesterfield Court House. William Davies was immediately up in arms. He protested to Governor Nelson that "if any officer of any rank whatever has the right to appropriate the stores of the state at his pleasure, at a time when our own men are in want of them, I think our situation must be truly deplorable." Nelson agreed, and he wrote Lafayette—as commander of the American forces in the state—a stiff letter. The action, he said, was "not to be tolerated" where civil government was established and regular modes of procurement laid down. Furthermore, he had heard that the Pennsylvania troops also had committed "Excesses . . . on the property of Individuals." Certainly, Nelson continued, this was done without the knowledge of their officers; but, whatever the case, in the future such action should be prevented. [19]

Lafayette at once wrote Wayne on the matter. This infuriated the fiery general, for he considered Nelson's complaint a reflection on the honesty of his officers and men. Lafayette tried in vain to act as peacemaker, and throughout August tempers remained high. [20]

Wayne eventually returned the clothing but not until he had the last word when he reminded Nelson, in strong terms, how inefficient the state had been in supplying the army. For two weeks, Wayne told the governor, his men had been forced to exist on "new Indian Corn and water," and it had been necessary for him "to take some Cornfields at Bottom's bridge to prevent [his] troops from starving, for which the owners rece[ive]d Certificates. . . ." He asked that Nelson remedy the situation, and then, casting his final barb, he mentioned his preference for procuring supplies "in a manner less troublesome to the people," but reminded Nelson that Congress had given him ample authority to appropriate needed provisions. [21]

Almost as difficult as the supply problem was that of keeping militia in the field. The militia of each county was usually divided into four groups and called up in rotation. Since a militiaman served only a two month's tour of duty, there was constant coming and going in the army. Toward the end of July a new group was ordered out. Those from the southern and western counties were to go to the aid of General Greene, the remainder to Lafayette. As always there was great difficulty in getting the men to report for duty, and in fact a uniform application of the militia law was difficult, not to say impossible. Men called for duty within the state spent much less time away from home than those who were sent to the Carolinas.[22]

One officer told Nelson that service in the south involved two months travel time in addition to the two months active duty. Because of this, the "horrors of the Southern climate," and the "fatigues of marching," his militia preferred to serve six months within Virginia than to be ordered to duty with General Greene. Yet, he complained, militia from southern counties had been ordered to the south on four different occasions and in addition had "done equal duty in the state with those of Northern Counties." Furthermore men were needed to ride express, to collect "Beeves," grind wheat and corn, transport provisions, and make and repair equipment for the army. Yet the only persons exempted by law from militia duty were artificers in iron works.[23]

Evidently Nelson and the Council occasionally allowed exemption for other public service, but the counties did not get credit for these persons when the next call for militia was issued. Bound by the law, the executive could do little to improve matters except to apply the rules as even-handedly as possible. In general, Nelson required strict adherence to the law, and made every attempt to enforce uniformly the provision providing six months of additional duty for those evading army service.[24]

Assuring that all men eligible for militia duty reported for service when called was much more difficult in areas distant from Richmond, particularly in the western part of the state. In counties to the west of the mountains, where the Indians were a greater threat than the British and where there were large pockets of loyalists, the evasion of militia duty in some instances reached the point of virtual insurrection. William Preston wrote from Montgomery County that one-half of the people were Tories and "cannot be drawn into the Service by any means whatever, and the Whigs who could render any service, are afraid to leave their property and connexions to the mercy of the former." He reported that in the previous year he had had to call for assistance from neighboring counties "to suppress an insurrection," and there was every reason to believe that he would have to contend with it again. He went on to say that he would issue orders as instructed for one-fourth of the militia to report for duty, but he was convinced that it would be to no avail.[25]

Earlier, in Hampshire, Rockingham, and Augusta counties, resistance to militia duty and taxes had resulted in several skirmishes with local authorities. A large number of these "unhappy," "deluded" people had been apprehended, and Nelson had called a Court of Oyer and Terminer to meet in Hampshire County on July 10, to try them. At the same time the Council, operating on the theory that the insurrections were "occasioned by the artifice of a few designing men," advised Governor Nelson to offer pardon to others involved, on condition that the ringleaders be delivered up. This device worked fairly well and by the end of July some of the disaffected were actually helping to apprehend a few of their more obstinate members who had fled to the mountains.[26]

Meanwhile the first group arrested was brought to the Hampshire courthouse for trial, amidst the wailing of "aged mothers, wives and children" who expected that "execution would be immediate. . . ." Fortunately for these unhappy persons, the judges appointed to try the case did not appear, and the prisoners were put on bail and allowed to go home. With the support of the county lieutenant, Peter Hogg, they then asked Nelson for indemnity, stating that due to their distant position they got little information and were misled by British agents in respect to militia service and taxes. Nelson was sympathetic but stated firmly that the constitution prevented him from interfering once the case came before the courts. He did assure them that "no further Process" would be issued until the next General Court. Eventually the whole group was pardoned. Unfortunately for Nelson the West was not the only area of discontent. The lower Tidewater and the Eastern Shore were also to give him trouble before his term ended.[27]

While Nelson struggled with the problems of administering the government of war-torn Virginia, military events took a turn for the better. After an indecisive victory over Lafayette near Jamestown early in July, Cornwallis moved across the James River and down to Portsmouth. Sir Henry Clinton had been requesting that Cornwallis send at least part of his forces in Virginia to New York or that they be employed in operations elsewhere. But Clinton had left the final decision to Cornwallis who decided to remain in the state with his entire army and establish a defensible base. After deciding against Old Point Comfort he settled on Yorktown; and on the morning of August 1, he landed fifteen hundred troops there and at Gloucester Point directly across the York River. The bulk of the British army was soon to follow.[28]

The reasons for Cornwallis's movements were unclear to Nelson and Lafayette, but since they might be the prelude to offensive action Nelson rescinded the order sending militia to General Greene. Nelson, ever alert to the possibility of ending the war, expressed to the county lieutenants his hope that the militia would, now that the harvest was in, turn out "with the greatest alacrity," for there "never was a Time when vigorous measures were more necessary, or when they promised greater Advantages." Offering the opinion that the British would now make great exertions, he declared that "a successful opposition on our Part, which the Strength of this State is very capable of making . . . will in all Probability . . . Put a happy Period to the War." [29]

The chance to defeat Cornwallis seemed to him a distinct possibility, as it did to Washington and Lafayette. Late in July the commander in chief had hinted to the marquis that he was considering moving his forces from New York to Virginia. With this in mind Lafayette wrote Nelson on August 8, stating that since a siege was now conceivable, he would like an estimation of how long Virginia would be able to support twelve thousand troops.[30]

From this point on, events moved rapidly. Washington learned on August 14 that the French Admiral de Grasse had already left the West Indies, with twenty-nine warships and more than three thousand troops, for operations in the Chesapeake Bay area. De Grasse signified that he would be able to remain only until October 15. If Washington was to take advantage of the naval superiority de Grasse could give him, he had to act swiftly.[31]

The American commander immediately pushed aside all plans for an attack on New York, and began preparations to move General Rochambeau's French army to Virginia along with the bulk of American forces. A courier was sent off within a few hours notifying Lafayette of the plans and admonishing him to take every precaution to keep Cornwallis from escaping. Several days later Lafayette told Nelson of the plans and urged him to prepare Virginia to give every "possible aid and assistance," particularly in respect to supplies. Nelson was overjoyed and replied to the general that "An event so unexpected, and so much wish'd cannot but be productive of the most happy consequences to this Country." Great events were underway.[32]

As the combined American and French forces began their move to the south, Nelson decided again to visit Lafayette's army, which was now bivouacked near West Point where the confluence of the Pamunkey and the Mattaponi form the York River. Plans had to be made for the coming campaign and Lafayette was still upset by what he considered lack of support on the part of Virginia. But on the way to camp Nelson again became ill and had to retire to Hanover, where he remained for most of the final two weeks in August.[33]

The burden of administering the government fell on the shoulders of Lieutenant Governor David Jameson, who was handicapped in the performance of his duties by the absence of a quorum of the Council. Here at this most critical time the executive was virtually paralyzed for two weeks because four out of eight Council members could not be brought together. Fortunately, both Jameson and William Davies in the War Office were extremely able men and they carried through with the plans made before Nelson's illness for gathering supplies and calling in militia.[34]

By the end of August Nelson was well enough to pay a brief visit to Lafayette, and by September 2 he was back in Richmond. There was now more need than ever for vigorous action on the part of the Virginia government, because de Grasse had arrived with a fleet of thirty-four vessels, largely ships of the line, and was landing three thousand troops at Jamestown.[35]

Nelson did not hesitate. He sent John Pierce, soon to be commissary general of the state in place of the incompetent John Brown,[36] to take personal charge of supplying the French army. He gave Thomas Newton the difficult job of procuring provisions in Princess Anne, Nansemond, and Norfolk counties for the French fleet, and authorized him to impress the needed supplies if necessary. At the same time the governor laid an embargo on the export of all beef, pork, bacon, peas, wheat, Indian corn, and other grain. He also sent urgent letters to the governors of Maryland and North Carolina requesting supplies of flour, beef, and salt. After issuing a call for a large body of the state militia the governor on September 5 announced that he was taking personal command of this force. The Council was to conduct the business of the executive in Nelson's absence, and he wrote each member requesting their presence in Richmond.[37]

Soon after Nelson's departure for the army, Lieutenant Governor Jameson wrote the governor pointing out the dangers of his absence from Richmond. Only himself and one other Council member were present, Jameson related, and most of the remaining members would not attend unless the governor came. The executive, he continued, was held in low enough repute before; but now, unable to do any business, it would become "quite contemptable," and he did not intend to stay in Richmond "to hear the daily complaints and reproaches of the people without the power of doing anything." In closing, Jameson told Nelson that "when you reflect on the injury done the Community by this want of government, and how soon the people will think themselves free from all restraint; I know you will do all in your power . . . [to] prevent the Evil; and that I think will not be but by returning to the Board." [38]

Jameson made a strong argument, but Nelson's reply was persuasive. He was concerned over the poor attendance of the Council members, but declared:

> It is . . . impossible for me to quit the Army at this Time, at least the bad Consequence which would result from it would not be compensated by any Good which might arise from my attending at the Council Board. The Wants of the Army which are many, & which require the most instant Attention, are here represented to me on the Spot, and the

most immediate Measures are fallen upon to supply or anticipate them. Not all the Exertions which could possibly have been made in Richmond, & by the Commissaries & others above, would have prevented the Army either from suffering extreme Distress, or seizing the little that remains to the People of the Neighborhood, to their utter ruin. It is my Opinion that nothing should come into Competition with our Endeavors to give Success to the present military Operation, because if they fail, we shall have but the Shadow of a Government, if even that, whereas if they succeed, the Hands of Government will be Stronger and it will be more respectable than ever.[39]

Nelson arrived in Williamsburg to take charge of the Virginia militia on September 11, and found supplies of food so low that on this particular day the militia had given up their corn meal so that the French troops would have something to eat. Incredulous, he wrote a friend: "Do you not think it curious that the Governor of Virginia should not know where to get a mouthful for his dinner? But that is literally the case." [40]

Nelson took immediate action. In order that provisions might be distributed equally among all the troops, French and American, he ordered all supplies of food to be located centrally and dispensed by himself on application. So that he could deal more efficiently with the French army he also chose as his aide St. George Tucker, who spoke the language. Then he began vigorous—almost desperate—efforts to procure supplies. In the next five weeks Nelson wrote over forty letters about supplies for the army. He urged commissioners of provisions in every county to impress if they could not obtain supplies otherwise. Some farmers refused to have their wheat ground unless they were to receive hard money, but this situation was remedied by taking unground wheat and then impressing mills and Negroes to do the grinding. Transportation remained a serious problem, but with the French fleet now giving the Americans control of the water, the state's extensive river system could be utilized, and boats and crew were impressed for this purpose. If the people resisted impressment, then militia were to be used to bring them into line.[41]

In almost all of these actions authorizing impressment, Nelson acted without consent of the Council, which under the law granting him extraordinary power and under the terms of the state constitution he was not authorized to do. To one state official he wrote that since he had "tried a variety of expedients for procuring provisions without success," and since this opportunity to defeat the British army "holds forth the most glorious consequences" for America:

> I think the trust my country has repos'd in me demands that I should stretch my powers to their utmost extent, regardless of the censures of the inconsiderate or any other evil that may result to myself from such a step [and] attain by the strongest methods of compulsion those necessaries which cannot otherwise be procur'd and from the want of which alone we can have any reason to fear that our enterprize will fail.

In closing he gave him his orders:

> You will therefore Sir without delay proceed to those parts of the country which are able to furnish any supplies of spirits wheat, flour, corn or any other specie of provision or forage, and if you observe that effectual methods have not already been taken to render them subservient to public use, you are hereby authorized and impowered to adopt such methods as you shall find necessary . . . the commanding officers of militia of all counties on whom you shall call for assistance are hereby order'd to lend you any aid you shall think necessary for the execution of your offices.[42]

At about four o'clock on the afternoon of September 14, Washington, accompanied by General Rochambeau and a few other officers, arrived in Williamsburg a few days ahead of their armies. Lafayette and Governor Nelson rode to greet them in a joyous reunion. Lafayette, particularly moved to see his beloved chief again, threw his arms around Washington's neck and embraced him warmly. Washington and Rochambeau reviewed both the French and the American armies, after which they attended a dinner held in the French camp in their honor.[43]

The coming of Washington spurred Virginians to renewed efforts to secure supplies for the army. A long dry spell, which had hurt the crops and lowered the streams to such an extent that many mills could not operate, hindered their efforts. Generally speaking, state officials had greater success in collecting supplies south of the James than in northern Virginia, where they met with greater resistance. Their difficulties arose in part from their having to compete with French agents who were paying cash for provisions. Nelson had tried to avoid this development, but the scarcity of food had caused the French to go out on their own rather than operate through the governor.[44]

Nelson wrote Jameson of his indignation at the difficulties the state officials were having. He conceded that part of the trouble was due to the French, but he attributed it also to "the unwillingness of the people to assist [a] Government from which former treatment gives them perhaps too little reason to expect Justice, and partly from that desire of handling Gold which has too often been found to prevail over every other consideration." Unbeknown to Nelson even his personal aide was hoping to profit from the situation. St. George Tucker wrote his wife instructing her to temporize with the public commissaries when they came seeking provisions because he had secret information that the French would soon be buying needed supplies with hard money.[45] Eventually Nelson was to appoint a state official to devote all his time to supplying the French, and through whose hands all provisions for them had to pass. By the middle of October this official, Richard Morris, had gone a long way toward solving the problem.[46]

About September 16, Nelson became ill again, for the fourth time in seven months. He remained inside, carrying on his business with the aid of his secretary, Robert Andrews, and his aide-de-camp, George Nicholas. Nevertheless, the efficiency of Nelson's administration is most evident during this period. Under severe pressure and immense responsibility he dealt with a multitude of problems both promptly and effectively.[47]

Aside from the question of supply, one of the main irritants continued to be the Loyalist problem. It was reported to Nelson from Princess Anne County, where Norfolk is located, that there was neither civil nor military law in operation and "murder is committed and no notice is taken of it. . . ." Nelson could not do much about the Norfolk area, but he did take vigorous action in other sections of the country.[48]

On September 18, he ordered Colonel James Innes to seize

Ralph Wormeley, Ralph Wormeley, Jr., Philip Grymes, James Mills, Simon Frazer, Robert Gilmore, Hugh Walker, and Jonathan Dennison, all of Middlesex County; a Dr. Brockenborough and Archibald Ritchie of Essex County; and Anthony McKittrick of Stafford County for conduct "which manifests Disaffection to this Government and the Interests of the United States. . . ." These Loyalists were to be conveyed to Richmond for trial. It must have pained Nelson to take this action for the Wormeleys were old acquaintances and Philip Grymes was his wife's brother.[49]

On the Eastern Shore the Reverend John Lyon and "part of his flock"—John Custis, William Garrison and Solomon Bunting—were seized for resisting militia duty and taken to Richmond. George Corbin, county lieutenant for Accomac, remarked that the "Parson" and his followers were showing marks of repentance for their action "but whether this is founded on a conviction that they have sined [*sic*] against their Country; or on the arrival of the fleet of our generous ally, I will not pretend to judge." The Reverend Mr. Lyon was eventually permitted to reside anywhere twenty miles above Richmond on giving security for good behavior. In these and other cases the Virginia government acted with firmness. Some of the disaffected people were released prior to Yorktown on showing the proper contriteness and giving security to furnish a soldier for the war. Even so, the Richmond jail was still crowded with Tories in December.[50]

The governor had his problems with the loyal Whigs in his militia as well as with the Loyalists. Colonel James Barbour of Culpeper seized twenty-nine boxes of arms being transported from the north to the American army and distributed them to the militia of his county. This was similar to the earlier action of Wayne, but Nelson considered Barbour's conduct more serious. "If we were to consider the Consequence of such Conduct," wrote the governor, "nothing could appear more criminal, or meriting more severe notice." If every county lieutenant, he continued, acted as Barbour had, there would be no arms for the army on "which the immediate salvation of the state depends. . . ." In a milder tone, Nelson stated that he was sure Barbour was only interested in putting his militia in good fighting order, yet if the colonel did not collect the arms and convey them to camp, he would have to "Exercise . . . those extensive Powers with which the late Laws have invested me." [51]

The predicament created by Barbour was only one of many militia problems with which Nelson had to deal. For example, in mid-September a body of Henrico County militiamen was detailed to patrol a portion of the James River; but after one trip they quit, causing Nelson to exclaim that "sure punishment should await their conduct." With the battle of Yorktown only days away one militia leader wrote asking that his men be discharged since they expected to serve only a fortnight "and some have urgent business in Richmond." And finally, in early October, when William Davies prepared to join Nelson before Yorktown, he found he could not because "the back [country] militia have stole my horses as well as those of everybody else they can lay their hands on." [52]

By September 22 the American and the French armies, which had been conveyed by water from the head of the Chesapeake Bay, were being landed on the James River side of the peninsula. Four days later all were ashore and had moved to Williamsburg. The increased need for provisions, which were still trickling in too slowly, put the governor "under the necessity of taking from the people of this ravaged Part of the Country, what humanity strongly inclined me to spare them." Nevertheless things were looking up. Governor Lee of Maryland promised two thousand barrels of flour immediately, with more to follow, and additional supplies were soon to come in from the Eastern Shore. [53]

In the dawn of September 28, the allied army got underway toward Yorktown. The French had about 7,800 troops, while the Americans totaled 8,845. Three thousand of the Americans were Virginia militia, divided into three brigades under Generals George Weedon, Robert Lawson, and Edward Stevens, and commanded by Governor Nelson, who was now up and around. The army arrived before Yorktown on the same day and formed camp in a great curve extending from York River above the town to Wormeley Creek below. The French held the left flank above Beaverdam Creek, which cut through the middle of the allied lines, while the Americans held the right. Nelson and his troops, stationed at the extreme right, made up a reserve for Lafayette's regulars. [54]

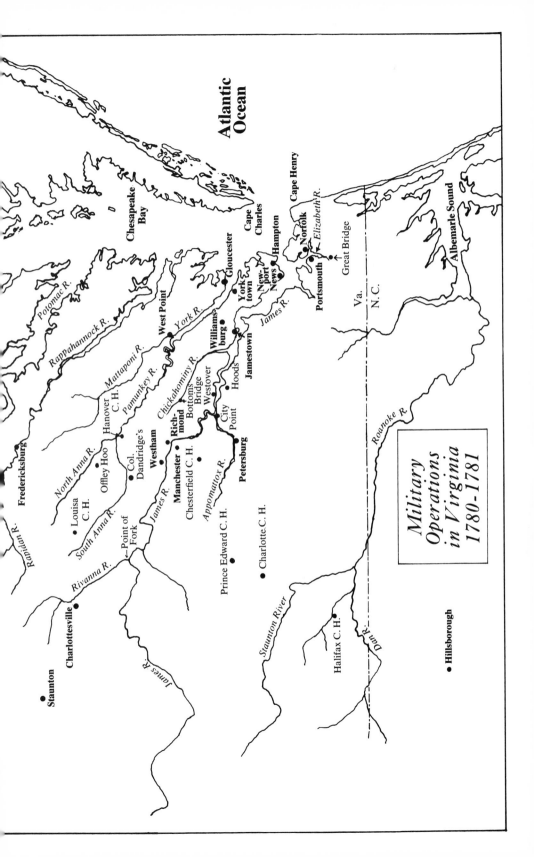

Atlantic Ocean

Chesapeake Bay

Cape Henry

Cape Charles

Hampton

Norfolk

Elizabeth R.

Portsmouth

Great Bridge

Albemarle Sound

Va.

N. C.

Gloucester

York town

New-port News

York R.

West Point

Mattaponi R.

Pamunkey R.

Hanover C. H.

Potomac R.

Rappahannock R.

Williams-burg

Chickahominy R.

Jamestown

Bottoms Bridge

Westover

Hoods

City Point

Appomattox R.

Richmond

Manchester

Chesterfield C. H.

Westham

Col. Dandridge's

Offley Hoo

North Anna R.

Louisa C. H.

South Anna R.

Point of Fork

Rivanna R.

Rapidan R.

Fredericksburg

Charlottesville

Staunton

Petersburg

Prince Edward C. H.

James R.

Charlotte C. H.

Staunton River

Roanoke R.

Dan R.

Halifax C. H.

Hillsborough

James R.

Military Operations in Virginia 1780-1781

On the night of September 30 the British evacuated three of their outlying posts, which the Americans quickly occupied, and for the next week the allies prepared for the siege.[55] The feelings Nelson harbored as he watched these preparations to bombard and starve the town of his birth must have been intensified by the fact that in Yorktown sat old Secretary Nelson, who had refused to be moved from his home, even by the arrival of the British.[56]

By October 9 the allied artillery was in place, and on that day the bombardment of Yorktown began at three o'clock in the afternoon. As the firing started, down on the American right General Nelson was asked to point out a good target toward which the artillerists could direct their fire. Nelson indicated a large house, which he suggested was probably Cornwallis's headquarters. The house was his own. Through this act of patriotic self-sacrifice, Nelson did much to wipe out Lafayette's feeling of irritation toward the Virginia government.[57]

Actually the governor's home was not the most prominent house in the town. The secretary's was the first to catch the eye, for it sat on an eminence near some of the most important British fortifications. Cornwallis actually made his headquarters in the secretary's house, which because of its location drew much of the fire from the allied cannon. The cannonade continued through the night and into the next day. At noon a flag of truce appeared on the British lines. At first the allies hoped that Cornwallis was going to ask for terms, but they soon learned that the flag was raised to allow Secretary Nelson to leave the beleaguered village.[58]

The old gentleman, suffering from an attack of gout, could not walk, and his two sons in the American army, Colonel William Nelson and Major John Nelson, went across and brought their father back to General Washington's headquarters. There the secretary recounted that the bombardment was producing great damage and had forced Cornwallis to seek safety in a "grotto" at the foot of his garden. It was his opinion "that the British were a good deal dispirited altho' . . . they affect to say they have no apprehensions of the Garrison's falling." [59]

Through the next week the bombardment of Yorktown continued. On October 14 two British redoubts close to the river on the east side of the town were taken by storm, allowing a tighter circle of trenches to be dug within two hundred yards of the British lines. Cannon could now bring an even more destructive fire to bear on the British. On the night of October 16 Cornwallis tried to escape across the York River to Gloucester, but a storm frustrated his plans. The next morning a British drummer mounted a parapet and beat a parley. Within a short while Washington received Cornwallis's note requesting a cessation of hostilities and a discussion of terms "for the surrender of the posts at York and Gloucester." Negotiations took place in the home of General Nelson's former business partner, Augustine Moore. Writing the Virginia delegates in Congress, on October 20, Nelson brought the story to a close:

> On the 17th at the Request of Lord Cornwallis Hostilities ceased, and yesterday the Garrison of York amounting to upwards of two thousand nine hundred Effectives, rank and file, marched out and grounded their arms. Their sick are about seventeen hundred. The Garrison of Gloucester and the men killed during the siege are computed at near two thousand, so that the whole loss sustained by the Enemy on this occasion must be between 6 and 7000 Men. This blow, I think must be a decisive one, it being out of the Power of G.[reat] B.[ritain] to replace such a number of good troops.[60]

The surrender of Yorktown raised Nelson's spirits, but it did not ease the load on his shoulders. The healthy British prisoners had to be moved to prison camps, the sick and wounded cared for, and all had to be fed. Washington urged that the Virginia military establishment be kept on a firm footing, while the men themselves tended to go home. The French, remaining in the state, created something of a problem, particularly in Yorktown, where they ousted some people from their homes to use them for winter quarters. The French occupied the governor's battered house among others, and would not, it was reported, give a friend of the governor's space there despite a written order from Nelson. Accounts had to be settled between the French and the state and between the state and the Continental Congress. Large numbers of cattle which had been collected had to be disposed of and other provisions stored. Still civil strife continued in the lower Tidewater. These and many other problems weighed heavily on the governor.[61]

Unfortunately Nelson was not a well man. He had been in ill health intermittently since 1777, and for the past year, especially since the serious respiratory ailment he had suffered in February and March, the spells of sickness increased. The physical and mental demands of the governorship in a period of crisis were obviously a serious drain on a not very vigorous constitution. He had held on through the Yorktown campaign, but now the burden was too much and late in October he withdrew, dangerously ill, to Offley Hoo in Hanover County.[62]

Through the first part of November, Nelson tried to conduct the business of the state through his secretary, Robert Andrews. But as the month wore on it became increasingly evident that he was not going to recover quickly. When the Assembly convened late in the month, he wrote the speaker of the House that "The very low state of health to which I am reduced, and from which I have little expectation of soon recovering, makes it my duty to resign the government, that the state may not suffer for want of an executive." [63] On November 30, the Assembly elected Benjamin Harrison over John Page and Richard Henry Lee to succeed Nelson.[64] Soon after this, a somewhat prejudiced Edmund Pendleton wrote James Madison of the governor's resignation: "The Governor has resigned, probably vexed to see his great popularity so suddenly changed into general execration, for having by his imprudent seizures, intercepted the specie that was about to flow amongst the people." [65] This was only the beginning of a storm of criticism that was to fall on Nelson.

The loudest complaint came from northern Virginia where, before Yorktown, state authorities had faced the most difficulty in collecting provisions. The inhabitants of Prince William County presented a petition of remonstrances against Nelson. They criticised the ex-governor in particular for issuing impressment warrants "without advice of Council" and "without limitation of kind quantity or proportion other than the arbitrary will and pleasure of the persons to whom they were directed. . . ." Further, they condemned him for not allowing the French to purchase provisions on the open market, and for laying an embargo on the export of certain commodities. There then began in the House a general discussion of Nelson's governorship, and as one observer commented, "his conduct is arraigned in the House with great freedom and asperity." [66]

News of the attack on his administration of course reached Nelson, and despite the fact that the weather was severely cold and snowy, on December 22 he journeyed to Richmond and requested a hearing before the House of Delegates. As Nelson phrased it, "I must beg the House [to] indulge me with half an hour today that I may lay before them a candid State[ment] of Facts and my reasons for adopting the measures that have given offense." The request was granted and Nelson appeared. [67] What he had to say in his own defense is not known. A few weeks later he wrote that the "critical situation of the army and the peculiar circumstances of the country, made vigorous exertions necessary; and I must acknowledge that I feel the truest satisfaction when I reflect that those exertions were crowned with success." [68]

Such an approach may well have formed the outline of his remarks, but whatever he said it must have been effective. On December 27 a bill was presented in the House to legalize the measures Nelson took while governor. After some debate, the House agreed unanimously to the bill, and the Senate took similar action. The bill stated that Nelson's acts were "productive of general good and warranted by necessity," and that they should be "held of the same validity . . . as if they had been executed by and with the advice of the Council, and with all formalities prescribed by law." Finally, it declared that "Thomas Nelson . . . be and hereby is, in the fullest manner indemnified and exonerated from all penalties and damages, which might have accrued to him from the same." [69]

Nelson had assumed office during a critical and awkward time. Virginia had been without a governor for three weeks; large enemy forces had been moving for six months, virtually at will, within her borders; and the state's resources had been strained for a much longer period of time as a result of British activity in the Carolinas. At his disposal were powers greater than those of any governor preceding him, and, except for a few days in June, he did not have the restraining influence of a legislature to deal with. A tremendous responsibility, which Nelson understood and accepted, thus rested with the executive. Although a more politically minded person would have shown caution, he used the power to its fullest extent. When it appeared necessary, in the six weeks before Yorktown, Nelson exceeded his authority. He made the decision to do so without regard to the effect it would have on his own career, for, as he said, he believed that duty forbade him to consider his "own interest when it was necessary to make it subservient to the public good." [70]

If the attempt to trap Cornwallis had failed it would have been easy to condemn Nelson, and, as it was, his vigorous actions and unconstitutional behavior caused widespread criticism. Certainly his periodic illnesses frustrated those who worked with him, and his unexplained absence from Richmond during part of July is a blemish on his administration. But one can hardly avoid the conclusion that his effort to supply the army at Yorktown was a crucial element in the victory. His correct estimate that the success of this military operation was absolutely essential to the American cause sustained him, and despite adverse circumstances, both personal and public, he accomplished his goal. Thomas Nelson proved himself the man for the time.

A promising future now faced America, but for Nelson the prospects were not so bright. He had jeopardized both his health and his fortune in the cause of American independence. Sickness and troubled attempts to re-establish himself economically marked the remainder of his career.

Chapter VIII

The Last Years

Through the winter of 1781-82 Thomas Nelson remained at Offley Hoo in an attempt to regain his health. Located far back in Hanover County, this plantation was an ideal place for Nelson to put the stresses and strains of the world behind him. Offley Hoo itself was not a pretentious dwelling, being described as merely "rather pretty" and "neither convenient nor spacious." In addition to the main house there was a kitchen, an overseer's dwelling and many Negro cabins. Only such buildings had been erected as were necessary for farming on part of this twelve-thousand-acre plantation.[1]

In the winter and spring of 1782 both General Rochambeau and Major General Chastellux of the French army visited Offley Hoo and were most hospitably entertained. Nelson was absent when Chastellux paid his visit but the Frenchman reported that he was received by the general's mother and wife "with all the politeness, ease and cordiality natural to this family. But as in America the ladies are never thought sufficient to do the honors of the house, five or six Nelsons were assembled to receive me. . . ." Chastellux observed that the secretary and two of Thomas Nelson's brothers were there, some of them being accompanied by their wives and children. This gathering was very confusing to the French general, as everyone was called Nelson, making it nearly impossible for him to establish their degrees of relationship.[2]

Chastellux stayed at Offley Hoo for a second day because of bad weather. During this time breakfast was at nine, dinner at two, and in the afternoon there was tea and punch followed by "an elegant little supper." After meals the men generally gathered in the parlor, where the conversation was noted as being agree-

124

able. The general was particularly impressed on discovering some books by good French and English authors, and agreeably surprised to find that during his entire stay, all indoors, there was no mention whatsoever of playing cards. He compared this with France where under similar circumstances the time almost certainly would have been occupied with tric trac, whisk and lotto. [3]

Baron Ludwig von Closen, who traveled with Rochambeau and whose visit preceded Chastellux's, described Nelson's family as "one of the happiest with which I am acquainted"; and Lucy Nelson whom he found "no longer young" fully lived up to his German standards in her excellent qualities as a mother and thrifty housekeeper. Nelson's generosity in providing Rochambeau with his four-horse carriage for a sightseeing trip of 160 miles on rather bad roads overwhelmed Von Closen. [4]

Nelson was elected to the House of Delegates from York County in May 1782, but he was not much involved in its activities. Several counties, "impressed with the embarassment of the times, elected the most able man, altho' they did not offer themselves." Nelson was probably in this category. He does not appear in the minutes for the session (the journals are not extant) until June 20, and by that time the meeting was drawing to a close. [5]

Nelson's health had improved by spring. During Chastellux's visit to Offley Hoo Nelson had been in Williamsburg, but it is likely that he was back in Hanover for the birth of Judith, his eleventh and last child, in May. Clearly private affairs were occupying his time, and in August he declined a request by Congress to serve as one of the commissioners to consider conflicting territorial claims of Connecticut and Pennsylvania. [6] In September he brought suit against Carter Braxton to recover the loan for which he had gone security in Philadelphia in 1776. Braxton agreed to give Nelson fifteen hundred acres of York County land if he did not repay the money before April 1, 1783. [7] He was also probably giving thought to reopening Thomas Nelson and Company, as a peace settlement appeared imminent. But the times were uncertain ones for businessmen. As one observer wrote Nelson, "the prospect of Peace and the uncertainty of it at the same time, has put all matters to a stand, every Person seems determined not to enter into an engagement of any kind til this matter is decided, the scarcity of money too forbids any expectation of selling any article to advantage for ready money. . . ." [8]

For Nelson business had been virtually at a standstill since the outbreak of the war, and even at that time he had been deeply in debt. In the meantime his family had continued to grow, placing further demands on his straitened finances—a situation not improved by his having pledged his own security for significant sums during the loan drives of 1780. Some of his creditors were already pressing him for payment, and as early as August 1782 he was advertising the sale of twenty to thirty Virginia-born Negroes. He sold more slaves in December and in January, and also delivered 184,000 pounds of tobacco to Benjamin Harrison and Company and David Ross and Company in payment of bonded debts. He was unable to satisfy other creditors, for in February he promised to pay a tobacco debt due in June— and could not make good. [9]

On the other hand Nelson was far from destitute. Substantial sums of money were owed him, and he still ranked among the ten largest property owners in Virginia. Nelson possessed well over twenty thousand acres spread through five counties: thirteen thousand acres in Hanover County, fifty-five hundred in Prince William, and lesser amounts in York, James City, and Loudoun. In addition he owned approximately four hundred slaves, five hundred head of cattle and one hundred horses and mules as well as sheep and hogs. To manage these holdings Nelson had in his hire at least six overseers, and probably others in James City and Loudoun counties. These were immense holdings, even for that time, but only the end of the war and the return of more normal business conditions could tell what he would be able to do with them. [10]

The times were critical not only for Nelson but also for Virginia. The state's public and private indebtedness was large. To retire the public debt some sort of realistic tax plan had to be put into operation. But with circulating money almost nonexistent collection of taxes was extremely difficult. Everyone hoped the resumption of trade would go a long way toward solving the problem, but that awaited the final signing of the treaty of peace, and no one knew whether Virginia's trade, even then, would resume its prewar patterns. These problems created a feeling of frustration among the public which found expression in bitter outbursts and sometimes violent action against Loyalists and those suspected of having British sympathies. English and Scottish merchants who had fled the state in the early years of the war, and who were now trying to return, were among the chief targets of this resentment.[11]

Along with the secretary and his brother Hugh, General Nelson returned to the York County Court in the fall of 1782, and in November he assumed his seat in the House of Delegates. Nelson was not active in this meeting of the Assembly; not until the May session of the following year did he begin to take on his usual share of the duties. His younger brother, William, who had just been admitted to the bar, was also present as a delegate from James City County.[12]

In this session and the one that followed in the fall, Nelson headed the Committee of Trade, served on the Committee of Propositions and Grievances and on various other committees dealing with the training of the militia and with defense, and chaired the Committee of the Whole when the questions of taxes and paying off the state debt to the central government were discussed. He was also among those representatives from the Tidewater who attempted but failed to return the capital to Williamsburg. Nelson was a hard-money advocate in these years. His being a creditor as well as debtor, coupled with Virginia's unhappy wartime experience with paper money, no doubt accounts for his stand. And despite his subsequent opposition to the new federal Constitution he favored giving the central government all the financial aid possible—a position which was not uncommon in Virginia.[13]

With autumn came peace and with peace some of the old amenities returned. Nelson ordered a stock of good Madeira that had washed his palate only in memory for the past few years. He need no longer resort to such makeshifts as cider and peach brandy. With the wine came other good things—pickles, new china, an enameled punch bowl, and an elegant tea urn.[14]

Peace also brought the reopening of the Nelson mercantile firm. Nelson was the principal partner, but certainly his brother Hugh and probably Augustine Moore were again his associates.

The firm did "considerable business" during the 1780s, but the actual extent or character of its activities cannot now be determined. The base of the mercantile operation continued to be Yorktown, but Nelson had made extensive repairs to his home on Francis Street in Williamsburg and was spending a good deal of time there. The house in Yorktown was, evidently, still in a state of disrepair as a result of the siege and its occupation by both French and British soldiers.[15]

Nelson's service in the fall session of the Assembly was cut short, after two weeks of attendance, by what appears to have been a recurrence of his previous illness. For a week in early December he was under the intensive care of Williamsburg physician John M. Galt. Dr. Galt prescribed a variety of medicines used at that time for the treatment of coughs and the removal of phlegm associated with "humoral asthmas." He also applied several plasters to Nelson's chest, including one that used cantharides (dried blister beetles) as the main specific. Nelson recovered from this attack, in spite of Dr. Galt's medications, and over a year passed before this particular ailment again plagued him. But his generally poor health seems to have convinced him that he should retire from public life, even though some of his friends were entreating him not to do so.[16]

In March 1784 William Lee wrote from James City County urging Nelson to work toward having "sound and true" men elected to the Assembly, for "believe me there is much Mischief in Contemplation and on you it depends more than any man I know to save the lower part, indeed the whole Country from Confusion and Ruin. A dark and mischievous Character is plotting to get into the next assembly, for no good purpose we may be assured, therefore I trust your patriotism will prevent you from retiring this year at least."[17] Nelson was not persuaded. Evidently he felt that since his health would not permit him to devote his time to both business and public matters he must give all his attention to his long neglected business. He did not return to the Assembly in the spring of 1784, but instead applied himself to mending his private affairs.

Business weighed heavily on Nelson during the next few years, but he remained a "generous, benevolent man" and a gracious host. Visitors came frequently to Williamsburg and Yorktown and none was more welcome than the marquis de Lafayette who arrived in the fall of 1784. Nelson entertained him on November 16 at his home in Williamsburg. Many of the town's notables came to meet the marquis at dinner, including Philip Mazzei, the Italo-American patriot, and James Madison, president of the College of William and Mary. The house was small and Nelson reportedly told his guests that they could blame their being overcrowded on the skill of the French artillery at the siege of Yorktown. It was a pleasant, memory-filled evening, concluded by the host remarking on the pleasure with which he had always served *"his young and brave* commander." Lafayette proceeded to Richmond the next day to meet General Washington and for a week that city bustled with "Feasting, balls, Illuminations, [and the] firing of cannon. . . ." [18]

Nelson must have treasured such a happy interlude as Lafayette's visit, but it afforded him only small respite from his increasingly serious financial situation. He remained deeply in debt, but if he could collect the money owed him, both by private individuals and the public, his circumstances would be much improved. In June 1784 he had petitioned the House of Delegates first to pay £91 owed him for board while commander of the state militia, and, more important, to repay the loans he had obtained by pledging his own security during the loan drive of February 1780. [19]

Declaring the first claim just, the House ordered the £91 paid at once. It referred the remainder of Nelson's petition to a committee charged with examining the state of public loans "due from the Commonwealth." [20] In the fall session of the Assembly the committee reported favorably on it, noting that "certain meritorious individuals" had loaned money and tobacco to Virginia "when the credit of the State was lost with every other person," and that neither the interest nor the principal of these loans had been paid. The committee stated further that though the sum in question was small, only £10,525 in tobacco and money, it had been supplied at a critical time and was a debt of "the first dignity," which should be paid. At the same time, the committee recommended that a variety of other loans should also be repaid. [21]

The House of Delegates agreed with the committee and ordered

it to prepare a bill or bills providing for payment. Two bills
were presented on December 30. One was "to amend and reduce
several laws for appropriating the public revenue into one act"
and the other directed the "liquidation of certain public accounts." The general appropriations bill passed on January 1,
but the Assembly postponed a vote on the public accounts bill
and adjourned without taking action.[22]

One cannot be positive about what happened next; evidence
is missing and the surviving record is unclear. Almost certainly
the public accounts bill included provision for the payment of
Nelson's claim. The general appropriations bill specifically provided for the payment of "money lent the public, on the requisi-
tion of the assembly in the session held in May, one thousand
seven hundred and eighty, or of Thomas Jefferson, esq. then governor of this commonwealth," and this seems to cover both the
May and February loan drives. Perhaps Nelson did not have
clear proof of his actions. That would explain why he personally
petitioned the state and why his appeal was handled separately
in a public accounts bill.[23]

Considering the unsettled state of affairs in Virginia at the
time, the crucial documents could easily have been lost. The procedure followed during the loan drive was for the collector to
deposit the money with the treasurer. The treasurer would then
deliver a list of those lending money to the auditors of the state,
who would in turn issue certificates or warrants to the lenders.
In 1831–32 the auditors who examined the claims of Nelson's
heirs against the state admitted that the original book in which
the certificates were listed was lost. Perhaps Nelson had also lost
crucial documents.[24]

In December 1785 legislation was again introduced that would
have provided for the payment of Nelson's claim against the state.
It was resolved that unpaid debts "due to the citizens of the commonwealth, upon liquidated accounts of agents or persons authorized to contract debts payable in tobacco, or for any other
just demand, and which have not heretofore been provided for . . .
either in part or whole" should be paid. But after being pushed
through the early stages of consideration the resolution was
permanently dismissed.[25]

The reason for this action on the part of the House of Delegates is in doubt. Perhaps the House, because of the lack of clear

documentation, did not want to leave itself open to a host of claims that might be less just than Nelson's. One other possible explanation turned up in the course of a violent political attack on Patrick Henry because of his opposition to the ratification of the Constitution. In this attack, which first emerged in 1789 as a series of letters in the *Virginia Independent Chronicle* and which later appeared as a pamphlet entitled *Decius's Letters on the Opposition To the New Constitution in Virginia,* Henry's entire political career was arraigned.[26]

Time and time again the author charged Henry, among other things, with profiting financially from his political position. At one point he was accused of appointing, while governor, one of his friends "commissioner of public stores," who in turn "passed a most fraudulent account on the state by means of his popular friends in [the] Assembly." The commissioner's friends were then "so barefaced as to nominate him among the committee to settle that very account."[27]

Decius then went on to charge that this action was taken "while one of the truest patriots in America, at the same time, was ruined for want of a bare reimbursement of what he had actually advanced out of his own private fortune for the promotion of our independence; and all because there was some public plunder to be shared in the first instance, and nothing but the good of the cause intended in the other." Thomas Jefferson wrote beside this passage, in his copy of the pamphlet, "Nelson."[28]

The commissioner of public stores *Decius* refers to was very probably David Ross, a friend of Henry's. Ross had been state commercial agent, or commissioner of public stores as the office was frequently called, from 1780 until 1782, when the office was abolished with approximately £10,000 being owed Ross and several other creditors. In 1784 the committee that considered Nelson's petition and recommended paying it, also urged that Ross be paid. Subsequently, the general appropriations bill of 1784 provided for paying Ross £6,000. It should be added that Ross was not in the Assembly at this time, nor is there any indication that his claim was fraudulent. And there is no evidence that Henry was involved in the affair. But the suspicion of collusion remains because none of Henry's defenders, who answered a wide variety of other charges, denied it.[29]

One other bit of seemingly unconnected information may have

bearing on the whole question. As Henry approached the end of his governorship in 1786 he wrote his daughter that he proposed to move "to Hanover to land I am like to get of Gen. Nelson." He did not obtain the land, which raises the possibility of ill will existing between the two men. But this cannot be verified either, and the reason why Nelson did not get his money must remain a mystery.[30]

The failure of the legislature to provide the money owed him was a crushing blow to Nelson. In common with most Virginians, he had very little liquid capital. But, unlike many of his fellow citizens, he was now taking steps to repay his prewar British debts, despite the fact that Virginia's courts were not open to the suits of British creditors, and would not be for a good many years. This action was consistent with his position on the payment of British debts before and during the war. It is further evidence of Nelson's integrity, but it certainly did not help to bolster his sagging fortunes.[31]

In 1784 he had finally sold the Nelsons' ancestral home in Penrith. The money from the sale probably went to the London firm of Thomas and Rowland Hunt as a first installment of what he owed it. Subsequently, in 1786, Nelson arranged either to pay outright or to give bonds for the remainder of his British debts. It seems that in most cases the debts were secured by bond, and he set aside land to be sold if money was not available for payment.[32]

Nelson had probably planned to get a substantial start towards meeting his obligations by using the money the state owed him. Failing here he sought desperately to obtain cash by other means. When General Horatio Gates mentioned to him the difficulty of depositing his money on security, Nelson offered to take it, pledging his "personal and landed security" for payment of the principal at a given time and 6 percent interest twice a year.[33]

Whether Gates accepted his offer is not known, but obviously Nelson did not obtain much money in this manner, for by August 1786 he was advertising the sale of land in Hanover and Gloucester counties. He also announced that he would have to sell about eighty of his Negroes unless persons indebted to him would "discharge their bonds, notes, and open accounts." Court action was promised against those who did not provide for payment.

He had already attached part of Carter Braxton's land to secure the loan of £2,000 he made to Braxton in 1776. In 1784 Nelson had asked the court to order the sale of this land, but as of April 1786 no action had yet been taken.[34]

Nelson's creditors were also taking him to court, and between the end of the war and his death in 1789 judgments against him amounted to £6,000. The pressures on him were obviously great and some measure of his frustration can be seen in a letter he wrote in 1787 to Edmund Berkeley. "I know by my own feelings," he confessed, "that nothing can be more disagreeable than to be dunn'd. I am however unfortunately reduc'd to the necessity of dunning, or parting with more property than I can spare from my numerous family. George Smith the young Man, who lives with me, will present your Bond and open account to you. . . . Do my Dear Sir give me all . . . the assistance in your power. If I do not raise a sum of money in the course of this Week, some of my Negroes will be sold on Monday next."[35]

Nelson's business affairs were further complicated by his executorship of the estate of Robert Carter Burwell, who died in 1779. Burwell had designated part of his lands to be sold to pay off his debts. This had been done, and Nelson, as executor, had loaned the proceeds to the state during the loan drive of 1780. The loan had been repaid but in currency so depreciated in value that it was insufficient to pay Burwell's sterling debts. Nelson explained that he had acted in 1780 to the best of his judgment, but "the Paper Money turning out a bubble deceiv'd me and thousands besides, for at the time I put the Money for which the Land was sold, into the Treasury, I also plac'd a considerable Sum of my own there." In explaining this situation to Nathaniel Burwell, the son and heir, he stated that the land would not "nearly have paid the debts, if it had been dispos'd of to the greatest advantage, but so as it was, the Sum amounts to nothing."[36]

Nelson intended, even though he had done what he thought best, to make up for the loss out of his own pocket. But substantial Burwell debts would remain to be paid, and the Burwell estate, with Nathaniel at its head, was not in any condition to meet these obligations, for Nathaniel had abandoned "himself totally to gaming and drinking" and had lost much of his property in the process. Nelson frankly told him, "You sold Land sufficient to have paid your Fathers Debts and to have made you happy for life. But nothing can stand an unfortunate throw of the Dice nor a run of ill luck at Cards." All of this caused the executor to comment that had he known what Burwell's imprudence was to involve him in, he would not have taken the "Executorship for several thousand pounds." The outcome of Nelson's involvement in the settling of the Burwell estate is not known, but it indicates the involved state of his own affairs, and suggests that his patriotism surpassed his business judgment.[37]

In the spring of 1786 Nathaniel Nelson, the general's younger brother, died suddenly of a disorder that "baffled the Effects of physic." The death was a blow to the whole Nelson clan. Since the elder Nelson's retirement from the legislature Nathaniel had been serving as one of the delegates from York County. Now Nelson determined to return to public life and that spring he was elected to the House of Delegates from York County.[38]

Economic conditions in the state were bad in 1786. Trade had not revived and money was scarce. In this situation petitions began to come in, especially from south of the James River, demanding a return to paper money and stay laws. Hard-money men everywhere were frightened and this may have been a factor in Nelson's decision to return to the legislature. James Madison wrote that he feared that they would not be able to parry the paper money threat, but he saw hope in the election of George Mason, Mann Page, and General Nelson, who will be "valuable fellow laborers" and serve as a counterpoise against "the popular cry." Madison's fears, arising in part from the defeat at the polls of such stalwarts as Benjamin Harrison, George Mercer, and James Monroe, proved to be greatly exaggerated. When the Assembly convened in the autumn it defeated the move to issue paper money, on the motion of Nelson, by the overwhelming margin of 85 to 17.[39]

More serious than the paper-money question was the near emptiness of the state treasury, partly as a result of the Assembly's postponement of tax collection during its previous session. Nelson headed a select committee that successfully pushed through a variety of measures to deal with this problem. The Assembly inaugurated a more efficient system of tax collection; it assessed new taxes, designed to weigh less heavily on hard-pressed Virginia planters, on clerks of the courts, attorneys, physicians, and retail merchants; it levied additional taxes on a variety of items including distilled liquors, wine, and salt; it also placed an increased duty on all imported items. The delegates hoped that this legislation would increase the state's income but, as one observer commented, "some time will elapse before any of . . . [the] arrangements can be productive." [40]

Meanwhile delegates from five states, including Virginia, had met in Annapolis to try to bring about more satisfactory commercial relations between the states. Out of this meeting came the very important recommendation for Congress to call a convention, composed of representatives of each state, to meet in Philadelphia in May 1787 and consider measures for revising the Articles of Confederation. The Virginia legislature unanimously accepted this recommendation and Nelson served on a committee to select delegates to the convention. They chose George Washington, Patrick Henry, Edmund Randolph, John Blair, James Madison, George Mason, and George Wythe. When Henry declined to serve because he "smelt a rat," Governor Edmund Randolph appointed Nelson in his place. The Council of State hoped that Nelson would accept. To make the trip north easier for him, as well as for Blair and Wythe, they arranged for the state boat *Liberty* to convey them to the head of the Bay. But Nelson also declined and eventually Dr. James McClurg filled the position. [41]

The sad state of his business affairs and continuing poor health probably account for Nelson's refusal to go to Philadelphia. Writing his son Tom from Yorktown in the summer of 1787, he remarked that he was packed and ready to "set out for Hanover . . . but my disorder attacked me last night as violently as ever." When the Assembly met in October he was not present, nor did he appear during the entire session. [42]

In the meantime the convention in Philadelphia was drafting a new frame of government. George Washington sent Nelson a copy of the completed document immediately on his return to Virginia. In a covering letter he told his friend that the Constitution was the "best that could be obtained at this time. . . ." The "political concerns of this country," he continued, are "suspended by a thread," and he was convinced that if the convention had not agreed on a plan "anarchy would soon have ensued. . . ."

Under these circumstances Washington thought "the adoption of it . . . desirable." Nelson, and a number of other Virginians, did not agree.[43]

It had been provided that the proposed frame of government would be voted on by conventions made up of delegates elected by the people. Some states held conventions that fall, and by the first of the year three—Delaware, New Jersey, and Pennsylvania —had ratified. In Virginia the convention was not to meet until June 2, 1788, but even so, opposing ranks formed early. James Madison reported that a decided majority of the Assembly and of the country at large favored the new Constitution; but individuals of "great weight both within and without the legislature" including "Mr. Henry, Genl. Nelson, W. Nelson, the family of Cabels, St. George Tucker, John Taylor and the Judges of the General Court except P. Carrington" were opposed to it.[44]

Madison did not know on what principle and to what extent Nelson opposed the document, nor is it known today. According to report, three parties had formed in Virginia: those who would ratify without amendments; those who did not "object to the substance of the Government" but favored "a few additional guards in favor of the Rights of the States and the people"; and those who opposed the "essence of the System" and preferred "an adherence to the principle of the existing Confederation." In the light of Nelson's career to this point it is reasonable to assume that he was one of the middle group, which included George Mason and Edmund Randolph.[45]

The election of delegates to the convention took place in March on the respective court days for each county. Whether Nelson stood for election from York County cannot be ascertained. One account states that Nelson ran as a Federalist but on election day withdrew because the oratory of an "aged voter" convinced him that the most capable men in the county should be elected and that George Wythe and John Blair were those men. It is true that Blair and Wythe were elected from York County, but Nelson certainly did not run as a Federalist.[46] He remained opposed to the Constitution and his feelings were so strong on the subject that when Washington sent him the proceedings of the convention, which told of Virginia's ratification of the Constitution, he interpreted it as an attempt to embarrass him. Washington hastened to correct this view, informing Nelson that he had not intended the communication to be interpreted "in any other light than as an instance of my attention and friendship.[47]

Nelson's reaction to Washington's first communication was out of character but not surprising, for in the summer of 1788 he was a very sick man. Early June found him too ill to attend to business, and from then on his condition grew progressively worse. Not only did recurrent attacks of what was probably asthma plague him, his whole physical condition seems to have deteriorated. Furthermore, the serious state of his business affairs contributed to his depression. For despite strenuous efforts he remained over £13,000 in debt and he had just recently been forced to sell 120 of his slaves in Prince William County. The fear that he would not be able to straighten out his affairs, and therefore be unable to provide for his numerous family, weighed on Nelson's mind. Late in December his condition had become so bad that he took the step of drawing up his last will and testament.[48]

Nelson had been able to keep most of his holdings intact, despite his misfortunes. In his will he provided that his wife Lucy should have, for the remainder of her life, his plantations in Hanover called Montair, Mallorys, Long Row, and Smiths, together with the slaves, stock, and farming equipment. She was also to get the bulk of his property in Yorktown. His son Robert was to get the Montair tract when Lucy died. The Yorktown holdings were to go to William, his first son, under similar conditions. William, who had earlier been given property in York and Hanover counties was also given another plantation in Hanover. Thomas, who had previously been given land in Hanover, was to receive a 2,500-acre addition to it, as well as the James City and Williamsburg property. The Offley Hoo plantation was to go to Philip, and the other two sons, Hugh and Francis, were each left a plantation in Hanover. Elizabeth Page, Nelson's eldest daughter, was to receive £1,000, and her sisters were each to get £600. The money was to be paid to the girls only after Nelson's debts had been settled. For the payment of his debts, he earmarked fifteen hundred acres in Hanover, plus his Prince William and Loudoun lands, and his two surveys on the Elizabeth River. The will also provided that Dr. Augustine Smith, who as a boy had lived with Nelson and whose medical education in Edinburgh he had paid for, was not to be charged "one shilling" for any of his maintenance or education. Finally, Nelson freed his Negro blacksmith named Harry, and provided that he should be given a good house and, for the rest of his life, clothes, three hundred pounds of pork, and five barrels of corn annually. The residue of the estate was to go to the eldest son, William.[49]

The will was signed on December 26. Less than two weeks later, on January 4, 1789, Thomas Nelson, fifty years of age, died at his plantation Montair in Hanover County.[50] Dr. Smith, who had just returned from Scotland, attended Nelson during the last weeks. His account of Nelson's death, though obviously colored by personal grief, conveys some of the despair that filled the old patriot's last days:

> From his unexampled patriotick exertions during the late war he had exhausted a fortune and at the time I mention saw his property arrested, and a prospect of sinking from affluence, almost to absolute poverty. My friend! you can easily conceive the poignant distress of a man in this situation, with an amiable wife and a dozen children around him. He cou'd not bear it. I attended him in his last illness and saw that the exquisite tortures of the mind were the disease that destroyed his body.[51]

The newspapers carrying accounts of his death were edged in black. One stated that as "a citizen there is but one to whom his country [Virginia] is more indebted." Another closed with Shakespeare's matchless words:

> His life was gentle, and the elements
> So mix'd in him that Nature might stand up
> And say to all the world 'This was a man!'[52]

Epilogue

History has not dealt adequately with Thomas Nelson. He is not remembered as a major political figure in Virginia during the era of the American Revolution. His image is that of a man who did no more than lose his fortune in the cause of American liberty. He is said to have expended large sums of his own money for Virginia's use during the war, and this plus other financial setbacks purportedly lead to his virtual bankruptcy. Even the sketch of Nelson in the *Dictionary of American Biography* tells how he "sacrificed his private means to pay his public debts, accumulated for Virginia's loan of 1780 and in fitting out and provisioning troops. This course . . . left him a poor man. . . ." And a recent history of Virginia asserts that "Nelson was to sacrifice his large fortune in the patriot cause. . . ." and to die in poverty.[1] That is, of course, a less than accurate portrayal.

The reasons for it can be found partly in the Revolution and its aftermath, partly in Nelson's own personal history, and partly in the character of Virginia's eighteenth-century elite. The Revolution altered economic, social, and political relationships and accelerated changes that were in process before it began. We "have not only had a revolution in Political Government" a Virginian wrote in 1784 "but also in many peoples private circumstances. . . ."[2] Nelson was not poor at the time of his death in 1789, but his circumstances were reduced. The mercantile firm had been in trouble as early as 1772–73 and when Nelson, during the Revolution, began to devote almost full time to public business it was forced to close its doors for the duration of the conflict. After 1783 the business could not regain its former strength. Nelson's health in the 1780s and his efforts, unlike many of his contemporaries, to repay his British debts were factors in the firm's problems. He was constantly short of hard money, and the failure of the state to repay the over £10,000 it owed him as a result of the loan drive of February 1780 did

139

not help. These were not circumstances conducive either to successful business operations or to the management of his extensive
holdings in land and slaves.

The demands placed on Nelson by his private affairs and
his persistent ill health meant that he did not devote so much
time to public life after 1781—it was impossible for him to do
so. His public exposure was limited and he was not involved,
in a major way, in the completion of independence. Nelson faded
from public view—a process that was probably hastened by his
dwindling fortune. His comparatively early death completed the
process.

Some remembered, however, that Virginia's legislature had
failed to repay him the loan drive money. This fact was given
some notoriety, immediately after his death, by the attack on
Patrick Henry in the *Decius Letters,* which pictured Nelson as
one who had suffered from Henry's political machinations. Years
later, when the family was petitioning the Virginia legislature to
repay the money that they alleged was owed them as heirs of
Thomas Nelson, they wrote various former associates asking for
useful information in support of their claim. The replies were
invariably vague concerning his financial contributions, but they
did nothing to destroy the developing image of Nelson as a man
who had given up his fortune for his country.

Thomas Jefferson said that he first "heard mention of his losses
by responsibilities for the public" when he returned from France
in 1789, "and knowing his zeal, liberality and patriotism, I
readily credited what I had heard, altho' I knew nothing of the
particulars or of their extent." [3]

James Madison's comments were similar. He was not in Virginia when Nelson's alleged financial sacrifices were made but
he could testify that "General Nelson . . . was excelled by no
man in the generosity of his nature, in the nobleness of his sentiments, in the purity of his Revolutionary principles, and in the
exalted patriotism that answered every service and sacrifice that
his country might need." [4]

Samuel Smith of Maryland was also vague. As far as he
could remember, Nelson, while governor, had expended large
amounts in behalf of the public which had involved his "private
estate" in great difficulties. "The General was in truth a Patriot"

Smith said. "In those days Patriotic men not only gave their time to the public but . . . Supplied the means necessary for the public Service for which there have ever been great difficulty to receive any remuneration."[5] Statements such as these and the eulogistic biography of Nelson in Sanderson's *Signers of the Declaration of Independence* in 1823, aided in creating a distorted image of a man who, despite important financial efforts, made his primary contribution in the political realm.

The fact that fortunes have been commonly shortlived in America—and that loss of wealth has not usually enhanced the loser's prestige—must also be considered as a reason for Nelson's misleading reputation. By eighteenth-century American standards the Nelsons were very wealthy. Virginians of the nineteenth century knew this. John Randolph of Roanoke, who was not far removed from the revolutionary generation, commented at one point on how "the Nelsons, and Pages, and Byrds, and Fairfaxes," had lived in their palaces and driven "their coaches and sixes."[6] By Randolph's time the Nelson fortune was a thing of the past, a situation that the family did not easily accept. Having once been rich, it was not easy, either economically or socially, to experience so rapid a decline. They knew, painfully so, what they had been. As proud people they reasoned that there was no deterioration in their talent. The cause of their straitened circumstances was the fact that their distinguished forebear had been poorly used by an ungrateful country.

Hugh Nelson wrote St. George Tucker in 1820, concerning the latter's manuscript biography of the general, urging him to do all in his "power to aid in redeeming" his father "from oblivion and in holding up to Posterity the character of a man who has been supposed, at least by his family, to have made" enormous "exertions in behalf of the Independence of this country."[7] The letter was written at the time that the family was first petitioning the legislature for recompense. If they were successful not only would Nelson's fame be restored but their own fortunes would also be enhanced—perhaps they could even, over time, regain their former status. For twenty years they were preoccupied with attempts to attain this goal. The family knew that an injustice of some sort had been committed. There were a few documents to give some credence to their belief.

As time wore on, as memories grew more vague, and as rising American nationalism caused Americans to develop more pride in the accomplishments of the past, the view began to prevail that Thomas Nelson was one revolutionary hero who had not only been slighted but had also received unwarranted injury. Not even the searching report of the auditors and treasurer in 1832, which denied that the state owed the family anything, destroyed this view.[8] What may have initially seemed a strong probability now hardened into firm conviction.

Finally the warped image of Nelson was influenced by the character of eighteenth-century Virginia's gentry. The society that produced Nelson emphasized a way of life and certain values, some admirable and some not, which did not prepare its members to survive economic, political, and social change. By the middle of the eighteenth century Virginia's aristocracy had arrived at a stable existence. The upper levels of the elite were clearly identifiable, social relationships and patterns of behavior were well established, and expensive living was the rule rather than the exception. Hard work was still evident among the generation that was coming of age in the 1750s and 1760s, but less so than among their fathers and grandfathers— Thomas Nelson is a good example. They approached things in a more relaxed manner—the good life was more important. They felt that Virginia society, though not perfect, was better than any other. And they reacted against change whether it was retrogressive or progressive.[9]

At its worst such a society produced men who were self-satisfied and who tended to dissipate their patrimony in easy, sometimes debauched, living. At its best it produced hospitable, gracious, and generous individuals who felt a responsibility to help their country and who believed the greatest contribution could be made through public service.

This frame of mind dictated the course the society followed in response to British innovation after 1760. Thomas Nelson was certainly among the best of the Virginia leadership. He epitomized much that was good in Virginia society, and as the Revolution approached and wore on he gave more and more time to public affairs. But it was not just the concept of public service that moved Nelson to devote an abnormal amount of time to the public. He also wanted to protect the political institutions that he considered the best in the world.

Nelson and other Virginia political leaders believed that these institutions provided the foundation for a freer, better way of life. After 1760 they had come to realize that something unique and worth fighting for had been created in America. Perhaps Nelson and his colleagues also wanted to protect their position of leadership—but if so, they left no record of that motive.

Nelson was, as early as 1774, resigned to losing his fortune. He did not, of course, seem to relish the hard work and constant attention that a successful business required, but the deciding factor in his neglect of the business and of his extensive landed estate was his desire to help his country in its struggle with Great Britain.

This neglect of his personal affairs resulted, for him, in debt, loss of property, and a generally weakened economic position. The mercantile firm does not seem to have survived him and the remnants of a great fortune were dissipated in the payment of his considerable debt and the parceling out of his estate among his many children. With their economic underpinning gone, none of Nelson's descendants attained his stature. His son, Hugh, served in Congress during the administrations of James Madison and James Monroe and was later minister to Spain, but he was the last in the line to have any real public importance. Of course the Nelson family retained a measure of its social standing—for having attained greatness a family was not immediately demoted because of loss of fortune. The past was something which Virginians might distort but they did not forget.

In some ways the Nelsons' loss of wealth and influence was part of a general decline that was effecting many, if not all, of the older and wealthier Virginia families. Hard work and business ability which had been so crucial in helping their forbears to build great estates did not seem to have been so common among the revolutionary generation. In addition, failure to diversify their agricultural activities, worn out soil, and lack of capital which would have allowed them to expand into new areas led to a static or deteriorating situation by the 1780s. Furthermore big families meant that large estates were subdivided. This was true of the Nelsons and many others. And new estates were not being created. An extensive class of *nouveaux riches* does not seem to have been present in Virginia. There were exceptions to be sure—one thinks of the Lees and the Randolphs—but the majority of the Virginia elite did not maintain into the nineteenth century the position they had held in the eighteenth.[10]

Thomas Nelson and his family were not, then, unique; there was a general reduction in the fortunes of Virginia's elite in the last quarter of the eighteenth century. But Nelson's exceptional public services during the Revolution do set him apart from the generality of the elite. Ironically, these achievements are obscured by the memory of his financial losses.

Appendix

THOMAS NELSON'S FINANCIAL SACRIFICE IN THE AMERICAN REVOLUTION AND THE CLAIMS OF HIS HEIRS

Thomas Nelson did, as has been shown, make a considerable financial sacrifice during the American Revolution. But time has distorted the picture and has given him credit for a greater financial contribution than he actually made. As early as 1790 he was being credited with an expenditure of "60 or 80 thousand pounds" in the war effort.[1] But it was not until 1821 that Nelson's heirs got around to petitioning the state "for the many great expenses incurred, and losses sustained, in consequence of his patriotic devotion to the public during the American Revolution." The petition stated that not only had he personally borne the expense of raising, equipping and marching a troop of cavalry to Philadelphia and back in the summer of 1778, but that during the state loan drive in June 1780, faith in state finances was so lacking that he had had to pledge his own security to obtain the needed money. The money, it was asserted, had not been paid by Virginia, and Nelson was forced to pay the debts out of his own pocket.[2]

This petition was referred to a select committee of the House of Delegates which, in February 1822, reported that the petition was reasonable, but for some unrevealed reason asked to be discharged from the duty of preparing a bill conformable with its report.[3] That killed the petition and the question was not to come up again for nine years.

In 1831 the heirs petitioned the state again. There were twenty-one separate claims in the new petition, totaling approximately £87,000. The claims of 1821 were included, amounting to £44,000; and there were new ones such as £10,974 for a loan

145

drive in February of 1780, and £2,200 for tobacco loaned the state.[4]

On March 26, 1831, the Committee on Revolutionary Claims presented its report to the House of Delegates. The committee found that during the Revolution, Nelson, in the capacity of a public officer, had borrowed money from private individuals and had either paid it into the state treasury or disbursed it "on account of the service." But the committee was unable to arrive at any decision as to how much money he had borrowed in this manner; how much of his own money he had contributed to the public service; or, for that matter, how much ought to be repaid by the state. Consequently, the committee recommended that the first and second auditors, as well as the treasurer of the state, examine the accounts and report exactly how much money Nelson had expended from his own funds while serving the state and how much of this had been repaid him.[5]

The report which the auditors and the treasurer presented to the committee in January 1832 was a devastating blow to the claims of Nelson's heirs. It was a long, detailed statement taking up ten pages in the legislative journals, and the evidence it set forth so demolished the case of the heirs that the Committee on Revolutionary Claims reported to the House of Delegates that it failed to "perceive that the Commonwealth . . . [was] under any obligation, either in law or justice to grant the prayer of the petitioners."[6] The auditors and the treasurer had dealt separately with each of the twenty-one claims of the heirs and in each case they were able to demonstrate to the satisfaction of the House that there was not enough evidence to substantiate the claims.

Part of this report can be verified today. For example, there is no evidence to show that Nelson bore the expense of marching a troop of cavalry to Philadelphia and back in the summer of 1778. The heirs were aware that the state had expended £2,500 on the troop, but they said that this was too little and asked for an additional £3,000. Since positive proof exists that over £8,000 was expended by the state, there seems to be no reason for thinking that the claims of the heirs were valid and every reason to believe that the findings of the auditors and the treasurer were correct.[7]

Further, and even more devastating than the other evidence,

information presented by the investigators showed that Nelson at various times had received a total of £15,491 to spend for public purposes. But there was no proof that he had spent this money for the use of the state. The auditors and the treasurer did not question Nelson's honesty, for they stated that "Nelson was acknowledged by all, to have been a man of high sense of honor. . . ."[8] They were merely trying to show, as forcefully as possible, that the evidence did not exist to substantiate the claims of the heirs.

The heirs' petition also included a claim based on Nelson's reimbursement of the creditors of the state as a result of the loan drive in February 1780. Nelson himself, as discussed in Chapter VIII, had petitioned the legislature in 1784 for recompense in connection with this loan drive, but interestingly enough neither the heirs in their petition nor the auditors and treasurer in their report referred to his claim. In fact it seems clear that neither the heirs nor the auditors were aware of Nelson's petition. It is not surprising that the auditors were ignorant of this fact, but it is strange indeed that the heirs were not aware of his action, despite the passage of forty-seven years. Had they known, it would have saved them a great deal of trouble. For Thomas Nelson never thought that the state owed him more than £10,525 and this in itself invalidates the claims of the heirs for £87,000. Knowledge of this one claim might also have changed the minds of the auditors. They admitted that Nelson had collected the money, but disputed the claim that it had not been repaid. At the same time they conceded that they could not prove that £5,286 of the total had been repaid, and knowledge of Nelson's petition might have caused them to give his heirs the benefit of the doubt.[9] At the very least it is likely that the auditors' knowledge of the petition would have thrown light on why Nelson's claim foundered in the legislature in 1784–85. But it is fruitless to pursue such speculation. By the 1830s most of the participants in the Revolution were dead, and among those still living memories were hazy. Even James Madison, when queried on Nelson's "advances and engagements for the public service," either had forgotten or chose not to mention that he had been a member of the committee which recommended Nelson's repayment and had framed a bill to that effect.[10]

In any case rejection of their claims in 1832 by the House of Delegates did not dissuade the heirs from continuing their efforts to gain repayment for Nelson's alleged financial sacrifices. In 1833 they petitioned Congress and though a bill was finally framed three years later which provided "that the heirs of General Nelson shall receive from the United States commutation pay and lands which he would have been entitled to as a major general of the Virginia line on continental establishment," it did not get beyond a second reading. Finally in 1839 Nelson's son Philip made one last try in the Virginia House of Delegates. On this occasion the petition asked only that the state repay the money Nelson had loaned the state in June 1780 "from the funds in his hands belonging to Robert Carter Burwell" and which "Has never been repaid." But the committee to which the petition was referred inflicted the final humiliation by rejecting even this much-reduced claim.[11]

It should be added that there is no reason to believe that in making these claims Nelson's heirs were aware that they might have no basis of fact. Time and circumstances conspired to make their claim seem just. After the Civil War balm was applied to their wounds by the decision to include the statue of Nelson among those which surround the equestrian statue of Washington on the state capitol grounds in Richmond. On the base of Thomas Nelson's statue is inscribed the word FINANCE.

Bibliographical Essay

There is no central collection of Nelson family papers. Both Thomas Nelson and his father William left a considerable body of papers but the bulk of them seem to have been destroyed by fire in the nineteenth century. As a result the material for a biography of Thomas Nelson has been gleaned from a large and varied source material. Only the most important sources will be discussed here; the notes give a full guide to all the material that has been used.

Manuscript collections have been relied upon heavily. The one significant remaining group of Nelson letters are to be found in the William and Thomas Nelson Letter Book, 1766–75, Virginia State Library, Richmond. Business correspondence makes up the bulk of this letter book, but the letters are not confined to business and there is a great deal of information included which throws light on family, political, and social affairs. There are a few eighteenth-century letters in the Nelson Box, Brock Collection, Huntington Library, San Marino, California. Some Nelson business records can be found in Auditor's Item 225, Virginia State Library. In the same depository William Allason's Letter Books, 1757–89 also have some helpful information. Roger Atkinson's Letter Book, 1769–77, the Berkeley Family of Barn Elm's Papers, Robert "King" Carter's Papers, Landon Carter's Journal and Diary, 1752–77, Harry Piper's Letter Book, 1767–76 and the Charles Yates Letter Book, 1773–83, in the Alderman Library, University of Virginia, Charlottesville, all include correspondence and/or related material of importance. At the Virginia Historical Society, Richmond, the Lee Papers, especially the William Lee Letter Books, 1769–89, were helpful. The Norton Papers, the Richard Corbin Letter Book, 1758–68, the Augustine Smith Papers and Susanna Nelson Page's manuscript biography of Lucy Grymes Nelson in the Research Library, Colo-

149

nial Williamsburg Foundation, were used with profit, as were the Francis Jerdone Papers and Account Books and the Tucker-Coleman Papers at the College of William and Mary. Helpful with respect to Nelson's revolutionary career were the John Page Papers and the Thomas Jefferson Page Papers at Duke University, the Emmett and Lennox Collections at the New York Public Library and the Steuben Papers at the New York Historical Society. For family background the Jones Family Papers at the Library of Congress proved valuable. Comment on Nelson and his family can also be found in the Robert Beverley Letter Book, 1761–93, Robert Honyman, Diary and Journal, 1776–82 and the William Reynolds Letter Book, 1772–83 all in the Library of Congress. In the same depository the Washington Papers include a substantial number of letters to and from Nelson. I was able to consult British material on microfilm as a result of the Virginia Colonial Record Project. Most useful were the Parker Family Papers, Liverpool Record Office; the Charles Steuart Papers, National Library of Scotland, Edinburgh; and the James Russell Papers, Coutts and Company, Bankers, London.

A large number of public manuscript records have also been used. Of the British material, Public Record Office, Colonial Office 5, 1317, 1318, 1331, 1333, 1334, 1335, 1345, 1347, 1349, 1352 and 1353 were of the most value. But use was also made of Treasury 79, Audit Office 13, and High Court of Admiralty 30, Papers. Extensive use was made of the Executive papers of the state of Virginia, 1776–81, Legislative Petitions, 1775–1815, Treasurer's Cash, Receipt, Ledger Book, and Journals; and Virginia Land Patent Books, all in the Virginia State Library. Virginia county records were also consulted, including Judgments and Orders, Deeds, Wills, Inventories, Personal Property Books and Land Tax Books, in the Virginia State Library. Less useful for Nelson material, but extremely useful for Virginia material in general, are the United States Circuit Court, Virginia District, Ended Cases, which are on deposit in the Virginia State Library.

Newspapers were the source of a great deal of incidental, and only occassionally important, information. Most helpful was the *Virginia Gazette* (Williamsburg) which covers the period up to and including the Revolution. For the 1780s the *Virginia Inde-*

pendent Chronicle, the *Virginia Gazette or American Advertizer,* and the *Virginia Gazette and Weekly Advertizer,* all published in Richmond, were consulted.

Among the published public documents John P. Kennedy and H. R. McIlwaine (eds.), *Journals of the House of Burgesses of Virginia* (13 vols., Richmond, 1905–15) need to be re-edited and brought up to date, but they are still extremely useful as are the *Journals of the House of Delegates of Virginia, 1776–90* (4 vols., Richmond, 1827–28). These should be used in conjunction with William W. Hening (ed.), *The Statutes at Large Being a Collection of All the Laws of Virginia,* 1619–1792 (13 vols., Richmond, Philadelphia, and New York, 1823). H. R. McIlwaine et al. (eds.), *Executive Journals of the Council of Colonial Virginia* (6 vols., Richmond, 1928–66) and H. R. McIlwaine et al. (eds.), *Journals of the Council of the State of Virginia* 1776–(4 vols., to date, Richmond, 1931–) give a good deal of supplementary material. Useful for Nelson's military and gubernatorial career was H. R. McIlwaine (ed.), *Official Letters of the Governors of the State of Virginia* (3 vols., Richmond, 1926–27). A bare outline of his Congressional service can be found in Worthington C. Ford, *et. al.* (eds.), *Journals of the Continental Congress* (8 vols., Washington, 1921). A report of the auditors and treasurer of the state of Virginia titled, "General Nelson's Heirs," Document 9, *Journal of the House of Delegates,* 1831–32, proved very useful with respect to Nelson's financial service.

An absolute must for any historian of Virginia is Julian P. Boyd (ed.), *The Papers of Thomas Jefferson* (19 vols. to date, Princeton, 1950–). The thoroughness of Mr. Boyd's editing is frequently amazing. John C. Fitzpatrick (ed.), *Writings of George Washington* (39 vols., Washington, 1931–44) was also of great aid. William T. Hutchinson and William M. E. Rachal (eds.), *The Papers of James Madison* (5 vols. to date, Chicago, 1962–), were useful as were the *Letters and Other Writings of James Madison,* Congressional Edition (4 vols., New York, 1884) which included important information for the period in the 1780s not yet covered by the new edition. David John Mays (ed.), *The Letters and Papers of Edmund Pendleton, 1734–1803* (2 vols., Charlottesville, 1967) provides crucial information. Of somewhat less aid was John C. Ballagh (ed.), *The Letters of*

Richard Henry Lee (2 vols., New York, 1911). For family background the William Byrd II diaries, especially Maude H. Woodfin and Marion Tinling (eds.), *Another Secret Diary of William Byrd, 1739–1741* (Richmond, 1942), were helpful. Of similar use was Jack P. Greene (ed.), *The Diary of Colonel Landon Carter of Sabine Hall, 1752–1778* (Charlottesville, 1965). Further light was thrown on Nelson's service in the Continental Congress by L. H. Butterfield (ed.), *Diary and Autobiography of John Adams* (4 vols., Cambridge, 1961) and by Edmund C. Burnett (ed.), *Letters of Members of the Continental Congress* (8 vols., Washington, 1921–36). A variety of relevant material can also be found in Frances N. Mason (ed.), *John Norton and Sons, Merchants of London and Virginia, Being the Papers from their Counting House for the Years 1750 to 1795* (Richmond, 1937).

Other writings by contemporaries which were of value were Evelyn Acomb (ed.), *The Revolutionary Journal of Baron Ludwig Von Closen, 1780–1783* (Chapel Hill, 1958); Reverend Andrew Burnaby, *Travels Through the Middle Settlements in North America In the Years 1759 and 1760* (London, 1775); Marquis de Chastellux, *Travels in North America In the Years 1780, 1781 and 1782*, edited by Howard C. Rice, Jr. (2 vols., Chapel Hill, 1963); George W. Corner (ed.), *Autobiography of Benjamin Rush* (Princeton, 1948); John Page, "Memoir," *Virginia Historical Register*, 3 (1850):144–45; Edmund Randolph, *History of Virginia*, ed. Arthur H. Shaffer (Charlottesville, 1970). Some insight into Virginia politics in the period 1776–90 is given by [James Montgomery?], *Decius's Letters on the Opposition to the New Constitution in Virginia* (Augustine Davis, Richmond, 1789), but it is highly polemical and must be used with care.

Among the best biographies of Nelson's contemporaries are Irving Brant, *James Madison, Virginia Revolutionist* (Indianapolis, 1941); Douglas S. Freeman, *George Washington* (6 vols., New York, 1948–54); Dumas Malone, *Jefferson the Virginian* (Boston, 1948); David J. Mays, *Edmund Pendleton 1721–1803, A Biography* (2 vols., Cambridge, 1952). Also of use were Robert D. Meade, *Patrick Henry* (2 vols., Philadelphia, 1957–69); William Wirt Henry, *Patrick Henry, Life, Correspondence, and Speeches* (3 vols., New York, 1891); William

Wirt, *Sketches of the Life and Character of Patrick Henry* (Philadelphia, 1818); and Kate M. Rowland, *The Life of George Mason* (2 vols., New York, 1892). A most helpful biography of Thomas Nelson, attributed to St. George Tucker, can be found in John Sanderson, *Biography of the Signers of the Declaration of Independence* (9 vols., Philadelphia, 1823–27). There is also some interesting information on Nelson and his family in William Meade, *Old Churches, Ministers and Families of Virginia* (2 vols., Philadelphia, 1857). A full discussion of the Nelson family can be found in Emory G. Evans, "The Nelsons: A Biographical Study of a Virginia Family in the Eighteenth Century" (Ph. D. dissertation, University of Virginia, 1957) and Emory G. Evans, "The Rise and Decline of the Virginia Aristocracy in the Eighteenth Century: The Nelsons," in Darrett B. Rutman (ed.), *The Old Dominion: Essays For Thomas Perkins Abernethy* (Charlottesville, 1964), 62–78. A full discussion of Thomas Nelson's house and its subsequent history can be found in Charles E. Hatch, Jr., *The Nelson House and the Nelsons* (U.S. Department of Interior, Office of History and Historic Architecture, Washington, 1969).

On Virginia politics, Hamilton J. Eckenrode, *The Revolution in Virginia* (Boston and New York, 1916) can still be used with profit as can Isaac S. Harrell, *Loyalism in Virginia* (Durham, 1926). But a great deal of research and writing done in the past twenty years throws new light on Virginia history in the revolutionary era, especially Charles S. Sydnor, *Gentlemen Freeholders: Political Practices in Washington's Virginia* (Chapel Hill, 1952); Robert E. Brown, *Virginia 1705–1786, Democracy or Aristocracy* (East Lansing, 1964); Thad W. Tate, "The Coming of the Revolution in Virginia: Britain's Challenge to Virginia's Ruling Class, 1763–1776," *William and Mary Quarterly*, 3rd ser., 19 (1962): 323–43; Joseph Albert Ernst, "The Robinson Scandal Redivivus: Money, Debts and Politics in Revolutionary Virginia," *Virginia Magazine of History and Biography*, 77 (April, 1969):146–73; Jack P. Greene, "Foundations of Political Power in the Virginia House of Burgesses, 1720–1776," *William and Mary Quarterly*, 3rd ser., 16 (1959):485–506, and "The Role of the Lower House of the Assembly in Eighteenth Century Politics," *Journal of Southern History*, 27 (1961):451–74; Emory G. Evans, "Planter Indebtedness and the Coming of the Revolution in Virginia," *William and Mary Quarterly,* 3rd ser., 19 (1962):511–33, and "Private Indebtedness and the Revolution in Virginia, 1776 to 1796," ibid., 3rd ser., 28 (1971):349–74; Jackson T. Main, "Sections and Politics in Virginia, 1781–1787," ibid., 3rd ser., 12 (1955):96–112. The above material should be used in conjunction with two trail-breaking articles by Jackson T. Main, "The One Hundred," *William and Mary Quarterly,* 3rd ser., 11 (1954):354–84, and "The Distribution of Property in Revolutionary Virginia," *Mississippi Valley Historical Review,* 41 (1954):241–58.

On economic matters Louis C. Gray, *History of Agriculture in the Southern United States to 1860* (2 vols., Washington, 1933) has much useable information. But as in the case of politics much additional work has been done on economic questions in recent years. See especially Jacob Price, "The Rise of Glasgow in the Chesapeake Trade, 1707–1775," *William and Mary Quarterly,* 3rd ser., 11 (1954):179–99; James Soltow, "Scottish Traders in Virginia, 1750–1775," *Economic History Review,* 2nd ser., 12 (1959–60):83–98, and "The Role of Williamsburg in the Virginia Economy, 1750–1775," *William and Mary Quarterly,* 3rd ser., 14 (1958):467–82; Samuel M. Rosenblatt, "The Significance of Credit in the Tobacco Consignment Trade: A Study of John Norton and Sons, 1768–1775," *William and Mary Quarterly,* 3rd ser., 19 (1962):382–99; Robert P. Thomson, "The Tobacco Export of the Upper James River Naval District, 1773–1775," *William and Mary Quarterly,* 3rd ser., 17 (1961):393–407; Joseph Albert Ernst, "Genesis of the Currency Act of 1764: Virginia Paper Money and the Protection of British Investments," *William and Mary Quarterly,* 3rd ser., 22 (1965):33–74.

For Nelson as a war governor see Margaret B. Macmillan, *The War Governors of the American Revolution* (New York, 1943). Military affairs as they relate to Nelson's career can be adequately followed in Christopher Ward, *The War of the Revolution* (2 vols., New York, 1952), and Louis Gottschalk, *Lafayette and the Close of the American Revolution* (Chicago, 1942). Also of help are John M. Palmer, *General Von Steuben* (New Haven, 1937), and Paul A. W. Wallace, *The Muhlenburgs of Pennsylvania* (Philadelphia, 1950).

LIST OF ABBREVIATIONS FOR NOTES

C.W.   Research Department, The Colonial Williamsburg Foundation, Williamsburg, Virginia

P.R.O., A. High Court of Admiralty Papers, Public Record Office, London, England

P.R.O., A.O. Audit Office, Public Record Office, London, England

P.R.O., C.O. Colonial Office, Public Record Office, London, England

P.R.O., T. Treasury Papers, Public Record Office, London, England

U.V.   Alderman Library, University of Virginia, Charlottesville, Virginia

V.G.   *Virginia Gazette.* Name or names in parentheses designate publishers of the various papers using the name "Virginia Gazette" during the eighteenth century

V.H.S. Virginia Historical Society, Richmond, Virginia

V.M.H.B. *Virginia Magazine of History and Biography*

V.S.L. Virginia State Library, Richmond, Virginia

W.M.Q. *William and Mary Quarterly*

155

Notes

Prologue

1. Robert Fairfax to Reverend Denny Martin, August 24, 1768. Kent Archives, Kent, England.

2. His service in the 1780s was intermittent because of ill health.

3. Thomas Nelson to Samuel Athawes, August 7, 1774, William and Thomas Nelson Letter Book (1766–75), V.S.L. (Cited hereafter as Nelson Letter Book.)

Chapter I

1. William Hugh Grove, Diary for 1732, p. 54; U.V.; Edward M. Riley, "The Founding and Development of Yorktown, 1691–1781" (Ph.D. diss., University of Southern California, 1942), pp. 212–20; *W.M.Q.*, 1st ser. 15 (1907–8):222.

2. *W.M.Q.*, 1st ser. 15(1907–8): 222; Thomas T. Waterman, *The Mansions of Virginia, 1707–1776* (Chapel Hill, 1946), p. 172; *V.G.* (Parks), February 10, 1738; *V.M.H.B.* 13 (1905):402–3; deposition of Thomas Nelson, November 18, 1728, York County, Orders and Wills, no. 3 (1713–29), pp. 558–59, V.S.L.; wills of grandfather William Nelson, father Hugh, and brothers John and Hugh, October 24, 1670, December 13, 1708, July 6, 1724, September 1, 1734, District Probate Registry, Carlisle, Cumberland, England; G. Watson, "The Nelsons of Penrith," *Transactions of the Cumberland and Westmoreland Antiquarian and Archaeological Society,* n. s. 1(1901):104–13; Louise Pecquet Du Bellet, "The Narrative of George Fisher," in *Some Prominent Virginia Families,* 4 vols. (Lynchburg, 1904), 2:764.

3. [Lord Adam Gordon], "Journal of an Officer's Travels in America,

1764-1765," Kings 213, British Museum, London; York County, Orders and Wills, no. 14(1709–16), pp. 43–44; Petition of Virginia Indian Company, April 23, 1716, and Virginia Indian Company to Board of Trade, April 24, 1717, P.R.O., C.O. 5/1317, 5/1318; Walter Stitt Robinson, "Indian Policy of Colonial Virginia" (Ph.D. diss., University of Virginia, 1950), pp. 181–90.

4. Robinson, "Indian Policy," pp. 181–90; Petition of Virginia Indian Company, April 23, 1716, P.R.O., C.O. 5/1317; York County, Deeds and Bonds, no. 3(1713–29), pp. 102–4, 402–3, 432–33, 487–88; York County, Deeds, no. 4(1729–40), pp. 559, 588, 597; York County, Orders and Wills, no. 18 (1732–40), pp. 478–79; Colonial Virginia Land Patents, Book 2(1719–24), pp. 10–11, V.S.L.

5. Bill of Thomas Nelson to Thomas Jones, November 7, 1732; Negroes mortgaged to Thomas Nelson, March 29, 1732; lands mortgaged to Thomas Nelson, March 29, 1732; Thomas Jones to [Thomas Nelson?], 1732; suit in Chancery of Thomas Nelson and Cole Digges against Thomas Jones, [1734?]; Bill of Thomas Nelson to Thomas Jones, February 7, 1735; Samuel Smith, Jr. to Thomas Nelson, November 24, 1738; Account of Thomas Jones with Thomas Nelson, November 11, 1738; Thomas Jones to Thomas Nelson, December 7, 1738; William Nelson to Thomas Jones, December 22, 1753; Thomas Nelson to Thomas Jones, December 24, 1753; all of the foregoing material is to be found in the Jones Family Papers, Library of Congress, Washington. Petition to the House of Commons of Jonathan Forward, April

19, 1745, in *Proceedings of British Parliaments Respecting North America*, ed. Leo Francis Stock, 5 vols. (Washington, 1941), 5:215.

6. Negroes imported into Virginia, March 25, 1718–March 25, 1727, P.R.O., C.O. 5/1320; Robert Carter to John Pemberton, March 15, 1727, March 16, 1727, Robert Carter Papers, U.V.; *V.G.* (Parks), April 8, 1737, June 8, 1739; *V.G.* (Hunter), June 25, 1752, July 3, 1752.

7. H. R. McIlwaine and Wilmer Hall, eds., *Executive Journals of the Council of Colonial Virginia*, 5 vols. (Richmond, 1928), 4:184; York County, Deeds and Bonds, no. 3 (1713–29), pp. 178–79, 394–95; York County, Orders and Wills, no. 16 (1720–29), pp. 574, 584, 599; York County, Orders and Wills, no. 14 (1709–16), p. 470; William Gooch to Thomas Gooch, March 27, 1728, William Gooch Letters, 1727–58, Benare Hall, Wrentham, Suffolk, England; John Spencer Bassett, ed., *The Writings of Colonel William Byrd of Westover in Virginia Esqr.* (New York, 1901), pp. 351-52.

8. *W.M.Q.*, 1st ser. 2(1893–95): 9–10n, 14(1905–6):117—23; Will of Thomas Reade, June 15, 1719, York County, Orders and Wills (1716–20), pp. 453, 478; Edward Jones, ed., *The Lower Norfolk County Antiquary*, 5 vols. (New York, 1951), 3:43; York County, Deeds, no. 5 (1741–54), p. 509; Richard Channing Moore Page, *Genealogy of the Page Family in Virginia* (New York, 1893), p. 158. Page incorrectly calls the daughter, whose name was Sarah, Sally. See *W.M.Q.*, 1st ser. 6(1897–98):143–45.

9. William Nelson's birth is calculated from the fact that he was sixty-one years old at his death on November 19, 1772, *V.M.H.B.* 33(1925): 189; Page, *Page Family*, p. 158; Hugh Jones, *The Present State of Virginia*, ed. Richard L. Morton (Chapel Hill,

1956), p. 82; Robert Carter to Lewis Burwell, August 22, 1727, Robert Carter to John Pemberton, September 15, 1727, Robert Carter Papers; William Nelson to William Cookson, November 26, 1767, William Nelson to Samuel Martin, July 2, 1772, Nelson Letter Book; John Symmer to Sir Hans Sloane, September 6, 1736, Sloane MSS, 4054, no. 304–307, British Museum; E. Alfred Jones, *American Members of the Inns of Court* (London, 1924), p. 163. The plantation which young Thomas received was in King William County and was called the Horn Quarter. See n. 4 and *W.M.Q.*, 1st ser. 6(1897–98):143–45. For William Nelson's early involvement in the business see Emory G. Evans, "The Nelsons: A Biographical Study of a Virginia Family in the Eighteenth Century" (Ph.D. diss., University of Virginia, 1957), chap. I.

10. Francis L. Berkeley, "The Berkeleys of Barn Elms" (M.A. thesis, University of Virginia, 1940), p. 39; Richard Morton, *Colonial Virginia*, 2 vols. (Chapel Hill, 1960), 2:413.

11. *W.M.Q.*, 1st ser. 2(1893–94): 221, 222, 223, 233, 5(1896-97): 149, 6(1897–98):135–36, 143–45, 165, 7 (1898–99):44–45, 14(1905–6): 258–61; Bernard Bailyn, "Politics and Social Structure in Virginia," in *Seventeenth Century America*, ed. James M. Smith (Chapel Hill, 1959), pp. 98–99; Page, *Page* Family, p. 149.

12. *V.M.H.B.* 11(1903–4):68; *W.M.Q.*, 1st ser. 6(1897–98):165.

13. A full-scale study of the Virginia aristocracy remains to be done. A fairly accurate picture of who they were can be gained from Jackson Turner Main, "The One Hundred," *W.M.Q.*, 3rd ser. 11(1954):354–84, and Jack P. Greene, "Foundations of Political Power in the Virginia House of Burgesses," ibid., 16(1959): 485–506. See also Charles Sydnor, *Gentleman Freeholders: Political Prac-*

tices in Washington's Virginia (Chapel Hill, 1952); Hunter D. Farish, ed., *The Journal and Letters of Philip Vickers Fithian 1773–1774: A Plantation Tutor of the Old Dominion,* new edn. (Williamsburg, 1957), pp. 26–27, 29, 161, 178; Jones, *Present State of Virginia,* chap. V; Marquis de Chastellux, *Travels in North America in the Years 1780, 1781 and 1782,* ed. Howard C. Rice, Jr., 2 vols. (Chapel Hill, 1963), 2:434–44; "The Journal of Ebenezer Hazard in Virginia, 1777," ed. Fred Shelley, *V.M.H.B.* 62 (1954):414; Grove, Diary for 1732, p. 56; Maude H. Woodfin and Marion Tinling, eds., *Another Secret Diary of William Byrd, 1739–1741* (Richmond, 1942), pp. 136, 139, 154, 155, 156.

14. Fithian, *Journal,* pp. 26–27; William Gooch to Thomas Gooch, May 26, 1735, Gooch Letters.

15. *V.G.* (Parks), October 10, 1745; Will of Thomas Nelson, August 6, 1745, *W.M.Q.,* 1st ser. 6(1897–98): 143–45.

16. York County, Wills and Inventories, no. 18(1732–40), p. 49; McIlwaine and Hall, *Executive Journals,* 4:421, 5:187; John P. Kennedy and H. R. McIlwaine, eds., *Journals of the House of Burgesses of Virginia,* 13 vols. (Richmond, 1905–15), 1742–49, pp. 67, 77, 78, 85, 88, 96, 103, 106, 107, 111, 115, 117, 129 140, 142, 144, 146, 150; Greene, "Political Power in the House of Burgesses," pp. 485–86, 489, 499.

17. William Gooch to the Board of Trade, August 27, 1741, P.R.O., C.O. 5/1325; List of Councillors and Persons Recommended to fill vacancies, June 1743, P.R.O., C.O., 324/48; Board of Trade to King, February 5, 1745, P.R.O., C.O. 5/1366.

18. Appointment of William Adair as Secretary of the Colony, January 7, 1743; P.R.O., C.O. 324/37; McIlwaine and Hall, *Executive Journals,* 5:96, 115, 283; William Gooch to Secretary of State, June 27, 1743, P.R.O., C.O. 5/1334; Philip A. Bruce, *Institutional History of Virginia in the Seventeenth Century,* 2 vols. (New York, 1910), 2:396–402; Robert Beverley, *The History and Present State of Virginia,* ed. Louis B. Wright (Chapel Hill, 1947), pp. 245, 248; *W.M.Q.,* 1st ser. 15(1906–7):223; Kennedy and McIlwaine, *Journals of Burgesses,* 1742–49, pp. viii, 163, 258; Greene, "Political Power in the House of Burgesses," p. 499.

19. Landon Carter, Diary, April 8, 9, 10, 11, 14, 16, 18, 1752, U.V.; Morton, *Colonial Virginia,* 2:603–5.

20. William Nelson to George Washington, February 22, 1753 in *Letters to Washington and Accompanying Papers,* ed. Stanislaus M. Hamilton, 5 vols. (Boston and New York, 1898), 1:1; "Proceedings of the Virginia Committee of Correspondence, 1759–1767," *V.M.H.B.* 11 (1903–4):10–25, 131–43; Graham Frank to Mrs. Ellen Frank, November 1, 1756, P.R.O., A. 30/258.

21. John Blair to George Washington, February 5, 1758, May 11, 1758 in *Letters to Washington,* ed. Hamilton, 2:262, 292–93.

22. Robert Carter to the Duke of Beaufort, October 9, 1770, Robert Carter to Hyndman and Lancaster, October 15, 1770, Robert Carter Letter Book, 1770, V.H.S.; William Nelson to Lord Hillsborough, October 15, 1770, November 9, 1770, P.R.O., C.O. 5/1348; *V.G.* (Rind), October 18, 1770; James Parker to Charles Steuart, December 1770, Charles Steuart Papers, National Library of Scotland, Edinburgh.

23. William Nelson to Samuel Athawes, November 12, 1770, December 6, 1770, May 16, 1771, William Nelson to Rowland Hunt, May 16, 1771, Nelson Letter Book; William Allason to John Gray, October 23, 1770, William Allason Letter Book,

1770–89, V.S.L. For Nelson's administration see Evans, "The Nelsons," chap. IV.

24. Dunmore to Secretary of State, June 25, 1775, P.R.O., C.O. 5/1353.

25. Charles Goore to Edmund Berkeley, Mar. 20, 1753, Berkeley Papers of Barn Elms, U.V.

26. T. West to Mrs. Esther West, November 12, 1756, P.R.O., A. 30/ 258; Francis Jerdone to Messrs. Buchanan and Hamilton, June 28, 1748, May 20, 1749, Francis Jerdone to Samuel Rickards, Israel Maudit and Co., December 14, 1754, *W.M.Q.* 1st ser., 11(1902-3):154, 155, 14 (19 05-6): 143-44; William Meade, *Old Churches and Families of Virginia,* 2 vols. (Philadelphia, 1857), 1:208; William Nelson to William Allen, September 10, 1748, MS. Historical Society of Pennsylvania, Philadelphia; *Pennsylvania Magazine of History and Biography,* 17 (1893): 265, 273; Livingston and Alexander to William Nelson, November 7, 1757, Nelson Letter Book; Francis Jerdone to William Nelson, October 28, 1758, Jerdone Letter Book, 1756-63, College of William and Mary, Williamsburg, Va. See also Evans, "The Nelsons," chaps. II, III, IV.

27. York County, Deeds, no. 5 (1741–54), pp. 232, 235; Francis Jerdone to Captain Hugh Crawford, April 25, 1757, Jerdone Letter Book; William Nelson to Edward and Samuel Athawes, September 13, 1766, December 23, 1766, Nelson Letter Book; List of Bonds and Mortgages due William Nelson, 1755-72 and 1768-73, Auditor's Item 225, V.S.L.; Note, June 20, 1751, Item 843, Jones Family Papers; York County, Judgments and Orders, (1752–54), pp. 158, 294–95, 296, 409, 422, 442, 484; York County, Deeds, no. 5 (1741–54), pp. 630–31, no. 6 (1755–63), pp. 6–7; Francis Jerdone to Samuel Rickard, Israel Mauduit and Co., Decem-

ber 14, 1754, *W.M.Q.*, 1st ser., 16 (1907–8): 144; Trading Accounts of William Davenport, 1747–61, 1769–88, University College, North Staffordshire, England. The volume of William Nelson's business was arrived at after a careful study of his business correspondence for the period June 1771 to August 1772. See Nelson Letter Book, pp. 192–93, 202, 213, 215, 221, 222, 225–26, 227, 228, 232, 233, 234, 235, 236, 242, 253, 254, 258.

28. Colonial Virginia Land Patents, Book 31 (1751–56), pp. 104–5, 526, 527, Book 32 (1752–56), p. 657, Book 33 (1756–61), pp. 115, 414; Louisa County, Deed Book B, pp. 229–34; Hanover County Rent Role, 1763, P.R.O., A.O. 13/30; William W. Hening, ed., *The Statutes at Large Being a Collection of All the Laws of Virginia, 1619–1792,* 13 vols (Richmond, etc., 1809-23), 8:54–56; Fauquier County, Deed Book 2, pp. 572–74, V.S.L.; York County, Deeds, no. 6 (1755–63), pp. 491–95; William Nelson to Edward and Samuel Athawes, August 14, 1767, William Nelson to Robert Cary and Co., August 14, 1767, Nelson Letter Book; Hanover County Quitrents, November 1, 1769, November 10, 1770, Morris Papers, U.V.; William Nelson to William Dabney, January 18, 1769, February 9, 1769, Charles W. Dabney Papers, Southern Historical Collection, University of North Carolina, Chapel Hill; Robert Beverley to Edward Athawes, March 3, 1762, Robert Beverley Letter Book, 1761–93, Library of Congress; William Nelson to Edward Hunt and Son, November 20, 1767, November 14, 1768, Nelson Letter Book.

29. Graham Frank to Mrs. Ellen Frank, November 1, 1756, Ann Butler to Mrs. John Routh, November 13, 1756, P.R.O., A. 30/258. Graham Frank had married William Nelson's housekeeper. He wrote his

mother that "except [for] the Governour, he [Nelson] is the greatest man in this Country" and he compared Nelson's style of living to "Ld Castlecomer." Policy No. 95, Mutual Assurance Society, Richmond, Virginia, photostat, V.S.L.

30. Francis Jerdone to Messrs. Buchanan and Hamilton, June 28, 1748, *W.M.Q.*, 1st ser. 11 (1902–3): 153; Mary Stephenson, "Nelson-Galt House, Lots 26–27," typescript, 1945, C. W.; Woodfin and Tinling, *Another Secret Diary*, pp. 136, 154–56.

31. Evans, "The Nelsons," chaps. I and II.

32. Francis Jerdone, Account Book, 1750–52, January 10, 1752, College of William and Mary; Charles E. Hatch, Jr., *Yorktown and the Siege of 1781*, National Park Service Historical Handbook Series, no. 14, (Washington, 1954), pp. 32–39; Riley, "Yorktown," chaps. IV, V, VI; Evans, "The Nelsons," chaps. I and II.

33. Evans, "The Nelsons," chaps. I and II.

34. William Nelson to John Norton, September 6, 1766, February 27, 1768, January 9, 1769, Nelson to Samuel Waterman, September 3, 1770, Nelson Letter Book; "Memoir of Colonel John Page of Rosewell," *Virginia Historical Register*, 3(1850): 144–46; George MacLaren Brydon, *Virginia's Mother Church*, 2 vols. (Philadelphia, 1947–52), 1:389, 2:321–23; Edward L. Goodwin, *The Colonial Church in Virginia* (Milwaukee and London, 1927), p. 319.

35. Meade, *Old Churches and Families*, 1:206–7; John Sanderson, *Biography of the Signers of the Declaration of Independence*, 9 vols. (Philadelphia, 1823), 7:266–67; William Sachse, *The Colonial American in Britain* (Madison, 1956), p. 51.

36. "Memoir of Colonel John Page," 144–45; Sanderson, *Signers*, 7:266–67; George W. Corner, ed., *The Autobiography of Benjamin Rush* (Princeton, 1948), p. 152. Sanderson says that Nelson's companion was Francis Corbin, but this cannot be because Francis was not born until 1759, see V.M.H.B. 30(1922):312, 315.

37. Meade, *Old Churches and Families*, 1:206–7; *V.M.H.B.* 35 (1927): 243; Sachse, *Colonial American in Britain*, p. 52; William Maitland, *A History of London . . . .*, 2 vols., (London, 1775), 2:1366–67; Sir Walter Besant, *London in the Eighteenth Century* (London, 1903), pp. 173, 230, 243; Rosamonde Bayne-Powell, *Travellers in Eighteenth-Century England* (London, 1951), p. 101.

38. George C. Brauer, *The Education of a Gentleman: Theories of Gentlemanly Education in England, 1660–1775* (New York, 1959), pp. 197, 201; Lucille Griffith, "English Education for Virginia Youth: Some Eighteenth-Century Ambler Letters," V.M.H.B. 69(1961):573.

39. Meade, *Old Churches and Families*, 1:207. There now can be seen in the Virginia Historical Society, Richmond, a gold snuffbox that belonged to Thomas Nelson. Oral tradition in the Nelson family relates that Lord Frederick North gave the snuffbox to Nelson, while he was in school in England, for having saved a young boy from drowning. The snuffbox was given to the society by Dr. Hugh T. Nelson of Charlottesville, Va. See statement spelling out the conditions of the gift by Roswell Page, November 3, 1930, V.H.S.

40. Meade, *Old Churches and Families*, 1:206–7; Sanderson, *Signers*, pp. 266–67; *W.M.Q.*, 1st ser. 3(1894–95):21, 39; 25 (1917):190; Beilby Porteus to [Thomas Dawson?], March 18, 1758, ibid., 2nd ser. 1(1921):20–21; *Dictionary of National Biography*, s.v. "Porteus, Beilby"; William M. Thackeray, *The Four Georges* (London and New York, 1912), p. 351.

41. Thomas D. Atkinson, *Cambridge Described and Illustrated* (London, 1897), pp. 406–14; Willard Connelly, "Colonial Americans in Oxford and Cambridge," *American Oxonian* 29(1942):75–77; *V.M.H.B.* 21(1913): 433–34.

42. A. W. Ward and A. R. Waller, eds., *Cambridge History of English Literature,* 15 vols (Cambridge, 1907–27), vol. 9, chap. 15; Meade, *Old Churches and Families,* 1:207.

43. Meade, *Old Churches and Families,* 1:207; Atkinson, *Cambridge Described,* pp. 406–14; John Frere to John Hatley Norton, April 1, 1768, in *John Norton and Sons, Merchants of London and Virginia: Being the Papers of Their Counting House, 1750–1795,* ed. Frances N. Mason (Richmond, 1937), p. 43; *Dictionary of National Biography,* s.v. "Frere, John."

44. *V.M.H.B.* 21(1913):433–34; Sanderson, *Signers,* 7:266–67; Meade, *Old Churches and Families,* 1:207; George W. Fairfax to Lord Fairfax, June 2, 1761, Fairfax of Cameron MSS, Gray's House, Holyport, Berkshire, England; Robert Beverley to Edward Athawes, July 11, 1761, Beverley to [?], November 10, 1761, Robert Beverley Letter Book.

45. William Nelson to John Norton, February 27, 1768, Nelson Letter Book; Robert Carter Nicholas to John Norton, November 30, 1772, Mason, *Norton and Sons,* pp. 285–86.

Chapter II

1. Carl Bridenbaugh, *Myths and Realities, Societies of the Colonial South* (Baton Rouge, 1952), chap. 1; Marquis de Chastellux, *Travels in North America in the Years 1780, 1781 and 1782,* ed. Howard Rice, Jr., 2 vols. (Chapel Hill, 1963), 2:176–204; "The Journal of Ebenezer Hazard in Virginia, 1777," ed. Fred Shelley, *V.M.H.B.* 62(1954):414; John F. D.

Smyth, *A Tour in the United States of America,* 2 vols. (London, 1784), 2:65–67, 70; Evelyn Acomb, ed., *The Revolutionary Journal of Baron Ludwig Von Closen* (Chapel Hill, 1958), p. 187; Charles Sydnor, *Gentlemen Freeholders: Political Practices in Washington's Virginia* (Chapel Hill, 1952), especially chaps. 5–8; Jackson Turner Main, "The Distribution of Property in Post Revolutionary Virginia," *Mississippi Valley Historical Review* 41 (1954): 241–58. Exact figures are hard to arrive at; but looking at the free members of society, the upper class perhaps made up 8 to 10 percent of the total, the middle class 40 to 45 percent, and the lower class 45 to 50 percent. For the Scots in the tobacco trade see Jacob M. Price, "The Rise of Glasgow in the Chesapeake Tobacco Trade, 1707–1775," *W.M.Q.,* 3rd ser. 11(1954):179–99; and James H. Soltow, "Scottish Traders in Virginia, 1750–1775," *Economic History Review,* 2nd ser. 12 (1959–60):83–98.

2. William Nelson to Capel and Osgood Hanbury, February 27, 1768, Nelson Letter Book.

3. John Wayles to [John T. Warre?], August 30, 1766, P.R.O., T. 79/30. See also Emory G. Evans, "Planter Indebtedness and the Coming of the Revolution in Virginia," *W.M.Q.,* 3rd ser. 19(1962):517–23.

4. For example see Richard Corbin to Philip Ludwell, August 13, 1764, Richard Corbin Letter Book, 1758–68, C.W.; Nathaniel L. Savage to [John Norton?], July 22, 1766; Norton-Dixon-Savage Papers, Huntington Library, San Marino, Calif.; Robert Carter to Ralph Wormeley, October 19, 1771, Robert Carter Letter Book, 1771, V.H.S.; Landon Carter Diary, February 12, 1774, U.V.; Ralph Wormeley, Jr., to [?], March 23, 1784, Robert Wormeley Letter Book, 1783–1800, U.V.; Report of W. W. Hening

on Claims of Glasford, Gordon, Montieth and Co., June 15, 1802, P.R.O., T. 79/73.

5. John P. Kennedy and H. R. McIlwaine, eds., *Journals of the House of Burgesses of Virginia,* 13 vols. (Richmond, 1905–15), 1761–65, pp. v, 77; York County, Judgments and Orders, 1759–63, pp. 307, 320, 1763–65, p. 12; Robert Carter Nicholas to John Norton, November 30, 1772, Frances N. Mason, ed., *John Norton and Sons, Merchants of London and Virginia: Being the Papers of Their Counting House, 1750–1795* (Richmond, 1937), pp. 285–86.

6. Susanna Nelson Page, "Lucy Grymes Nelson," MS, April 10, 1835, Smith-Digges Papers, 1789-1843, C.W.; "Peter Pelham," MS, C.W.; Jane Carson, *Colonial Virginians at Play,* (Williamsburg, 1958, 1965), pp. 30–33; Andrew Burnaby, *Travels Through the Middle Settlements in North America in the years 1759 and 1760* (London, 1775), pp. 21–22.

7. *V.M.H.B.* 27(1919):184–87, 403, 413, 28(1920):91–96; Page, "Lucy Grymes Nelson."

8. Page, "Lucy Grymes Nelson"; Birth records in Nelson family Bible, photostat, V.H.S.; W. A. R. Goodwin, *The Record of Bruton Parish Church,* ed. Mary F. Goodwin (Richmond, 1941), 141; John Sanderson, *Biography of the Signers of the Declaration of Independence,* 9 vols. (Philadelphia, 1823), 7:267; [Lord Adam Gordon], "Journal of an Officer's Travels in America, 1764–1765," Kings 213, British Museum, London.

9. William Nelson to John Norton, July 25, 1766, February 27, 1768, Nelson to Cousin William Cookson, September 12, 1766, November 26, 1767, Nelson to John Tucker, November 24, 1767, Nelson to Graham Frank November 28, 1767, Thomas Nelson to William Cookson, January 27, 1773, Nelson Letter Book; Page,

Page Family, p. 171; Nelson family Bible.

10. Nelson family Bible; William Nelson to William Cookson, September 12, 1766, Nelson to John Norton, February 27, 1768, Thomas Nelson to Samuel Athawes, June 6, 1774, Nelson Letter Book; *V.G.* (Purdie and Dixon), October 27, 1774; Page, "Lucy Grymes Nelson"; Jacob Hall, Jr. to Mrs. Hannah Nice, [1775?], *W.M.Q.,* 1st ser. 22 (1913–14), 158–59.

11. York County, Deeds, no. 6 (1775–63), pp. 318–23; York County, Judgments and Orders, 1772–74, p. 209; William Nelson to Capel and Osgood Hanbury, February 27, 1768, Nelson to Edward Hunt and Sons, November 17, 1769, Nelson Letter Book; Julian P. Boyd, ed., *The Papers of Thomas Jefferson* (Princeton, 1950–), 1:156–58.

12. Thomas Nelson to Thomas and Rowland Hunt, July 9, 1774, Nelson to Robert Cary and Co., January 20, 1773, Nelson to John Norton, January 15, 1774, Nelson to Samuel Athawes, September 7, 1774, Nelson to Samuel Martin, August 16, 1774, William Nelson to Cousin William Cookson, November 19, 1768, and to Samuel Athawes, November 19, 1771, Nelson Letter Book; Robert Beverley to Beilby Porteus, November 25, 1784, *V.M.H.B.,* 21 (1913): 98; Robert Carter Nicholas to John Norton, November 30, 1772, and John Frere to John Hatley Norton, April 1, 1768, Mason, *Norton and Sons,* pp. 285, 43; "Character of Leading Men and Description of Places in Virginia Given to the Commander in Chief [1779?]," Peter Russell Collection, Baldwin Room MSS, Toronto Public Library, Toronto, Canada; *V.G.* (Purdie), March 21, 1775; ibid., (Dixon), March 25, 1775, February 10, 1776.

13. Thomas Nelson to Samuel Athawes, October 8, 1774, Nelson Letter Book.

14. Robert Fairfax to Reverend Denny Martin, August 24, 1768, Culpeper-Fairfax-Martin Letters, Wykeham-Martin MSS, Archives of Kent, Maidstone, England; List of Foreign Debtors, John Norton and Sons, July 31, 1770, July 30, 1773, Norton Papers, C.W.

15. William Nelson to Samuel Athawes, August 14, 1772, Thomas Nelson to William Cookson, January 27, 1773, Nelson Letter Book; *V.G.* (Purdie and Dixon), November 19, 1772; Peter Lyons to John Norton, November 25, 1772, Robert Carter Nicholas to John Norton, November 30, 1772, Mason, *Norton and Sons,* pp. 281, 285–86; Notice of the Death of the Honourable William Nelson, November 19, 1772, Washington Collection, Mount Vernon, Va.; William Reynolds to John Norton, November 28, 1772, William Reynolds Letter Book, 1771–79, Library of Congress; Lord Dunmore to the Earl of Dartmouth, December 18, 1772, P.R.O., C.O. 5/1351; Thomas and Rowland Hunt to Robert Carter, February 22, 1773, Robert Carter Papers, 1772–85, V.H.S.

16. Will of William Nelson, October 6, 1772, *V.M.H.B.,* 33 (1925): 190–92; for Hanover County land see Hanover County, Land Book, 1782, V.S.L.; List of Debts, May 18, 1773, Auditor's Item 225, V.S.L.; Robert Carter Nicholas to John Norton, November 30, 1772, Mason, *Norton and Sons,* pp. 285–86; Sanderson, *Signers,* 7:266.

17. Thomas Nelson to Thomas and Rowland Hunt, December 2, 1772, January 21, 1773, Nelson to Dobson and Daltera, January 15, 1773, Nelson to Maurice Griffith, January 15, 1773, Nelson to Hyndman and Lancaster, January 15, 1773, Nelson to Robert Cary, January 20, 1773, Nelson to John Norton, January 20, 1773, Nelson Letter Book.

18. John Norton to Robert Carter Nicholas, July 9, 1772, August 8, 1772, Wilson Cary Nicholas Papers, 1765–72, U.V.; Alexander McCaul to Thomas Jefferson, July 8, 1772, Boyd, *Jefferson Papers,* 1:93; John Clapham, *The Bank of England, A History* (Cambridge, 1945), 1:244ff.

19. *V.G.* (Purdie and Dixon), June 10, 1773; List of Debts, April 10, 1775, Auditor's Item 225; Evans, "Planter Indebtedness," pp. *523–25.*

20. Thomas Nelson to Thomas and Rowland Hunt, February 16, 1773, May 20, 1773, Nelson Letter Book; John Norton to John Hatley Norton, May 29, 1773, Norton Papers.

21. Thomas Nelson to Thomas and Rowland Hunt, July 29, 1773, Nelson Letter Book.

22. Thomas Nelson to Thomas and Rowland Hunt, December 7, 1773, Nelson Letter Book.

23. For tobacco shipments see Nelson Letter Book, pp. 282, 284, 287, 290.

24. Louis C. Gray, *History of Agriculture in the Southern United States to 1860,* 2 vols. (Washington, 1933), 1:278; Thomas Nelson to John Norton, August 7, 1773, Nelson to Robert Cary, August 19, 1773, December 7, 1773, Nelson to Thomas and Rowland Hunt, November 7, 1773, Nelson Letter Book; *W.M.Q.,* 1st ser. 2(1893–94):14n, 15; John Norton to John Hatley Norton, September 25, 1773, Norton Papers; York County, Orders and Judgments (1772–74), pp. 426, 451; Louisa County, Deed Book, D, pp. 133–34.

25. Thomas Nelson to William Cookson, January 27, 1773, Nelson to Samuel Martin, January 27, 1773, September 15, 1773, December 2, 1773, December 7, 1773, Nelson to Thomas Cookson, September 15, 1773, Nelson Letter Book.

26. List of Foreign Debtors John Norton and Co., July 30, 1773, Nor-

ton Papers; Thomas Nelson to Thomas and Rowland Hunt, December 7, 1773, Nelson to John Norton, January 15, 1774, Nelson to Samuel Athawes, September 14, 1775, Nelson Letter Book; York County, Deeds, no. 8(1769–77), pp. 302–3, 350–51, 424.

27. Thomas Nelson to Thomas and Rowland Hunt, May 3, 1774, Nelson Letter Book.

28. Thomas Nelson to Thomas and Rowland Hunt, May 31, 1774, October 10, 1774, Nelson Letter Book.

29. Thomas Nelson to Samuel Martin, August 16, 1774, November 16, 1774, Nelson to Samuel Athawes, October 8, 1774, Nelson Letter Book. Cookson, first cousin to William Nelson, was a "grocer" in Penrith.

30. Thomas Nelson to Thomas and Rowland Hunt, July 9, 1774, Nelson Letter Book; for tobacco shipment see ibid., pp. 313, 319, 320, 321, 322, 325.

31. Thomas Nelson to Thomas and Rowland Hunt, October 10, 1774, July 15, 1775, Nelson Letter Book.

32. Thomas Nelson to Samuel Athawes, July 15, 1775, Nelson to Thomas and Rowland Hunt, July 15, 1775, Nelson Letter Book; Auditor's Item 225; for tobacco shipment see Nelson Letter Book, pp. 326, 327, 329.

Chapter III

1. William Meade, *Old Churches and Families of Virginia,* 2 vols. (Philadelphia, 1857), 1:207; John P. Kennedy and H. R. McIlwaine, eds., *Journals of the House of Burgesses of Virginia,* 13 vols. (Richmond, 1905–15), 1761–65, pp. 77, 230.

2. Governor Fauquier to Board of Trade, Fauquier to Earl of Shelburne, April 27, 1767, P.R.O., C.O. 5/1331; Fauquier to Secretary of State, June 14, 1765, P.R.O., C.O. 5/1345. For the best analysis of Virginia politics in the aftermath of the Robinson affair see Joseph Albert Ernst, "The Robinson Scandal Redivivus: Money, Debts and Politics in Revolutionary Virginia," *V.M.H.B.* 77 (1969):146–73.

3. Meade, *Old Churches and Families,* 1:206–15; Lyman H. Butterfield, ed., *Diary and Autobiography of John Adams,* 4 vols. (Cambridge, Mass., 1961), 2:172; "Character of the Leading Men and Description of Places in Virginia Given to the Commander in Chief, [1779?]," Peter Russell Collection, Baldwin Room MSS, Toronto Public Library, Toronto, Canada; Thomas Nelson to Thomas and Rowland Hunt, July 29, 1773, July 9, 1774, Nelson Letter Book.

4. William Nelson to Cousin William Cookson, November 26, 1767, Nelson to John Backhouse, November 27, 1767, Nelson Letter Book.

5. William Nelson to Farrell and Jones, November 19, 1768, ibid.

6. *V.G.* (Purdie and Dixon), May 25, 1769; Kennedy and McIlwaine, *Journal of Burgesses,* 1766–69, pp. xxxvii–xlii, 15, 118, 147, 158, 164, 188, 190, 211, 214–18, 227, 228, 257, 265, 272, 289, 297, 309, 314, 318, 339; Jack P. Greene, "Foundations of Political Power in the Virginia House of Burgesses," *W.M.Q.,* 3rd ser. 16 (1959):499.

7. Kennedy and McIlwaine, *Journal of Burgesses,* 1770–72, pp. xxvii–xxxi; William Nelson to Lamar, Hill and Bisset, April 24, 1769; Nelson to Charles Goore, September 2, 1769, Nelson to Thomas Lamar, September 16, 1769, Nelson to John Norton, November 18, 1769, January 24, July 19, 1770, Nelson to Robert Cary, July 20, 1770, Nelson to Edward Hunt and Son, November 12, 1769, September 26, November 12, 1770, Nelson Letter Book.

8. Douglas Southall Freeman, *George Washington,* 6 vols. (New

York, 1948–54), 3:222–23; Copy of Virginia Association Resolves, May 17, 1769, Parker Papers, Liverpool Record Office, Liverpool, England; Harry Piper to Dixon and Lidderdale, June 8, 1769, Harry Piper Letter Book, 1767–76, U.V.; Lord Botetourt to Hillsborough, May 23, 1769, P.R.O. 5/1347; James Parker to Charles Steuart, June 22, 1769, August 5, 1770, Steuart Papers, National Library of Scotland, Edinburgh; John Baylor to John Backhouse, July 21, 1769, U.S. Circuit Court, Virginia District, Ended Cases, Backhouse Admx. vs. Baylor's Exors., 1798, V.S.L.; M. Jacqueline to John Norton, August 14, 1769, Francis N. Mason, *John Norton and Sons, Merchants of London and Virginia: Being the Papers of Their Counting House, 1750–1795* (Richmond, 1937), p. 103.

9. William Nelson to John Norton, January 24, May 17, July 19, 1770, Nelson Letter Book; John Norton to Robert Carter Nicholas, April 21, 1770, William Cary Nicholas Papers, U.V.; William Nelson to Lord Hillsborough, December 19, 1770, P.R.O., C.O. 5/1349; *V.G.* (Purdie and Dixon), July 18, 1771.

10. *V.G.* (Purdie and Dixon), September 26, 1771, November 19, 1772; Lord Dunmore to Earl of Dartmouth, December 12, 1772, P.R.O., C.O. 5/1334.

11. James Parker to Charles Steuart, April 19, 1771, May 19, 1773, Steuart Papers; William Allason to Andrew Sproull, August 5, 1771, Allason Letter Book, V.S.L.; William Reynolds to Courtenay Norton, October 19, 1771, William Reynolds Letter Book, Library of Congress; *South Carolina Gazette,* September 10, 1772 as quoted in Rutherford Goodwin, *A Brief and True Report Concerning Williamsburg in Virginia* (Williamsburg, 1941), p. 64; Robert Carter Nicholas to John Norton, November 30, 1772, George

F. Norton to John Hatley Norton, January 30, 1773, Mason, *Norton and Sons,* p. 299; Dunmore to Hillsborough, November 1, 1771, P.R.O., C.O. 5/1349; Dunmore to Dartmouth, December 12, 1772, P.R.O., C.O. 5/1334; Dartmouth to Dunmore, February 3, 1773, P.R.O., C.O. 5/1351; John Norton to John Hatley Norton, February 16, 1773, Norton Papers, C.W.; Thomas Nelson to Earl of Stamford, July 21, 1773, Nelson Letter Book.

12. Virginia Council Journals, 1752–76, June 9, 1773, photostat copy, U.V.; Robert Carter Nicholas to John Norton, November 30, 1772, Mason, *Norton and Sons,* pp. 285–86.

13. Kennedy and McIlwaine, *Journal of Burgesses,* 1773–76, pp. viii–xii, 4, 22, 28, 35–36; William W. Hening, ed., *The Statutes at Large Being a Collection of All the Laws of Virginia, 1619–1792,* 13 vols. (Richmond, etc., 1809–23), 8:645–52; James Parker to Charles Steuart, February 20, 1773, Steuart Papers.

14. Kennedy and McIlwaine, *Journal of Burgesses,* 1773–76, pp. viii–xiv.

15. Freeman, *Washington,* 3:349–50; Kennedy and McIlwaine, *Journal of Burgesses,* 1773–76, pp. 124, 132; Resolution of the House of Burgesses, May 24, 1774, Julian P. Boyd, ed., *The Papers of Thomas Jefferson* (Princeton, 1950–) 1:105–7.

16. Kennedy and McIlwaine, *Journal of Burgesses,* 1773–76, pp. xii–xiv, 139, 145–48.

17. "Proceedings of a Meeting of Representatives in Williamsburg," May 30, 1774, and Peyton Randolph and others to members of the Late Burgesses, May 31, 1774, Boyd, *Jefferson Papers,* 1:109–12.

18. Nelson's correspondence from Yorktown picks up on May 31, see Nelson Letter Book, pp. 308–9; Landon Carter Diary, June 3, 1774, U.V.

19. *V.G.* (Purdie and Dixon), July 21, 1774.

20. Ibid.

21. Ibid., supplement.

22. Ibid.

23. Ibid.

24. David J. Mays, *Edmund Pendleton, 1721–1803,* 2 vols. (Cambridge, Mass., 1952), 1:274–75; William Carr to James Russell, June 6, 1774, James Russell Papers, Coutts and Company, Bankers, London, England.

25. William Carr to James Russell, May 26, 1774, Russell Papers; James Parker to Charles Steuart, June 17, 1774, September 26, 1774, Steuart Papers; William Reynolds to George F. Norton, June 3, 1774, Reynolds Letter Book; Harry Piper to Dixon and Lidderdale, June 9, 1774, Piper Letter Book.

26. Harry Piper to Dixon and Lidderdale, June 9, 1774, Piper Letter Book; Council to Lord Dunmore, June 10, 1774, P.R.O., C.O. 5/1352; Dunmore to Secretary of State, December 24, 1774, P.R.O., C.O. 5/1353; William Carr to James Russell, June 15, 1774, Russell Papers; James Parker to Charles Steuart, June 17, 1774, Steuart Papers; William Allason to Walter Peter, July 1, 1774, Allason Letter Book; Charles Yates to Harry Ellison, July 21, 1774, Charles Yates Letter Book, 1773–1783, U.V.; Williamson Ball to Duncan Campbell, July 25, 1774, American Loyalist Claims, P.R.O., T. 79/12; John Tayloe to Duncan Campbell, July 20, 1774, ibid.

27. James Parker to Charles Steuart, June 17, 1774, Steuart Papers; *V.G.* (Purdie and Dixon), supplement, July 21, 1774; George Washington to Bryan Fairfax, July 4, 1774, July 20, 1774, John C. Fitzpatrick, ed., *Writings of George Washington,* 39 vols. (Washington, 1931–44), 3:227–29, 230–34.

28. Robert Beverley to Landon Carter, August 28, 1774, Robert Beverley Letters, 1763–74, U.V.

29. Landon Carter Diary, June 8, 1774, August 8, 1774, September 20, 1775.

30. Freeman, *Washington,* 3:367; "Resolutions and Association of Virginia Convention of 1774," August 16, 1774, and "Instructions by the Virginia Convention to their Delegates in Congress, 1774," Boyd, *Jefferson Papers,* 1:137–43.

31. The only remaining record of the vote for delegates to the 1774 Congress was written down by Edmund Berkeley on a blank page of the *Virginia Almanac* for 1774, now in the Berkeley Papers, U.V.; Dunmore to Secretary of State, December 24, 1774, P.R.O., C.O. 5/1353.

32. Thomas Nelson to Samuel Athawes, August 7, 1774, Nelson Letter Book.

33. Thomas Nelson to Thomas and Rowland Hunt, August 7, 1774, Nelson Letter Book.

34. *Proceedings of the Massachusetts Historical Society,* 1st ser., 3 (1859):259–61.

35. Kennedy and McIlwaine, *Journal of Burgesses,* 1773–76, pp. xvi, 165–72.

36. Thomas Nelson to Earl of Stamford, October 8, 1774, Nelson to Samuel Athawes, October 8, 1774, Nelson to John Norton, October 8, 1774, Nelson Letter Book.

37. James Parker to Charles Steuart, October 14, 1774, Steuart Papers; Lord Dunmore to Secretary of State, December 24, 1774, P.R.O., C.O. 5/1353.

38. Lord Dunmore to Secretary of State, December 24, 1774, P.R.O., C.O. 5/1353; *V.G.* (Rind), November 24, 1774.

39. *V.G.* (Rind), November 24, 1774; James Parker to Charles Steuart, November 27, 1774, Steuart Pa-

pers; William Reynolds to John Norton, December 24, 1774, May 16, 1775, Reynolds to George F. Norton, December 24, 1774, May 25, 1775, Reynolds Letter Book; Charles Yates to Gales and Fearon, December 2, 1774, Yates Letter Book; Lord Dunmore to Secretary of State, December 24, 1774, P.R.O., C.O. 5/1353; William Lee to Richard Lee, May 19, 1775, William Lee Letter Book, 1774–75, V.H.S.

40. William Carr to James Russell, September 27, 1774, October 23, 1774, December 8, 1774, January 9, 1775[6?], Russell Papers; William Reynolds to John Norton, August 6, 1774, Reynolds Letter Book; see also Charles Yates to Samuel Martin, September 28, 1774, Yates to Harry Fletcher, February 16, 1775, Yates Letter Book.

41. James Russell to Thomas Jones, November 25, 1774, Jones Family Papers, Library of Congress; William Lee to Francis Lightfoot Lee, December 24, 1774, Lee to John Lidderdale, January 2, 1775, Lee Letter Book.

42. William Lee to John Lidderdale, January 2, 1775, Lee to Richard Lee, January 6, 1775, Lee to Edward Browne, January 30, 1775, Lee to Thomas Adams, March 18, 1775, Lee Letter Book.

43. Lord Dunmore to Secretary of State December 24, 1774, P.R.O., C.O. 5/1353.

44. *V.G.* (Purdie), February 3, 1775; ibid, (Dixon and Hunter), March 25, 1775; Charles Yates to Harry Fletcher, February 16, 1775, Yates Letter Book.

45. *V.G.* (Purdie), February 24, 1775; ibid, (Dixon and Hunter), April 1, 1775.

46. *The Proceedings of the Convention and Corporations of the Colony of Virginia Held at Richmond . . . on the 20th of March 1775* (Richmond, 1816)—this volume also includes the proceedings for the conventions that met in July 1775, December 1775 and May 1776; William Wirt, *Life and Character of Patrick Henry* (Philadelphia, 1816), pp. 115–23; Edmund Randolph, *History of Virginia,* ed., Arthur H. Shaffer (Charlottesville, 1970), p. 213.

47. Dumas Malone, *Jefferson the Virginian* (Boston, 1948), p. 195; James Parker to Charles Steuart, April 6, 1775, Steuart Papers; Wirt, *Henry,* pp. 115–23.

48. *V.G.* (Dixon and Hunter), April 1, 1775; Mays, *Pendleton,* 2:12.

49. William Reynolds to George F. Norton, April 20, 1775, Reynolds Letter Book; H. J. Eckenrode, *The Revolution in Virginia* (Boston and New York, 1916), pp. 47–49.

50. Lord Dunmore to Lord Dartmouth, May 1, 1775, May 15, 1775, Kennedy and McIlwaine, *Journal of Burgesses,* 1773–76, pp. xvii–xix, xxi–xxiii; Peter Force, ed., *American Archives,* 9 vols. (Washington, 1837–53), 4th ser., 2:371; Malone, *Jefferson the Virginian,* p. 198n.

51. Charles Yates to Samuel Martin, May 11, 1775, Yates Letter Book; Gustavius B. Wallace to Michael Wallace, May 14, May 15, 1775, Wallace Family Papers, U.V.; George Washington to Albemarle County Company, Gilmer Papers, V.H.S.; Wirt, *Henry,* pp. 136–43; Freeman, *Washington,* 3:414.

52. Kennedy and McIlwaine, *Journal of Burgesses,* 1773–76, p. xvi; *V.G.* (Purdie), supplement, May 5, 1775, May 12, 1775; ibid. (Dixon and Hunter), May 6, 1775; Wirt, *Henry,* pp. 143–44; William Reynolds to John Norton, May 16, 1775, Reynolds to George F. Norton, May 25, 1775, Reynolds Letter Book.

53. Randolph, *History of Virginia,* p. 220; James Parker to Charles Steuart, May 7, 1775 (note appended to letter of June 6), Steuart Papers.

There is a possibility that Secretary Thomas Nelson was the one who rode out to meet Henry. But James Parker (letter above) stated that it was Thomas Nelson, Jr., and there is no evidence contradicting him.

54. Kennedy and McIlwaine, *Journal of Burgesses,* 1773–76, pp. xx–xxi, 174–75, 186–88.

55. Ibid., pp. 189, 193–94, 201.

56. Ibid., pp. xxiii, 206–7; William Lee to Landon Carter, June 14, 1775, Lee Letter Book; see also Charles Yates to Samuel Martin, June 20, 1775, Yates Letter Book.

57. *Proceedings of the July 1775 Convention,* pp. 5, 11; Force, *American Archives,* 4th ser., 4:1519–20.

58. *Proceedings of the July 1775 Convention,* pp. 11, 19.

59. Jefferson had been elected the previous April to fill the unexpired term of Peyton Randolph who had gone home for personal reasons; *V.G.* (Purdie), August 18, 1775; *Proceedings of the July 1775 Convention,* pp. 14, 16, 17, 19.

60. Claim of Bernard Carey, October 18, 1783, P.R.O., A.O. 12/54; for John Randolph Grymes see Virginia Loyalist Claims, August 10, 1784, P.R.O., T. 29/124 and Certificate of Clerk of General Court, Negative of Inquisitions, March 22, 1787, PJ.R.O., T. 78/72.

61. "Character of Leading Men and Description of Places in Virginia Given to the Commander in Chief, [1779?]," Peter Russell Collection, Baldwin Room MSS, Toronto Public Library, Toronto, Canada; *V.G.* (Purdie and Dixon), supplement, July 21, 1774.

Chapter IV

1. Thomas Nelson to Samuel Athawes, August 7, 1774, Nelson Letter Book.

2. *V.G.* (Purdie), September 1, 1775; ibid., (Pinckney), September 14, 1775. For the route from Williamsburg to Philadelphia see Arthur P. Gray, "Washington's Burgess Route," *V.M.H.B.* 46(1938):299–315; David J. Mays, *Edmund Pendleton, 1721-1803,* 2 vols. (Cambridge, Mass., 1952), 1:280–82; and Philip Padelford, ed., *Colonial Panorama 1775, Dr. Robert Honeyman's Journal . . . .* (San Marino, 1939), pp. 1–13.

3. "Diary of Richard Smith [1775–1776]," *American Historical Review* 1(1895–96):289; Thomas Jefferson to Thomas Nelson, May 16, 1776, Julian P. Boyd, ed., *The Papers of Thomas Jefferson* (Princeton, 1950–), 1:292; Dumas Malone, *Jefferson the Virginian* (Boston, 1948), p. 211; *Journals of the Continental Congress,* 34 vols. (Washington, 1904–36), 3:302–34. Randolph was buried in Philadelphia, but his body was brought back to Williamsburg a year later, see *Journals of the House of Delegates of Virginia, 1776–1790,* 4 vols. (Richmond, 1828), 1:70.

4. *V.G.* (Purdie), supplement, October 6, 1775; Wyndham B. Blanton, *Medicine in Virginia in the Eighteenth Century* (Richmond, 1931), pp. 60–66; Malone, *Jefferson the Virginian,* pp. 99–100; Page, "Lucy Grymes Nelson," Smith-Digges Papers, C.W. Inoculation against smallpox was quite a serious undertaking at this time because the better Jennerian method had not yet been developed and the mortality rate was high from "variolation" as it was sometimes called.

5. Page, "Lucy Grymes Nelson"; David Hawke, *In the Midst of Revolution* (Philadelphia, 1961), chap. II; Carl Bridenbaugh, *Cities in Revolt* (New York, 1955), p. 217n. Thomas Nelson to John Page, February 13, 1776, copy Manuscripts Division, Swem Library, College of William and Mary. The original is in the hands of a private collector.

6. Lyman H. Butterfield, ed., *Diary and Autobiography of John Adams,* 4 vols. (Cambridge, Mass., 1961), 2:172, 179–81, 3:376.

7. *Journals of Continental Congress,* 2:250, 3:262, 328, 475, 4:151–57; John Sanderson, *Biography of the Signers of the Declaration of Independence,* 9 vols. (Philadelphia, 1823–27), 7:276.

8. Edmund C. Burnett, *The Continental Congress* (New York, 1941), pp. 112, 120; E. James Ferguson, *The Power of the Purse, A History of Public Finance 1776–1790* (Chapel Hill, 1961), chap. II.

9. For some of Thomas Nelson's other activities in Congress see for example, *Journals of Continental Congress,* 3:471–73; Edmund C. Burnett, *Letters of the Members of the Continental Congress,* 8 vols. (Washington, 1921–38), 1:275, 726; Thomas Nelson to John Page, January 22, 1776, February 13, 1776, Sanderson, *Signers,* 7:277, 278. The February 13 letter of Nelson to Page is incomplete in Sanderson. A full copy is in the library of the College of William and Mary. Early in Nelson's first term in Congress he and Peyton Randolph were accused of being willing to furnish a British man-of-war with supplies in the Rappahannock River. In the light of Nelson's feelings toward England and the fact that nothing further was said about the accusation it is safe to assume that there was no basis to the charge. See *V.G.* (Purdie), September 15, 1775.

10. Thomas Nelson to Thomas Jefferson, February 4, 1776, Jefferson to Nelson, May 16, 1776, Boyd, *Jefferson Papers,* 1:285–86, 292–93; "Thomas Nelson in Account with the Commonwealth of Virginia, 1775–1777," Emmett Collection, New York Public Library. Carter Braxton was to replace the deceased Peyton Ran-

dolph. It was common practice for members of Congress to return home periodically. Since each colony had only one vote, every delegate did not need to be present at all times.

11. *V.G.* (Purdie), March 8, 1776; *Journal of Convention of May, 1776,* p. 5.

12. Peter Force, ed., *American Archives,* 9 vols. (Washington, 1837–53), 4th ser. 6:1511, 1518; "Landon Carter Diary," *W.M.Q.,* 1st ser. 13 (1904–5): 13, 14; John P. Kennedy and H. R. McIlwaine, eds., *Journals of the House of Burgesses of Virginia,* 13 vols. (Richmond, 1905–15), 1773–76, p. 283. Curtis P. Nettels makes a convincing case for the influence of the military on the movement for independence. Charles Lee had been sent south to command the newly created southern department and his presence strengthened the hand of Virginia radicals. Whether there was any connection between Nelson's return to Virginia and Lee's presence there is impossible to determine. But certainly the two men were of the same persuasion. See Nettels, *George Washington and American Independence* (Boston, 1951), pp. 240–43, 256–61.

13. Mays, *Pendleton,* 2:106–8; Force, *American Archives,* 4th ser., 6:1511; Thomas Jefferson to Thomas Nelson, May 16, 1776, Boyd, *Jefferson Papers,* 1:292.

14. Thomas Nelson to [?], May 8, 1776, Charles Campbell, *History of the Colony and Ancient Dominion of Virginia* (Philadelphia, 1860), pp. 645–46. The original of this letter has not been found and the recipient is not known. I suspect it was Patrick Henry, but that is only a suspicion.

15. Thomas Nelson to [?], May 8, 1776, Campbell, *History of Virginia,* pp. 645–46.

16. For a full discussion of Henry's stand on independence see Robert D.

Meade, Patrick Henry, 2 vols. (Philadelphia, 1957–69), 1:102–11; Mays, *Pendleton*, 2:106–8; and Irving Brant, *James Madison, Virginia Revolutionist* (Indianapolis, 1941), pp. 215–33; Patrick Henry to Richard Henry Lee, May 20, 1776, *Southern Literary Messenger*, 8:260; Edmund Randolph, *History of Virginia,* ed., Arthur H. Shaffer (Charlottesville, 1970), pp. 250–51. Hugh Blair Grigsby, *The Virginia Convention of 1776* (Richmond, 1855), pp. 203–4.

17. William Wirt Henry, *Patrick Henry, Life, Correspondence and Speeches,* 3 vols. (New York, 1891), 1:395.

18. Randolph, *History of Virginia,* pp. 250–51.

19. Mays, *Pendleton,* 2:106–7; Boyd, *Jefferson Papers,* 1:290–91.

20. *V.G.* (Purdie), May 17, 1776; Thomas Ludwell Lee to Richard Henry Lee, May 18, 1776, Patrick Henry to John Adams, May 20, 1776, John H. Hazelton, *The Declaration of Independence, Its History* (New York, 1906), p. 401; Henry to Richard Henry Lee, May 20, 1776, *Southern Literary Messenger* 8:260; Boyd, *Jefferson Papers,* 1:298; George Mason to Richard Henry Lee, May 18, 1776, Lee-Ludwell Papers, V.H.S. There has been some debate over whether Nelson carried the Virginia Resolutions to Philadelphia or not, due to his attendance record. In his expense account Nelson billed Virginia from June 9, two days after the motion for independence was made. But this is not conclusive evidence, for in the previous year Nelson's bill began with September 20, whereas he was actually in attendance as early as September 3 (see Nelson Expense Account, Emmett Collection, and "Diary of Richard Smith," p. 289). More telling is the fact that the resolutions were supposedly received and read on May 27 and on the following day

Richard Henry Lee wrote Thomas Ludwell Lee that Nelson had not yet arrived and was not expected for about a week. But Lee did not mention the resolutions and spoke of returning home when Nelson arrived. Further the *Journals of Continental Congress* state only that "Certain instructions" to the Virginia delegates were received and read. Possibly these were not the instructions ordering the move for independence. (See *Journals of Continental Congress,* 4:397 and James C. Ballagh ed., *The Letters of Richard Henry Lee,* 2 vols. [New York, 1911], 1:196.) On the other hand there is substantial contemporary testimony that he did carry the resolutions and I must conclude that this is correct (see letters above of Thomas Ludwell Lee, Patrick Henry, and George Mason).

21. Thomas Jefferson, "Notes of Proceedings in the Continental Congress, 7 June–1 August 1776," Boyd, *Jefferson Papers,* 1:309–13; *Journals of Continental Congress,* 5:433.

22. For a complete view of the evolution of the Virginia constitution of 1776, see Boyd, *Jefferson Papers,* 1:329–86.

23. Richard Henry Lee to Edmund Pendleton, May 12, 1776, Ballagh, *Letters of Lee,* 1:192; Randolph, *History of Virginia,* p. 260.

24. Randolph, *History of Virginia,* p. 260; *Journal of Convention of May 1776,* pp. 78–79, 80; Mays, *Pendleton,* 2:123–24; H. R. McIlwaine et al., eds., *Journals of the Council of State of Virginia, 1776–1781,* 4 vols. to date (Richmond, 1931–), 1:86. After his defeat by Henry, Secretary Nelson was elected to the Council but declined for reasons of "age and infirmities." Nevertheless he continued to fill his old post as secretary, which was little changed under the new order of things.

25. *Journal of Convention of May*

1776, pp. 58, 81; George W. Corner, ed., *The Autobiography of Benjamin Rush* (Princeton, 1948), p. 52; Chancery Suit between Thomas Nelson and Carter Braxton, York County Loose Papers, V.S.L. Harrison's absence from Congress was to be temporary as he was re-elected in the fall.

26. For a thorough discussion of when the Declaration of Independence was signed see Boyd, *Jefferson Papers,* 1:299–308.

27. Merrill Jensen, *The Articles of Confederation, An Interpretation of the Social-Constitutional History of the American Revolution, 1774–1781* (Madison, 1959), chaps. V–VIII; Burnett, *Continental Congress*, pp. 213–29. Merrill Jensen, in making his case for the political conservatism of the majority of the committee, places Nelson in this camp. That Jensen errs respecting Nelson is obvious—for the Virginian neither opposed independence nor "when this appeared inevitable" did he try "to delay a declaration of independence until a government could be created for thirteen colonies and foreign alliances could be obtained." It is true that Nelson, as one who labored for the "good of the whole" in a congress with no power, favored the creation of a central government which could act with authority. His position suggests that the lines between radical and conservative are not as clear cut as Jensen believes.

28. Jensen, *Articles of Confederation,* chaps. V–VIII; Burnett, *Continental Congress*, pp. 213–29.

29. St. George Tucker to Thomas Nelson, September 1, 1776, Tucker-Coleman Papers, College of William and Mary; Thomas Nelson to John Page, September 17, 1776, Burnett, *Letters,* 2:95; Nelson to Page, September 18, 1776, Emmett Collection.

30. Nelson's Expense Account, Emmett Collection; *Journal of Delegates,*

October 1776 session, p. 10; McIlwaine, *Journals of Council of State,* 1:133–34, 2:440, 464, 468; Appointment of John Nelson to rank of Captain, 6th Virginia Troop of Horse, June 19, 1776, Executive Papers, V.S.L.; *V.G.* (Purdie), January 17, 1777, September 26, 1777; ibid. (Dixon and Hunter), February 18, 1777; Lucy Nelson to Thomas Jefferson, October 13, 1777, Boyd, *Jefferson Papers,* 2:33.

31. Roger Atkinson to Samuel Pleasants, November 20, 1776, Roger Atkinson Letter Book, 1769–76, U.V.

32. Earl G. Swem and John W. Williams, *A Register of the General Assembly of Virginia and of the Constitutional Conventions* (Richmond, 1918), pp. 1–3; Jack P. Greene, "Foundations of Political Power in the Virginia House of Burgesses," *W.M.Q.*, 3rd ser. 16(1959):493–502; *Journal of Delegates,* 1776, October 1776 session, pp. 10, 13; Nelson family Bible.

33. *Journals of Continental Congress,* 6:992, 1038; Force, *American Archives*, 5th ser., 3:1599.

34. Burnett, *Continental Congress,* pp. 232–33; Thomas Nelson to Thomas Jefferson, January 2, 1777, Boyd, *Jefferson Papers,* 2:3–4.

35. Thomas Nelson to Robert Morris, January 25, 1777, Burnett, *Letters,* 2:225–26.

36. Rhadamanthus was one of the three judges in classical mythology who decided the fate of souls of the departed in the lower world. William Hooper to Robert Morris, February 1, 1777, Burnett, *Letters,* 2:232n.

37. Nelson family Bible; *V.G.* (Purdie), April 11, 1777.

38. Nelson's Expense Account, Emmett Collection; Mann Page, Jr. to John Page, May 6, 1777, Lloyd Smith Collection, Morristown, N.J., National Park; Richard Henry Lee to Patrick Henry, May 13, 1777, Bal-

lagh, *Letters of Lee,* 1:290; Edmund Pendleton to William Woodford, May 20, 1777, Southern Historical Collection, University of North Carolina; Sanderson, *Signers,* 7:279; *Journal of Delegates,* 1777–80, May 1777 session, pp. 4, 19; *Journals of Continental Congress,* 7:335; Thomas Nelson to George Wythe, May 16, 1777, Burnett, *Letters,* 2:363. Pendleton referred to Nelson's sickness as his "former appoplectic visit," while Mann Page reported that any application to business "affects his head" and unless Nelson got some rest "he must inevitably die."

39. Thomas Nelson to George Wythe, May 16, 1777, Burnett, *Letters,* 2:363.

Chapter V

1. Thomas Nelson to Benjamin Harrison, August 15, 1777, Nelson to George Washington, November 28, 1779, Washington Papers, Library of Congress; *V.G.* (Purdie),, April 11, 1777, May 2, 1777; York County, Orders and Judgments, 1777–84, p. 142; H. R. McIlwaine et al., eds., *Journals of the Council of State, of Virginia, 1776–1781,* 4 vols. to date (Richmond, 1931–) 1:453.

2. *Journal of the House of Delegates of Virginia, 1776–1790,* 4 vols. (Richmond, 1827–28), May 1777 session, p. 32.

3. Nicholas Cresswell, *Journal, 1774–1777* (New York, 1924), pp. 206–7.

4. *Journal of Delegates,* 1777–80, May 1777 session, pp. 38–40; *V.G.* (Purdie), May 30, 1777.

5. *Journal of Delegates,* 1777–80, May 1777 session, pp. 109, 111; Irving Brant, *Madison, Virginia Revolutionist* (Indianapolis, 1941), pp. 313–14.

6. McIlwaine, *Journals of Council of State,* 1:463–64, 467, 470.

7. *V.G.* (Purdie), August 22, 1777.

8. Thomas Nelson to Benjamin Harrison, August 15, 1777, Nelson to George Washington, August 22, 1777, Washington Papers; Washington to Nelson, September 2, 1777, John C. Fitzpatrick, ed., *Writings of George Washington,* 39 vols. (Washington, D. C., 1931–44), 9:163–64.

9. *V.G.* (Purdie), August 22, 1777; B. Danridge to Washington, August 22, 1777, Washington Papers; John Page to John Norton, September 18, 1777, Norton Papers, C.W.; Treasurer's Receipt Book, 1777–78, November 17, 1777, V.S.L.; McIlwaine, *Journals of Council of State,* 1:463–64, 467.

10. Circular to County Lieutenants, August 23, 1777, Emmett Collection, New York Public Library; McIlwaine, *Journals of Council of State,* 1:470, 476, 484; Nelson to Washington, August 22, 1777, Washington Papers; Washington to Nelson, September 2, 1777, Fitzpatrick, *Writings of Washington,* 9:163–64.

11. Nelson to Washington, September 5, 1777, Washington Papers; *Journals of Council of State,* 2:2.

12. Nelson to Washington, September 12, 1777, Washington Papers; *Journals of Council of State,* 1:486, 488.

13. *Journals of Council of State,* 1:489, 491, 497, 499.

14. Nelson to Washington, September 5, October 24, 1777, Washington Papers; *Journals of Council of State,* 2:1, 5; Washington to Nelson, September 27, 1777, Fitzpatrick, *Writings of Washington,* 9:163–64.

15. Nelson to General George Weedon, October 28, 1777, MS, American Philosophical Society, Philadelphia, Pennsylvania.

16. Nelson to Washington, October 24, November 21, 1777, Washington Papers; Nelson to General George Weedon, October 28, 1777, MS, American Philosophical Society; *Jour-*

nal of *Delegates,* 1777–80, October 1777 session, p. 6.

17. *V.G.* (Dixon), October 30, 1777.

18. William W. Hening, ed., *The Statutes at Large Being a Collection of All the Laws of Virginia, 1619–1792,* 13 vols. (Richmond, etc., 1809–23), 9:286–89, 10:349–68; *Journal of Delegates,* 1777–80, October 1777 session, pp. 37, 77–78; Treasurer's Cash Book, 1777–79, August 1, 1777, V.S.L.

19. *Journal of Delegates,* 1777–80, May 1777 session, p. 10, October 1777 session, p. 113; Hening, *Statutes,* 9:377–80; "Bill for Sequestering British Property," Julian P. Boyd, *The Papers of Thomas Jefferson* (Princeton, 1950–), 2:168–71; Isaac S. Harrell, *Loyalism in Virginia* (Durham, 1926), pp. 81–89. Jefferson's colleagues on the committee that framed this act were Edmund Pendleton, Robert Carter Nicholas, Joseph Jones, Cuthburt Bullitt, and Joseph Prentis. Prices were rising tremendously in Virginia at this time. Cotton was a dollar a pound; salt, five pounds a bushel; English broadcloth, four pounds a yard; honey, twenty-five shillings a gallon; peach brandy, formerly two shillings and six pence per gallon, now twenty-five shillings; and whisky, twenty shillings per gallon. See Robert Honyman Diary, 1776–81, November 2, 1777, Library of Congress.

20. John Sanderson, *Biography of the Signers of the Declaration of Independence,* 9 vols. (Philadelphia, 1823–27), 7:282; William Meade, *Old Churches and Families of Virginia,* 2 vols. (Philadelphia, 1857), 1:211.

21. *Journal of Delegates,* 1777–80, October 1777 session, pp. 119, 125, 126.

22. Washington to Nelson, November 8, December 10, 1777, Fitz-

patrick, *Writings of Washington,* 10:27–28, 147–48.

23. *Journal of Delegates,* 1777–80, October 1777 session, pp. 37, 55.

24. Nelson to Washington, October 24, November 21, 1777, Washington Papers; Hening, *Statutes,* 9:275.

25. Hening, *Statutes,* 9:275; Nelson to Washington, October 24, 1777, Washington Papers.

26. Hening, *Statutes,* 9:337–45.

27. Washington to Nelson, November 8, 1777, Fitzpatrick, *Writings of Washington,* 10:27–28; Nelson to George Weedon, December 19, 1777; MS, American Philosophical Society.

28. *Journal of Delegates,* 1777–80, October 1777 session, pp. 55, 59, 78, 81, 82, 84, 85, 86, 88, 89, 92, 102, 107, 112; Hening, *Statutes,* 9:345–49.

29. *Journal of Delegates* 1777–80, October 1777 session, p. 94; Nelson to Washington, January 20, 1778, Washington Papers.

30. "Bill concerning Inoculation for Smallpox," Boyd, *Jefferson Papers,* 2:122–24.

31. Nelson to Washington, January 20, 1778, Washington Papers; Washington to Nelson, February 8, 1778, Fitzpatrick, *Writings of Washington,* 10:432.

32. Hening, *Statutes,* 9:345–49; McIlwaine, *Journals of Council of State,* 2:73.

33. Washington to Nelson, February 8, 1778, Fitzpatrick, *Writings of Washington,* 10:431–33.

34. Washington to Nelson, February 8, 1778, ibid; on Nelson's desire to lead troops in the field see Nelson to Washington, September 12, 1777, November 28, 1779, Washington Papers, and Nelson to George Weedon, October 28, December 19, 1777, MS, American Philosophical Society.

35. Nelson to Washington, May 5, 1778, Washington Papers; Sanderson, *Signers,* 7:284; *V.G.* (Dixon), April 24, 1778, ibid. (Purdie), May 1, 1778.

36. *V.G.* (Purdie), June 5, 12, 1778; McIlwaine, *Journals of Council of State,* 2:144, 152; *Journal of Delegates,* 1777–80, May 1778 session, p. 9; Hening, *Statutes,* 9:449–51; Honyman Diary, June 26, 1778; "Account of Robert Bolling," *V.M.H.B.,* 12 (1904–5):154. After Thomas Nelson's death his heirs petitioned the state and later the federal government for recompense, stating that Nelson had borne all the expense of raising, equipping, and marching this troop of horse to Philadelphia and back. There is no evidence to support this petition. See Appendix.

37. Nelson to Washington, June 30, 1778, Washington Papers.

38. Washington to Nelson, May 15, July 22, 1778, Fitzpatrick, *Writings of Washington,* 11:392–93; 12:203–4; Honyman Diary, July 3, 1778; Sanderson, *Signers,* 7:285; "Account of Robert Bolling," p. 154.

39. Washington called the horse "Nelson," and used it for the remainder of the war. See *Quebec to Carolina in 1785–1786, Being the Travel Diary and Observations of Robert Hunter, Jr., a Young Merchant of London,* eds. Louis B. Wright and Marion Tinling (San Marino, 1943), p. 196; Nelson to Washington, August 11, 1778, Washington Papers; Washington to Nelson, August 20, 1778, Fitzpatrick, *Writings of Washington,* 12:203–4, 341–42; Honyman Diary, August 20, 1778; "Account of Robert Bolling," p. 154; Sanderson, *Signers,* 7:285; *Journals of the Continental Congress,* 34 vols. (Washington, 1904–36), 11:766–77; John Almon, ed., *The Remembrancer or Impartial Repository of Public Events for the Year 1778* (London, 1778), p. 302.

40. Honyman Diary, February 22, September 29, 1778; Albemarle County, Deeds, Book 7, pp. 258–59; *V.G.* (Dixon and Hunter), November 13, 1778; William Nelson to George Washington, October 13, 1777, MS, Historical Society of Pennsylvania, Philadelphia; Lucy Nelson to Thomas Jefferson, October 13, 1777, Boyd, *Jefferson Papers,* 2:33.

41. *Journal of Delegates,* 1777–80, October 1778 session, pp. 5, 6, 9, 10, 13, 20, 24, 30, 75, 79, 80, 91, 95, 101, 104; Alexander Purdie to Thomas Nelson, October 10, 1778, Executive Papers, 1776–79, V.S.L.; Nelson family Bible.

42. George Washington to Benjamin Harrison, December 18, 1778, Fitzpatrick, *Writings of Washington,* 13:466–67.

43. *Journal of Delegates,* 1777–80, October 1778 session, pp. 102, 105, 107; Edmund Pendleton to George Washington, December 26, 1778, and Pendleton to William Woodford, April 26, 1779, David J. Mays, ed., *The Papers of Edmund Pendleton, 1734–1803,* 2 vols. (Charlottesville, 1967), 1:277, 280. Pendleton told Woodford that Nelson had accepted the appointment "to serve only 'til May. . . ." Pendleton was usually an accurate reporter and I see no reason to question his statement. York County, Deeds, no. 6 (1777–91), p. 21.

44. *Journals of Continental Congress,* 13:195; Honyman Diary, February 15, 24, 1779.

45. For the general problems that faced Congress see Edmund C. Burnett, *The Continental Congress* (New York, 1941), chaps. 21–23; for some of the shortcomings of Congress see Douglas Southall Freeman, *George Washington,* 6 vols. (New York, 1948–54), 5:91n, 92–95.

46. *Journals of Continental Congress,* 13:195; Nelson to Washington, March 23, 1779, Washington Papers; E. James Ferguson, *The Power of the Purse, A History of Public Finance 1776–1790* (Chapel Hill, 1961), pp. 45–46.

47. *Journals of Continental Congress,* 13:195, 245, 336, 346–52, 369–73, 436; Burnett, *Continental Congress,* pp. 433–38.

48. Washington to Nelson, March 15, 1779, Fitzpatrick, *Writings of Washington,* 14:246–47.

49. *Journal of Delegates,* 1777–80, May 1779 session, p. 4; Nelson to Washington, November 28, 1779, Washington Papers; Edmund Pendleton to William Woodford, April 26, 1779, Mays, *Papers of Pendleton,* 1:280.

50. Sanderson, *Signers,* 7:289; Honyman Diary, May 13, 1779; Colonel [?] Marshall to Nelson, *V.G.* (Dixon), May 26, 1779; H. R. McIlwaine, ed., *Official Letters of the Governors of the State of Virginia,* 3 vols. (Richmond, 1926–31), 1:366, 368, 369–70, 371–72, 374; Philip Mazzei, *Récherches Historiques et Politiques sur les Etats-Unis de l'Amérique Septentrionale,* 4 vols. (Paris, 1788), 2:199–201; *Journals of the Council of State,* 2:253. Official response to this invasion is scarce because the Council journals for this period are either destroyed or illegible. See ibid., 2:250.

51. *Journal of Delegates,* 1777–80, May 1779 session, p. 4; Edmund Pendleton to William Woodford, April 26, 1779, Mays, *Papers of Pendleton,* 1:280. Evidence that Nelson's return to Virginia had been planned earlier appears in the above letter of Pendleton to Woodford. Pendleton wrote that Nelson would resign his position in May "and will be chosen at a 2d election."

52. J. J. Pringle to Arthur Lee, August 18, 1779, Lee Papers, UV; Dumas Malone, *Jefferson the Virginian* (Boston, 1948), pp. 302–3; *Journal of Delegates,* 1777–80, May 1779 session, p. 29.

53. Nelson to Washington, November 28, 1779, Washington Papers;

Journal of Delegates, 1777–80, May 1779 session, p. 34.

54. *Journal of Delegates,* 1777–80, May 1779 session, p. 56; Honyman Diary, June 1, 12, 1779; Malone, *Jefferson the Virginian,* pp. 314–19; Hening, *Statutes,* 10:66–71.

55. *V.G.* (Dixon), July 31, 1779.

56. *Journal of Delegates,* 1777–80, October 1779 session, pp. 35–36; Ferguson, *Power of the Purse,* p. 46.

57. Nelson to Washington, November 28, 1779, Washington Papers; James Madison to James Madison, Sr., December 8, 1779, William T. Hutchinson and William M. E. Rachal, eds., *The Papers of James Madison,* 5 vols. to date (Chicago, 1962–), 1:315–16; Hening, *Statutes,* 10:165–72, 182–89.

58. British Debts paid in Virginia Currency during War, 1778–80, P.R.O., C.O. 5/1344; *Journal of Delegates,* 1777–80, October 1779 session, pp. 9, 13, 14, 26, 36, 40, 43, 60, 75, 78, 79, 87, 108; Harrell, *Loyalism in Virginia,* pp. 92–93.

59. Harrell, *Loyalism in Virginia,* pp. 93–98, 111; Hening, *Statutes,* 10:153–56; the legislature admitted the failure of the debt-paying provision of the Sequestration Act and repealed it in May 1780.

60. Honyman Diary, January 10, 13, 14, 1780; William Reynolds to John Ball, January 6, 1780, Reynolds Letter Book, Library of Congress; George Washington to Thomas Jefferson, December 11, 1779, December 25, 1779, "Notes on Threatened Invasion," December 1779, Jefferson to Theodorick Bland, January 18, 1780, Boyd, *Jefferson Papers,* 3:217, 243, 252–53, 263. The Virginia debt figure includes the state's share of the Continental debt.

61. Information on the loan drive in February 1780 is scarce, but there is no question that it took place. See Honyman Diary, February 28, 1780;

Journal of Delegates, 1777–80, May 1780 session, p. 86.

62. For Nelson's role see "Account of Monies Received in Consequence of Governor's Address," Treasurer's Office, Ledger Receipts, December 31, 1779—April 6, 1782, July 16, 1780 and Treasurer's Office, Journal of Receipts, March 2, 1780—April 2, 1782, pp. 119–21, V.S.L.; Petition of Thomas Nelson, June 8, 1784, Legislative Petitions, 1775–1815, York County, 1090-A, V.S.L.; "General Nelson's Heirs," *Journal of Delegates,* 1831–32, document 9, items 3 and 4. Nelson's heirs were to later claim that he was not repaid by the state for the sums he guaranteed. See Appendix.

63. Honyman Diary, February 29, March 16, April 15, 1780.

64. Ibid., May 29, July 4, 1780; *Journal of Delegates,* 1777–1780, May 1780 session, p. 4; Richard Henry Lee to Henry Laurens, May 16, 1780, James C. Ballagh, *The Letters of Richard Henry Lee,* 2 vols. (New York, 1911), 2:181; *Journals of Continental Congress,* 16:263.

65. *Journal of Delegates,* 1777–1780, May 1780 session, pp. 6, 7, 14, 15, 20.

66. Samuel Huntington to Thomas Jefferson, May 19, 1780, Jefferson to Benjamin Harrison, June 8, 1780, Jefferson to Samuel Huntington, June 9, 1780, June 30, 1780, Boyd, *Jefferson Papers,* 3:378–80, 423, 425–27, 471–72; *Journal of Delegates,* 1777–80, May 1780 session, pp. 27, 28–30, 62.

67. Sanderson, *Signers,* 7:289–91; Petition of Thomas Nelson, June 8, 1784, Legislative Petitions, 1775–1815, York County, 1090-A; "General Nelson's Heirs," items 4, 13; Treasurer's Office, Ledger Receipts, 1779–82, June 16, 1780; Treasurer's Office, Journal of Receipts, 1780–82, p. 128. In the Treasurer's Ledger and Journal Nelson is credited for only £30,350.4 in

one and £30,354.4 in the other. But in the petition of his heirs in 1831 he is credited for £41,601 which the auditors said was correct. I accept the latter figure because the auditors did verify it and they may have had access to information that is now lost. Furthermore if there is added, to the £30,350 figure, £7,162 from the estate of Robert Carter Burwell which he controlled as executor, and £2,837 from the same estate for which he may well have been responsible, the total is £40,349. See also an undated appeal in the John Page Papers at Duke University. This is clearly in support of this loan drive for it mentions the need to help the French army in America. The conclusion to this appeal states that "We the undersigned do therefore engage to furnish the Treasurer with the Sum annexed to our respective names, or do engage to repay Int[erest] to any person who will lend to the Treasurer the said sums." Thomas Nelson is listed for £5,000 for six months and this does not appear in the treasurer's records. It should be added that on May 16, he placed in the State Loan Office £17,500 from the estate of Robert C. Burwell. Add to this the almost £10,000 he subscribed, as executor, to the June loan drive and the sum is very large indeed. One wonders what the Burwells felt about this. See Treasurer's Office, Journal of Receipts, 1780–82, p. 81. See Appendix.

Chapter VI

1. H. R. McIlwaine et al., eds., *Journals of the Council of State of Virginia, 1776–1781,* 4 vols. to date (Richmond, 1931–), 2:264; Francis Mallory to Jefferson, June 30, 1780, Jefferson to Samuel Huntington, July 2, 1780, Julian P. Boyd, *The Papers of Thomas Jefferson* (Princeton, 1950–),

3:475, 477–88; Nelson to John Page, July 8, 1780, John Sanderson, *Biography of the Signers of the Declaration of Independence,* 9 vols. (Philadelphia, 1823–27), 7:290.

2. Robert Honyman Diary, August 21, 31, 1780, Library of Congress; Thomas Jefferson to James Callaway and Jefferson to Charles Lynch, August 1, 1780, William Preston to Jefferson, August 8, 1780, Jefferson to John Nelson, September 8, 1780, Boyd, *Jefferson Papers,* 3:519–20, 523, 533–34, 607.

3. Nelson family Bible. Thomas was now responsible for thirteen children, having recently accepted the guardianship of Augustine and Thomas Smith, sons of the deceased Robert Smith. Very little is known about the Smith family but Nelson did pay for Augustine Smith's medical education at the University of Edinburg. See *W.M.Q.,* 1st ser., 2:14n; Dr. Augustine Smith to W. Erskine, May 16, 1789, Smith Letter Book, C.W.

4. *V.G.* (Dixon and Nicolson), October 25, 1780; Nelson to Jefferson, October 21, 1780, Jefferson to Samuel Huntington, October 22, 1780, Jefferson to George Washington, October 22, 1780, Jefferson to Edward Stevens, October 22, 1780, Jefferson to Horatio Gates, October 28, 1780, Jefferson to Thomas Sim Lee, November 2, 1780, Boyd, *Jefferson Papers,* 4:54, 58, 59–60, 77, 89–90.

5. Nelson to Jefferson, October 21, 1780, Jefferson to Washington, October 22, 1780, Edward Stevens to Jefferson, October 30, 1780, Jefferson to Horatio Gates, October 28, 1780, Jefferson to James Wood, November 1, 1780, Jefferson to Thomas Sim Lee, November 2, 1780, Jefferson to Samuel Huntington, November 3, 1780, Boyd, *Jefferson Papers,* 4:54, 59–60, 81–82, 77, 87–88, 89, 92–93; Nelson to [?], October 22, 1780, MS,

Pierpont Morgan Library, New York, New York.

6. Jefferson to George Weedon, October 22, 1780, Jefferson to J. P. G. Muhlenberg, October 28, 1780, Boyd, *Jefferson Papers,* 4:61, 78; Nelson to George Weedon, November 3, 4, 1780, MS, American Philosophical Society; "General Nelson's Heirs," *Journal of Delegates,* 1831–32, document 9, item 20.

7. Alexander Leslie to Lord Cornwallis, November 4, 1780, Jefferson to Robert Lawson, November 22, 1780, Jefferson to Benjamin Harrison, November 24, 1780, Boyd, *Jefferson Papers,* 4:110, 142, 151; Peter Muhlenburg to Jefferson, November 18, 1780, Executive papers; Nelson to George Weedon, November 22, 1780, MS, American Philosophical Society; John R. Alden, *The South in the Revolution, 1763–1789* (Baton Rouge, 1957), pp. 250, 291.

8. General Von Steuben to Jefferson, November 27, 1780, Nathanael Greene to Jefferson, December 14, 1780, Boyd, *Jefferson Papers,* 4:163, 206; Honyman Diary, December 2, 1780.

9. Washington to Jefferson, December 9, 1780, Steuben to Jefferson, December 15, 1780, Boyd, *Jefferson Papers,* 4:195, 209; John M. Palmer, *General Von Steuben* (New Haven, 1937), pp. 243–44.

10. Jacob Wray to Nelson, December 30, 1780, Brock Collection, Huntington Library, San Marino, Calif.; Jefferson to Steuben, December 31, 1780, "Jefferson's Diary of Arnold's Invasion," December 31–January 2, 1781 (1796? version), William Tatham to William A. Burwell, June 13, 1805, Nathaniel Burwell to Jefferson, January 2, 1781, Jefferson to Jacob Wray, January 15, 1781, Boyd, *Jefferson Papers,* 4:254, 258, 273–76, 294, 377–88; Dumas Malone, *Jefferson the Virginian* (Boston, 1948), pp. 336–41.

11. Criticism of the state government and especially Jefferson subsequently became widespread. Edmund Pendleton wrote Washington that it was disgraceful to have "Our Metropolis, at 100 miles distance from the Sea Coast, Supprized and taken without resistance by an handful of Banditti." "I am sure his [Jefferson's] Intentions are the very best, but he was Incredulous and not sufficiently attentive on this Occasion." Pendleton to Washington, February 16, 1781, David J. Mays, ed., *The Papers of Edmund Pendleton, 1734–1803,* 2 vols. (Charlottesville, 1967), 1:340; see also Honyman Diary, January 29, 1781.

12. McIlwaine, *Journals of Council of State,* 2:269; "Jefferson's Diary of Arnold's Invasion" (1816 version), January 3, 1781, Jefferson to Nelson, January 2, 1781, Jefferson to Steuben, January 4, 1781, Boyd, *Jefferson Papers,* 4:262, 297, 308; Malone, *Jefferson the Virginian,* p. 338; Christopher Ward, *The War of the Revolution,* 2 vols. (New York, 1952), 2:868; Palmer, *Von Steuben,* pp. 246–47; *V.G.* (Dixon and Nicolson), January 13, 1781.

13. Boyd, *Jefferson Papers,* 6:109n; Nelson to [Jefferson or Steuben?], January 3, 4, 1781, John Dixon to Nelson, January 4, 1781, Steuben Papers, New York Historical Society.

14. "Jefferson's Diary of Arnold's Invasion" (1816 version), William Tatham to William A. Burwell, January 13, 1805, Boyd, *Jefferson Papers,* 4:262, 273–76; *V.G.* (Dixon and Nicolson), January 13, 1781; Palmer, *Von Steuben,* pp. 246–47.

15. *V.G.* (Dixon and Nicolson), January 13, 1781; "Jefferson's Diary of Arnold's Invasion" (1816 version), Boyd, *Jefferson Papers,* 4:262–63; Thomas Nelson to [Jefferson or Steuben?], January 4, 6, 7, 1781, Steuben Papers; Palmer, *Von Steuben,* pp.

246–47; Malone, *Jefferson the Virginian,* pp. 338–39.

16. Steuben to Jefferson, January 6, 7, 1781, "Jefferson's Diary of Arnold's Invasion" January 8, 1781, George Muter to Jefferson, January 7, 1781, Jefferson to Steuben, January 7, 1781, Nelson to Jefferson, January 8, 1781, Boyd, *Jefferson Papers,* 4:312, 316, 317–18, 259–60, 263, 314–15, 316–17, 321; Palmer, *Von Steuben,* pp. 249–50.

17. Nelson to [Jefferson or Steuben?], January 6, 7, 1781, Steuben Papers; Nelson to Jefferson, January 8, 1781, Boyd, *Jefferson Papers,* 4:321.

18. Jefferson to George Muter, January 7, 1781, Steuben to Jefferson, January 7, 1781, Jefferson to Steuben, January 9, 1781, Jefferson to George Weedon, January 11, 1781, Boyd, *Jefferson Papers,* 4:313–14, 317–18, 326, 339.

19. Nelson to Steuben, January 10, 12, 15, 1781, Steuben Papers; Jefferson to Steuben, January 10, 1781, Nelson to Jefferson, January 13, 15, 16, 1781, Jefferson to Nelson, January 15, 1781, Steuben to Jefferson, January 21, 1781, Boyd, *Jefferson Papers,* 4:332, 351, 373, 382–83, 371–72; Palmer, *Von Steuben,* pp. 249–50.

20. [Steuben?] to Nelson, January 21, 1781, Steuben Papers; Steuben to Jefferson, January 21, 1781, Boyd, *Jefferson Papers,* 4:422–23; Palmer, *Von Steuben,* pp. 245–50.

21. Palmer, *Von Steuben,* pp. 250–51; Steuben to Jefferson, January 21, 1781, Jefferson to Nelson, January 25, 1781, Boyd, *Jefferson Papers,* 4:422–23, 449–51.

22. Nelson to Jefferson, January 22, 1781, February 7, 1781, Boyd, *Jefferson Papers,* 4:427, 554.

23. Nelson to Jefferson, January 8, 20, 22, 1781, Jefferson to Nelson, January 25, 1781, Boyd, *Jefferson Papers,* 4:321, 419, 427, 449–50.

24. Steuben to Nelson, February 2,

1781, Boyd, *Jefferson Papers,* 5:687; Nelson to Steuben, February 2, 3, 1781, Steuben Papers. Nelson had moved his family to his Hanover County estate Offley Hoo during the Leslie invasion of the previous fall. Sometime during the winter he sent his two eldest sons, who had been at the College of William and Mary, to study under David Rittenhouse in Philadelphia. See William Meade, *Old Families and Churches of Virginia,* 2 vols. (Philadelphia, 1857), 1:424.

25. Jefferson to Nelson, January 16, 1781, Boyd, *Jefferson Papers,* 4:382; Reverend Robert Andrews to James Maxwell, January 18, 1781, Executive Papers, V.S.L.

26. Nelson to Jefferson, February 7, 1781, *Jefferson Papers,* 4:553–54; Nelson to Captain Joel, February 8, 1781, MS, Pierpont Morgan Library.

27. Jefferson to Nelson, February 13, 1781, Beesly Edgar Joel to Jefferson, February 9, 1781, Boyd, *Jefferson Papers,* 4:602, 569–70.

28. Paroled persons were those who had signed a parole with the British, in many cases under duress, agreeing not to take up arms against them. Honyman Diary, January 29, 1781, Nelson to Steuben, February 14, 15, 1781, Steuben Papers; Nelson to Jefferson, February 18, 1781, Boyd, *Jefferson Papers,* 4:650–51, 651n. At the same time that attempts to take Arnold were developing, the intense feeling against the British was increased by what has come to be known as "The Affair at Westover." Westover was the home of Mary Willing Byrd, widow of William Byrd III, and Nelson, as military commander in the area, was directly involved. An outward attempt by Mrs. Byrd to regain slaves and horses seized by Arnold's forces in his raid up the James River in January also concealed illegal commerce with the enemy. In mid-February forces under Nelson's command detained Lieutenant Hare, of Arnold's army, who was bringing back one of Mrs. Byrd's horses under a flag of truce. It was discovered that the lieutenant was also transporting a great deal of merchandise, including wine, brandy, china, linen, and broad cloth, which was evidently intended for Mrs. Byrd. During his detention the lieutenant leveled what Jefferson described as "calumnies on individuals of this state. . . ." Having found "one scoundrel in America . . . they would pretend to beleive [*sic*] all are so." In any case, Nelson sent the evidence concerning the incident to Jefferson on February 18, and a trial of Mrs. Byrd was planned. In the confusion of the following months the trial never took place; nor, it should be added, did Mrs. Byrd recover the property seized by the British. See Nelson to Jefferson February 18, 1781, Jefferson to Nelson, February 21, 1781, and Appendix I, ibid., 4:650–51, 677, 5:671–705.

29. Nelson to [Jefferson?] February 15, 1781, Nelson to Steuben, February 15, 1781, Steuben Papers. Jefferson to Nelson, February 16, 1781, Nelson to Jefferson, February 18, 1781, Boyd, *Jefferson Papers,* 4:631, 650–51.

30. Nelson to Steuben, February 18, 1781, Boyd, *Jefferson Papers,* 4:650–51; Palmer, *Von Steuben,* p. 254; Louis Gottschalk, *Lafayette and the Close of the American Revolution* (Chicago, 1942), p. 196.

31. Nelson to Jefferson, February 19, 20, 1781, Jefferson to Nelson, February 21, 1781, Boyd, *Jefferson Papers,* 4:658–59, 677; Gottschalk, *Lafayette,* p. 196. The state had gone to great pains to accommodate the French. Work was begun at Yorktown, under Nelson's direction, to provide a safe anchorage for their warships, but the only vessels that used the facility were eight "prizes,"

which had been taken by de Tilly. It appears that after the departure of the French, plans were resumed to capture Arnold, but, perhaps because of Nelson's illness, they did not mature. Jefferson to Nelson, February 16, 1781, February 21, 1781, Sans to Nelson, February 21, 1781, Boyd, *Jefferson Papers,* 4:631, 677–78, 678n, 678–79.

32. Nelson to [Steuben?], February 18, 1781, [Steuben?] to Nelson, February 2, 15, 1781, Steuben to Nelson, February 20, 1781, Steuben Papers; James Innes to Jefferson, February 21, 1781, Jefferson to Nelson, February 21, 1781, Boyd, *Jefferson Papers,* 4:675, 677–78, 678n. Nelson called his illness in the winter of 1781 "Rhumatism," which at that time meant catarrh or an inflammatory infection of the mucous membrane, especially of the nose and air passages. See Nelson to Jefferson, April 10, 1781, ibid., 15:607. This was probably the respiratory ailment that was to plague him the rest of his life. Contemporaries called it asthma and said that it was "contracted by exposure during the war . . . ." See "A Colonial and Revolutionary Family," MS, Thomas Jefferson Page Papers, Duke University.

33. James Innes to Jefferson, February 21, 1781, Nelson to Jefferson, February 19, 1781, Boyd, *Jefferson Papers,* 4:675–76, 659.

34. Nelson to [Steuben or Jefferson?], February 21, 1781, George Weedon to Steuben, March 28, 1781, [Steuben?] to Nelson, March 10, 1781, Steuben Papers. Internal evidence suggests that the March 10 letter was from Steuben. Ward, *Revolution,* 2:870.

35. Gottschalk, *Lafayette,* p. 221; Order by Thomas Nelson to impress horses, May 4, 1781, United States Revolution Collection, Library of Congress; Nelson to Jefferson, May

10, 1781, Boyd, *Jefferson Papers,* 5:631.

36. Steuben to Jefferson, March 26, 1781, Jefferson to Steuben, April 3, 1781, Boyd, *Jefferson Papers,* 5:250, 332–33; Ward, *Revolution,* 2:870; Gottschalk, *Lafayette,* pp. 201–6; Palmer, *Von Steuben,* pp. 256–58, 262–63.

37. Palmer, *Von Steuben,* pp. 263–65; Ward, *Revolution,* 2:871–72.

38. Lafayette to Jefferson, April 27, 1781, Boyd, *Jefferson Papers,* 5:564, and 550n; Gottschalk, *Lafayette,* pp. 219–23; Palmer, *Von Steuben,* p. 267.

39. Gottschalk, *Lafayette,* pp. 224–26; Palmer, *Von Steuben,* p. 267.

40. *Journals of the House of Delegates of Virginia, 1776–1790,* 4 vols. (Richmond, 1828) May 1781 session, p. 3; Gottschalk, *Lafayette,* pp. 226–27, 232–33; Ward, *Revolution,* 2:872–73; Lafayette to Washington, [May 4, 1781?], Washington Papers, Library of Congress.

41. Jefferson to James Innes, May 2, 1781, William Langborn to Jefferson, May 12, 1781, Order to those Appointed by Lafayette to remove Horses out of the Route of the Enemy, May 15, 1781, Rueben Mitchell to Jefferson, May 16, 1781, John Nelson to Jefferson, May 25, 1781, Lafayette to Jefferson, May 31, 1781, Boyd, *Jefferson Papers,* 5:593–94, 637–38, 638n, 655–56, 656n, 658–59, 6:15–17, 52; Thomas Nelson to [Jefferson?], May 9, 1781, MS, Pierpont Morgan Library. In May the Assembly did establish martial law within twenty miles of both the British and American camps. See W. W. Hening, *The Statutes at Large Being a Collection of All the Laws of Virginia, 1619–1792,* 13 vols. (Richmond, etc., 1809–23), 10:411.

42. Ward, *Revolution,* 2:873; Gottschalk, *Lafayette,* pp. 238–42; Palmer, *Von Steuben,* pp. 273–74; Honyman Diary, May 28, 1781, May 31, 1781.

43. Ward, *Revolution,* 2:873–74; Gottschalk, *Lafayette,* pp. 242–43; Palmer, *Von Steuben,* pp. 274–82; Malone, *Jefferson the Virginian,* pp. 352–61.

44. Malone, *Jefferson the Virginian,* pp. 352–61; "Jefferson's Diary of Arnold's Invasion," Boyd, *Jefferson Papers,* 4:260–61.

Chapter VII

1. *Journals of the House of Delegates of Virgiina, 1776–1790,* 4 vols. (Richmond, 1828), 1781–85, May 1781 session, p. 15.

2. Ibid., p. 10; Henry Young to William Davies, June 9, 1781, Richard Henry Lee to Virginia Delegates in Congress, June 12, 1781, Julian P. Boyd, *The Papers of Thomas Jefferson* (Princeton, 1950–), 6:84–85, 85–86n, 90–93, 93n; Richard Henry Lee to George Washington, June 12, 1781, James C. Ballagh, *The Letters of Richard Henry Lee,* 2 vols. (New York, 1911), 2:234; Honyman Diary, June 11, 1781, Library of Congress.

3. "Jefferson's Diary of Arnold's Invasion," Boyd, *Jefferson Papers,* 4:260, see also 6:78–79n; H. J. Eckenrode, *The Revolution in Virginia* (Boston, 1916), pp. 226–27; Dumas Malone, *Jefferson the Virginian* (Boston, 1948), p. 360; John Tyler in *Richmond Enquirer,* September 10, 1805; *Journal of Delegates,* 1781–85, May 1781 session, p. 15.

4. Archibald Cary to Jefferson, June 19, 1781, Boyd, *Jefferson Papers,* 6:96; Christopher Ward, *The War of the Revolution,* 2 vols. (New York, 1962), 2:874; Thomas Nelson to George Washington, July 27, 1781, H. R. McIlwaine, ed., *Official Letters of the Governors of the State of Virginia,* 3 vols. (Richmond, 1926-31), 3:13.

5. Archibald Cary to Jefferson,

June 19, 1781, Boyd, *Jefferson Papers,* 6:96; H. R. McIlwaine et al., eds., *Journals of the Council of State of Virginia, 1776–1781,* 4 vols. to date (Richmond, 1931–) 2:348; Edmund Pendleton to James Madison, December 3, 1781, David J. Mays, *The Papers of Edmund Pendleton, 1734–1803,* 2 vols. (Charlottesville, 1967), 2:381–82; John Cropper, Jr., to Nelson, August 25, 1781, William P. Palmer, ed., *Calendar of Virginia State Papers,* 11 vols. (Richmond, 1875–93), 2:359–61; Washington to John Parke Custis, July 25, 1781, John C. Fitzpatrick, ed., *Writings of George Washington,* 39 vols. (Washington, 1931–44), 22:415.

6. W. W. Hening, ed., *The Statutes at Large Being a Collection of All the Laws of Virginia, 1619–1792,* 13 vols. (Richmond, etc. 1809–23), 10:411, 413–16, 419–21, 423, 437.

7. For a clear discussion of wartime administration see Margaret Burnham Macmillan, *The War Governors in the American Revolution* (New York, 1943), especially chaps. V and VI.

8. See notes in Boyd, *Jefferson Papers,* 6:36–38, 77–79, for a strong defense of Jefferson; Louis Gottschalk, *Lafayette and the Close of the Revolution* (Chicago, 1942), p. 250, is also sympathetic, but the most balanced account is to be found in Malone, *Jefferson the Virginian,* pp. 349–69. For an opposing point of view see Eckenrode, *Revolution in Virginia,* pp. 195–231.

9. Nelson to Capt. John Randolph, [n.d., summer 1781?], *Calendar of Virginia State Papers,* 2:689–90; Nathanael Greene to Nelson, July 18, 1781, MS, William M. Clements Library, University of Michigan; Nelson to George Weedon, July 2, 1781, MS, American Philosophical Society. Jefferson's own statement concerning his retirement can be found in "Jeffer-

son's Diary of Arnold's Invasion," Boyd, *Jefferson Papers,* 4:260.

10. Auditor's Item 144, Account Vouchers, 1780–82, V.S.L., "Report on exchange rate of Virginia paper money" by David Ross, July 22, 1781, Robert Claiborne to Nelson, June 24, 1781, Executive Papers, V.S.L.; David Ross to William Davies, June 29, 1781, William Davies to Lafayette, June 25, 1781, War Office Letter Book (War 54), January 1781–September 1781, V.S.L.; Nathanael Greene to Jefferson, June 29, 1781, Virginia Delegates in Congress to Governor, May 22, 1781, Boyd, *Jefferson Papers,* 6:103–4, 9–10; Nelson to Daniel Morgan, June 20, 1781, McIlwaine, *Official Letters,* 3:5.

11. Much of the outgoing mail is missing for the first month and a half of Nelson's term. See McIlwaine *Official Letters,* 3:vi–vii. But it is clear that Nelson took forceful action. For example see his order to impress horses June 20, 1781, United States Revolution Collection; Nelson to General George Weedon, July 2, 1781, MS, American Philosophical Society; Nelson to Lafayette, June 28, 1781, Nelson to Daniel Morgan, June 20, 1781, McIlwaine, *Official Letters,* 3:6–7, 5; Gottschalk, *Lafayette,* p. 250.

12. Gottschalk, *Lafayette,* pp. 256–59; Nelson to George Washington, July 27, 1781, McIlwaine, *Official Letters,* 3:13–14.

13. William Davies to Major Forsythe, June 26, 1781, War Office Letter Book, January 1781–September 1781; Nelson to General George Weedon, July 2, 1781, MS, American Philosophical Society; Thomas Anburey, *Travels Through the Interior Parts of America,* 2 vols. (London, 1789), 2:317.

14. Nelson to General George Weedon, July 2, 1781, MS, American Philosophical Society; Nelson to General Cornwallis, July 3, 1781, Nelson to Auditors of the State, July 19, 1781, McIlwaine, *Official Letters,* 3:7, 9; McIlwaine, *Journals of Council of State,* 2:353, 356; Samuel Giddens to Nelson, July 16, 1781, Executive Papers.

15. William Davies to Steuben, July 12, 1781, Boyd, *Jefferson Papers* 6:78n; Robert Honyman Diary, July 22, 1781, Library of Congress; William Davies to [County Lieutenants?], July 15, 17, 1781, War Office Letter Book, January 1781–September 1781. Davies did not approve of many of Nelson's actions and a veiled dislike runs through much of his correspondence. See for example Davies to Nelson, August 14, 1781, Davies to Lafayette, August 15, 1781, Davies to Captain James Anderson, August 24, 1781, ibid.

16. Hening, *Statutes,* 10:399–400, 429–31. The amount of money expended during Nelson's administration has been computed from McIlwaine, *Journals of Council of State,* 2:356–404.

17. Hening, *Statutes,* 10:426–29; Garrett Van Meter to Nelson, July 28, 1781, Adam Stephen to Nelson, August 3, 1781, C. Jones to Nelson, August 16, 1781, Executive Papers; Nelson to Richard Claiborne, July 28, 1781, Nelson to Lafayette, August 15, 1781, McIlwaine, *Official Letters,* 3:15, 23–24; William Davies to Nelson, August 14, 1781, *Calendar of Virginia State Papers,* 2:328–30.

18. Honyman Diary, August 3, 1781; Nelson to William Davies, July 31, 1781, Executive Papers. The Executive Papers, particularly the group for July 18 to July 31, 1781, contain many vouchers for the impressment of horses, corn, and other supplies from the people of the Virginia countryside.

19. William Davies to Nelson, July 25, 28, 1781, Executive Papers; William Davies to Anthony Wayne, Au-

gust 1, 1781, War Office Letter Book, January 1781–September 1781; Nelson to Lafayette, August 3, 1781, McIlwaine, *Official Letters*, 3:20–21; Gottschalk, *Lafayette*, pp. 281–82.

20. Gottschalk, *Lafayette*, pp. 281–82.

21. Anthony Wayne to Nelson, August 19, 1781, Executive Papers; William Davies to Major Richard Call, August 21, 1781, War Office Letter Book, January 1781–September 1781.

22. Nelson to County Lieutenants, July 31, 1781, McIlwaine, *Official Letters*, 3:17; George Skillern to Nelson, July 10, 1781, Turner Southall to Nelson, July 24, 1781, Lewis Burwell to Nelson, July 30, 1781, Executive Papers; Hening, *Statutes*, 10:416–21, 425.

23. Robert Lawson to Nelson, July 26, 1781, Thomas Clayton to Nelson, July 26, 1781, William McCraw to Nelson, August 7, 1781, E. Simpson to Nelson, August 8, 1781, Executive Papers.

24. John Watson to Nelson, July 23, 1781, Nelson to James Innes, July 30, 1781, Executive Papers.

25. William Preston to Nelson, July 26, 28, 1781, Executive Papers.

26. Garrett Van Meter to Jefferson, April 11, 20, 1781, George Moffett to Jefferson, May 5, 1781, Samuel McDowell to Jefferson, May 9, 1781, Boyd, *Jefferson Papers*, 5:409–10, 513–14, 603–4, 621–22; McIlwaine, *Journals of Council of State*, 2:350, 351.

27. Garrett Van Meter to Nelson, July 28, 1781, Peter Hogg to Nelson, August 2, 1781 (appended to this letter is the petition of the disaffected people), Executive Papers; Nelson to Peter Hogg, August 9, 1781, McIlwaine, *Official Letters*, 3:21; Eckenrode, *Revolution in Virginia*, p. 248.

28. Ward, *Revolution*, 2:876–78; Don Higginbotham, *The War of American Independence . . . 1763–1789* (New York, 1971), pp. 377–79;

James Barron to Nelson, July 30, 1781, John Nelson to Nelson, August 3, 1781, John Page to Nelson, August 7, 1781, Executive Papers; Nelson to Virginia Delegates in Congress, August 3, 1781, McIlwaine, *Official Letters*, 3:19.

29. Nelson to County Lieutenants, July 31, 1781, Executive Papers; William Davies to County Lieutenants, August 1, 1781, War Office Letter Book, January 1781–August 1781; McIlwaine, *Journals of Council of State*, 2:369.

30. Washington to Lafayette, July 30, 1781, Fitzpatrick, *Writings of Washington*, 22:431–32; James McHenry (aide-de-camp to Lafayette) to Nelson, August 8, 1781, Executive Papers.

31. Douglas Southall Freeman, *George Washington*, 6 vols. (New York, 1948–54), 5:309–11.

32. Washington to Lafayette, August 15, 1781, Washington to Nelson, August 27, 1781, Fitzpatrick, *Writings of Washington*, 22:501–2, 23:55–56; Nelson to [Washington?] September 2, 1781, Emmett Collection.

33. Lafayette to Nelson, August 6, 1781, *V.M.H.B.* 5(1897–98):382–83; James McHenry to Nelson, August 8, 1781, Executive Papers; David Jameson to Nelson, August 24, 28, 1781, Jameson to Lafayette, August 30, 1781, McIlwaine, *Official Letters*, 3:26, 26–27; Gottschalk, *Lafayette*, pp. 282, 291.

34. David Jameson to Commodore Barron, August 31, 1781, McIlwaine, *Official Letters*, 3:27–28; William Davies to County Lieutenants, August 21, September 1, 1781, Davies to Colonel Bannister, August 24, 1781, Davies to Captain Deportiere, Davies to Captain Prejor, August 31, 1781, Davies to Colonel Charles Lynch, September 1, August 29, 1781, Davies to Lafayette, September 1, 1781, War

Office Letter Book, January 1781–September 1781.

35. Lafayette to Nelson, September 2, 1781, *V.M.H.B.*, 6(1898–99):59; Nelson to Comte de Grasse, September 2, 1781, Nelson to Governor Thomas Lee, September 2, 1781, Executive Papers.

36. There had been trouble with Brown since early August. See John Brown to Nelson, August 11, 1781, William Davies to Nelson, August 14, September 6, 1781, Executive Papers; McIlwaine, *Official Letters,* 3:29n; McIlwaine, *Journals of Council of State,* 2:387.

37. Lafayette to Nelson, September 2, 1781, *V.M.H.B.*, 6 (1898–99):59; Nelson to John Brown, September 2, 1781, Nelson to Governor Thomas Lee, September 2, 1781, Nelson to John Pierce, September 2, 1781, Nelson to Thomas Newton, September 4, 1781, Proclamation of Thomas Nelson, September 5, 1781, Nelson to Governor Thomas Burke, September 13, 1781, Nelson to absent members of Council, September 5, 1781, David Jameson to Nelson, September 15, 1781, Executive Papers; Nelson to William Fleming, September 5, 1781, Signers of the Declaration of Independence Collection, Wisconsin State Historical Society, Madison; McIlwaine, *Journals of Council of State,* 2:379–81, 383. William Davies disagreed with Nelson's calling up so many militia. He did not feel "that there should be a man more in the field than can be useful especially as General Washington says himself he does not require the aid of the militia. I am sure the worst consequences will follow from the number of useless mouths there will be. . . ." Davies to Major Pryor, September 4, 1781, War Office Orders [Letters], August 15–November 1, 1781 (War 55), V.S.L. In a similar vein see also James Hendricks to Davies, Septem-

ber 11, 1781, *Calendar Virginia State Papers,* 2:414. Ultimately 3,100 Virginia militia served at Yorktown which does not seem to have been an excessive number out of a total of almost 20,000 allied soldiers. Freeman, *Washington,* 5:414. Militia were also used in a variety of other ways; for example see letter of Nelson to County Lieutenants in northern Virginia, September 13, 1781, ordering the militia to make the roads passable for Washington's army. McIlwaine, *Official Letters,* 3:47.

38. David Jameson to Nelson, September 15, 1781, Executive Papers.

39. Nelson to David Jameson, September 21, 1781, McIlwaine, *Official Letters,* 3:65.

40. Nelson to [?], September 11, 1781, Accession 20364, V.S.L.

41. Nelson to John Pierce, September 13, 14, 1781, Nelson to Captain Callendar, September 12, 1781, Nelson to David Ross, September 12, 1781, Nelson to James Hendricks, September 14, 1781, [George Nicholas?] to Captain Roberts, September 14, 1781, [Nelson?] to Croppert Avery, September 18, 1781, [Nelson?] to William Ronald, September 19, 1781, Executive Papers; Nelson to St. George Tucker, September 16, 1781, Tucker-Coleman Papers, College of William and Mary; David Jameson to Colonel John Banister, September 13, 1781, McIlwaine, *Official Letters,* 3:44. For the volume of Nelson's correspondence concerning supply see ibid., 3:41–84. There is also a mass of material to document the actions of Nelson in the Executive Papers. The manuscripts cited have been selected because they point out most clearly the means he used.

42. Nelson to Major Hubbard, September 20, 1781, Hubbard-Bolling Family Papers, U.V.

43. Nelson to David Jameson, September 14, 1781, McIlwaine, *Official*

Letters, 3:51; St. George Tucker to Frances Tucker, September 15, 1781, Tucker-Coleman Papers; Freeman, *Washington,* 5:330–32.

44. Nelson to David Jameson, September 14, 1781, John Pierce to Nelson, September 27, 1781, Executive Papers; Honyman Diary, September 15, 1781.

45. David Jameson to Nelson, September 15, 18, 1781, John Pierce to Nelson, September 18, 27, 1781, John Hendricks to Nelson, September 29, 1781, Executive Papers; St. George Tucker to Frances Tucker, September 23, 1781, Tucker-Coleman Papers; William Davies to Nelson, September 28, 1781, War Office Orders [Letters], August 15–November 1, 1781; David Jameson to Nelson, September 18, 26, 1781, Nelson to Jameson, October 1, 1781, McIlwaine, *Official Letters,* 3:57–58, 67–68, 74–75.

46. Nelson to Richard Morris, October 6, 1781, McIlwaine, *Official Letters,* 3:80; De Tarle to Nelson, October 23, 1781, Executive Papers. De Tarle, who was handling supply for the French army, requested in this letter that the regulations against buying on the open market be rescinded— testimony to the effectiveness of Nelson's arrangement.

47. Nelson to George Washington, September 16, 1781, Emmett Collection, New York Public Library; Robert Andrews to General Weedon, September 26, 1781, McIlwaine, *Official Letters* 3:68. That an army of around 20,000 was adequately fed and partially supplied from the resources of Virginia and the neighboring states is proof of Nelson's able administration. But there are numerous incidents to demonstrate his promptness and good sense. For example, in September a question arose with respect to when the rate of exchange should be set on certificates the public was being issued in return for provisions. On Sep-

tember 23, William Davies wrote Nelson suggesting that the state's citizens would more readily provide food if they were allowed the exchange rate that was current at the time the certificate was presented to the auditors for settlement, rather than at the time when it was issued. In an inflationary situation this was to the public's advantage. Nelson received this letter on the twenty-sixth and the following day he approved of the procedure as one "which not only Justice recommends, but Policy & even necessity." (Davies to Nelson, September 23, 1781, War Office Orders [Letters], August 15–November 1, 1781; Nelson to David Jameson, September 27, 1781, McIlwaine, *Official Letters,* 3:70–71).

48. Thomas Newton to Nelson, September 18, 1781, Executive Papers.

49. Nelson to James Innes, September 18, 1781, McIlwaine, *Official Letters,* 3:55–56.

50. George Corbin to Nelson, September 30, 1781, Executive Papers; Nelson to George Webb, October 17, 1781, McIlwaine, *Official Letters,* 3:86; Eckenrode, *Revolution in Virginia,* pp. 259–60.

51. Nelson to William Davies, September 19, 1781, Nelson to James Barbour, September 19, 1781, McIlwaine, *Official Letters,* 3:59, 60–61; William Davies to Nelson, September 15, 1781, War Office Orders [Letters], August 15–November 1, 1781.

52. William Davies to Nelson, September 15, October 10, 1781, War Office Orders [Letters], August 15–November 1, 1781. Nelson to William Davies, September 19, 1781; McIlwaine, *Official Letters,* 3:59; James Clay to Nelson, September 13, 1781, Executive Papers.

53. Nelson to David Jameson, September 21, 1781, Nelson to de Tarle, October 4, 1781, McIlwaine, *Official*

Letters, 3:65, 77; Nelson to David Jameson, September 26, 1781, Thomas Lee to Nelson, September 25, 1781, James Hendricks to Nelson, October 11, 1781, Executive Papers; Freeman, *Washington,* 5:338–39.

54. Freeman, *Washington,* 5:345; Ward, *Revolution,* 2:886–87; Gottschalk, *Lafayette,* pp. 315–16.

55. Nelson to David Jameson, October 1, 1781, Nelson to Virginia Delegates in Congress, October 5, 1781, McIlwaine, *Official Letters,* 3:74–75, 78–79.

56. John Pryor to William Davies, October 2, 1781, *Calendar of Virginia State Papers,* 2:518.

57. Nelson to William Davies, October 8, 1781, MS, New York Public Library; Page, "A Colonial and Revolutionary Family"; Marquis de Lafayette, "Genl. Nelson of Virginia," MS, Sparks Transcripts, 32:147–48, Houghton Library, Harvard University. Nelson's house was hit several times, but the extent of damage is not known. His property was among those subsequently listed by the state as having been damaged. Baron Von Closen reported that "most of the houses [in Yorktown were] riddled by cannon fire, and [there were] almost no window-pains in the houses." See *Calendar of Virginia State Papers,* 3:132; Evelyn Acomb, ed., *The Revolutionary Diary of Baron Ludwig Von Closen, 1780–1783* (Chapel Hill, 1958), p. 155.

58. Marquis de Chastellux, *Travels in North America in the Years 1780, 1781 and 1782,* ed. Howard C. Rice, Jr., 2 vols. (Chapel Hill, 1963), 2:385.

59. "Diary of Captain John Davis," *V.M.H.B.* 1(1893–94):11; St. George Tucker, "Journal of the Siege of Yorktown," Edward M. Riley, *W.M.Q.,* 3rd ser. 6(1948):386–87; Richard Butler, "Journal of the Siege of Yorktown," *Historical Magazine,* 2nd ser., 8

(1869):108–9; Chastellux, *Travels,* 2:385.

60. Nelson to George Webb, October 17, 1781, Nelson to Virginia Delegates in Congress, October 20, 1781, McIlwaine, *Official Letters,* 3:86–87, 88–89; Freeman, *Washington,* 5:376–77; Ward, *Revolution,* 2:894.

61. Nelson to Robert Lawson, October 20, 1781, David Jameson to Benjamin Harrison, November 26, 1781, McIlwaine, *Official Letters,* 3:88, 98–100; George Weedon to Nelson, October 21, 1781, Colonel Blaine to Nelson, October 25, 1781, John Jones to Nelson, October 30, 1781, John Pierce to Nelson, November 1, 1781, Thomas Newton to Nelson, November 2, 10, 1781, William Reynolds to Nelson, November 16, 1781, Executive Papers; George Washington to Nelson, October 27, 1781, Fitzpatrick, *Writings of Washington,* 23:271–72.

62. Chastellux, *Travels,* 2:382; Vicomte de Rochambeau, "Journal", in Jean-Edmund Weelen, *Rochambeau, Father and Son* (New York, 1936), pp. 249–50; George Webb to David Jameson, November 2, 1781, Nelson to David Ross, November 3, 1781, McIlwaine, *Official Letters,* 3:92–93; John Nelson to Thomas Nelson, November 3, 1781, Executive Papers.

63. Nelson to Speaker of the House, November 20, 1781, John Sanderson, *Biography of the Signers of the Declaration of Independence,* 9 vols. (Philadelphia, 1823–27), 7:298; John Breckenridge to William Preston, November 26, 1781, Preston Papers, Draper Collection, Wisconsin State Historical Society, Madison.

64. Nominations for Governor, November 29, 1781, Executive Papers; *Journal of Delegates,* 1781–85, October 1781 session, pp. 17, 21, 22.

65. Edmund Pendleton to James

Madison, December 3, 1781, Mays, *Papers of Pendleton,* 2:381–82.

66. *Journal of Delegates,* 1781–85, October 1781 session, p. 34; Honyman Diary, December 23, 1781. The petition was written by George Mason. See a full discussion in Robert A. Rutland, ed., *The Papers of George Mason, 1725–1792,* 3 vols. (Chapel Hill, 1970), 2:701–11.

67. Honyman Diary, December 5, 1781; Nelson to John Tyler, December 22, 1781, Brock Collection, Huntington Library, San Marino, Calif.; *Journal of Delegates,* 1781–85, October 1781 session, p. 53.

68. Nelson to Senate, January 12, 1782, in *Virginia Gazette or American Advertizer,* June 15, 1782.

69. *Journal of Delegates,* 1781–85, October 1781 session, pp. 58, 62, 63, 65; Hening, *Statutes,* 10:478. Prior to the passage of the bill exonerating Nelson, Edmund Pendleton commented that there would probably be an approval of Nelson's conduct "from a conviction that what he did wrong was imputable to a mistake in his judgment and not to a corrupt heart." Pendleton to James Madison, December 31, 1781; Mays, *Papers of Pendleton* 2:383.

70. Nelson to Senate, January 12, 1782 in *Virginia Gazette or American Advertizer,* June 15, 1782.

Chapter VIII

1. Marquis de Chastellux, *Travels in North America in the Years 1780, 1781 and 1782,* ed. Howard C. Rice, Jr., 2 vols. (Chapel Hill, 1963), 2:382–83; Evelyn Acomb, ed., *The Revolutionary Diary of Baron Ludwig Von Closen, 1780–1783* (Chapel Hill, 1958), p. 180; Hanover County Land Book, 1782, V.S.L. All county land and personal property books hereafter cited are in V.S.L.

2. Robert Honyman Diary, February 22, 1782, Library of Congress; Chastellux, *Travels,* 2:383.

3. Chastellux, *Travels,* 2:383–84.

4. Acomb, *Von Closen Diary,* p. 180. Von Closen reported that before the war Nelson had seven hundred slaves, but that in 1782 he had only eighty or one hundred. As will be shown subsequently Nelson had many more than this. It should also be stated that although Lucy Nelson looked "no longer young" to Von Closen she outlived her husband by forty-one years, dying in 1830 at the age of eighty-seven. See Page, "Lucy Grymes Nelson," Smith-Digges Papers, C.W. At the time of Von Closen's visit, Lucy Nelson was five months pregnant—a fact he chose not to mention.

5. Earl G. Swem and John W. Williams, *A Register of the General Assembly of Virginia, 1776–1918 and the Constitutional Conventions* (Richmond, 1918), pp. 15–16; Edmund Randolph to James Madison, May 5, 1782, William T. Hutchinson and William M. E. Rachal, *The Papers of James Madison,* 5 vols. to date (Chicago, 1962–), 4:208; Minute Book, House of Delegates, May 1782, p. 76, V.S.L.

6. Chastellux, *Travels,* 2:382; Nelson family Bible; Julian Boyd, ed., *The Papers of Thomas Jefferson* (Princeton, 1950–), 6:478n.

7. Chancery Suit of Thomas Nelson against Carter Braxton, York County Loose Papers, V.S.L.; York County, Deeds, no. 6 (1777–91), pp. 147–48.

8. [?] to Thomas Nelson, March 22, 1783, MS, Massachusetts Historical Society, Boston. Nelson was the recipient of a half-bale of table cloths in the spring of 1782 which were certainly for the store. It is probable that Nelson did not order these in violation of the nonimportation provisions, but that they were sent at the risk of the British merchant. See

William Reynolds to David Eyman, February 1, 1782, Reynolds Letter Book, 1772–83, Library of Congress.

9. William Reynolds to James Jarvis, February 26, 1783, Reynolds to Samuel Browne, April 15, 1783, July 1, 1783, Reynolds Letter Book; *Richmond Virginia Gazette or the American Advertizer,* August 10, 1782; "Nelson's Heirs," *Journal of the House of Delegates of the Commonwealth of Virginia* . . . , session of December 1831, (Richmond, 1831), document 9, item 2.

10. Hanover County, Land Book, 1782; Hanover County, Personal Property Book, 1782; Prince William County, Land Tax Book, 1782–1805; Prince William County, Personal Property Book, 1782; York County, Land Book, 1782; York County Personal Property, Book, 1788; Will of Thomas Nelson, December 26, 1788, York County Wills and Inventories, no. 23(1783–1811), pp. 171–75; Jackson T. Main, "The One Hundred," *W.M.Q.,* 3rd ser. 11(1954):364, 379. Main's figures for Nelson's landed property are somewhat lower than mine because he did not use Nelson's will.

11. William Hay to James Baird, December 12, 1783, Claim of John Hay and Co. P.R.O., T. 79/27; Peter Lyons to Samuel Gist, December 1, 1783, August 1, 4, 1784, Virginia Claims, G (II) Samuel Gist, P.R.O., A.O. 13/30; Ralph Wormeley, Jr. to Welch and Son, February 23, 1784, September 20, 1785, Robert and Ralph Wormeley Letter Book; Robert Beverley to William Beverley, June 1783, Beverley Letter Book; *Journal of Delegates,* 1781–85, May 1783 session, pp. 46, 55, October 1783 session, pp. 41, 43; *Virginia Gazette or the American Advertizer,* December 21, 1782, May 24, 1783, July 5, 1783, September 27, 1783, November 1, 1783; Statement of Spencer Roane,

William Wirt Henry, *Patrick Henry, Life, Correspondence, and Speeches,* 3 vols. (New York, 1891), 2:244–45; William Lee to Richard Henry Lee, [November 1783?], Lee Papers; [?] to Richard Corbin, Jr., September 5, 1786, Extract of Letters lately received from Virginia, P.R.O., A.O. 13/34. See also Jackson Turner Main, "Sections and Politics in Virginia, 1781–1787," *W.M.Q.,* 3rd ser. 12 (1955):96–112.

12. York County, Orders and Judgments, 1774–84, p. 305; H.R. McIlwaine et al., eds., *Journals of Council of the State of Virginia, 1776–1781,* 4 vols. to date (Richmond, 1931–), 3:145; *Journal of Delegates,* 1781–85, November 1782 session, p. 10.

13. *Journal of Delegates,* 1781–85, May 1783 session, pp. 8, 11, 12, 13, 14, 18, 47, 53, 59, 66, 82, 92, 97, October 1783 session, pp. 23–24; James Madison to James Monroe, June 4, 1786, *Letters and Other Writings of James Madison,* Congressional Edition, 4 vols. (New York, 1884), 1:238–39; Main, "Sections and Politics," pp. 104–6. Nelson was also beginning to again perform a variety of other public duties. He was a trustee of the towns of Williamsburg and Yorktown, on the Board of Visitors of the College of William and Mary and a director of the insane asylum in Williamsburg. McIlwaine, *Journals of Council of State,* 3:273; W. W. Hening, ed., *The Statutes at Large Being a Collection of All the Laws of Virginia, 1619–1792,* 13 vols. (Richmond, etc., 1809–23), 11:405–6, 473; William P. Palmer, ed., *Calendar of Virginia State Papers,* 11 vols. (Richmond, 1875–93), 3:558; Dudley Digges to St. George Tucker, January 15, 1783, Tucker-Coleman Papers; *The History of William and Mary College From Its Foundation, 1693, to 1870,* (Baltimore, 1870), p. 66.

14. William Lee to Thomas Nelson, October 1783, May 4, 1784, William Lee Letter Book, V.H.S. Unfortunately the wine proved to be bad.

15. William Lee to Thomas Nelson, January 1784, MS, C.W.; Humphrey Harwood, Ledger B, p. 51, ibid.; "General Nelson's Heirs," item 20; Bill of Thomas Nelson to Edmund Berkeley, December 15, 1785, Berkeley Papers, U.V. The latter bill suggests that the store in Yorktown was doing the same type of business that it had done before the war. Items that Berkeley was billed for included flannel, linen, kersey, sugar, and Hyson tea.

16. *Journal of Delegates,* 1781–85, October session, pp. 13, 18. John M. Galt, Apothecary-Surgeon, Account Book, 1783–85, C.W.

17. William Lee to Thomas Nelson, March 1784, William Lee Letter Book.

18. Robert Beverley to Beilby Porteus, November 25, 1784, *V.M.H.B.,* 21(1913):98; Philip Mazzei, *Récherches Historiques et Politiques sur les Etats-Unis de l'amérique Septentrionale,* 4 vols. (Paris, 1788), 2:201–2; Louis Gottschalk, *Lafayette Between the American and French Revolution* (Chicago, 1950), pp. 125–26; William Anderson to Thomas Massie, November 20, 1784, Massie Family Papers, V.H.S. For an example of other visitors see Louis B. Wright and Marion Tinling, eds., *Quebec to Carolina in 1785–1786, Being the Travel Diary and Observations of Robert Hunter, Jr., a Young Merchant of London* (San Marino, 1943), pp. 231–32.

19. Nelson's petition and the subsequent reports of the House of Delegates are not specific, but almost certainly this was the February loan drive, for Jefferson requested that Nelson, along with others, collect this money for state use and the other loan drive of this year was for the purpose of getting money to support the French army in America; and further, the sums which Nelson collected in the June loan drive greatly exceeded what he asked for in connection with this loan drive. "General Nelson's Heirs," items 3 and 4; Petition of Thomas Nelson, June 8, 1784, Legislative Petitions, 1775–1815, York County, 1090A, V.S.L.; *Journal of Delegates,* 1781–85, June 1784 session, p. 44.

20. *Journal of Delegates,* 1781–85, June 1784 session, p. 46.

21. Ibid., October 1784 session, pp. 86–87, 90–91.

22. Ibid., October 1784 session, pp. 96, 98, 100, 104, 109–10; Hening, *Statutes,* 11:434.

23. Hening, *Statutes,* 11:434.

24. "General Nelson's Heirs," items 3 and 4.

25. *Journal of Delegates,* 1781–85, October 1785 session, p. 123.

26. *Virginia Independent Chronicle,* January 28, 1789; [Dr. James Montgomery?], *Decius's Letters on the Opposition to the New Constitution in Virginia* (Richmond, Augustine Davis, 1789).

27. *Decius's Letters,* letter no. 3.

28. Ibid.

29. Ibid.; *Journal of Delegates,* 1781–85, October 1784 session, p. 91; Hening, *Statutes,* 11:133, 436; McIlwaine, *Journals of Council of State,* 2:278; H. R. McIlwaine, ed., *Official Letters, of the Governors of the State of Virginia,* 3 vols. (Richmond, 1926–27), 3:234n.

30. Patrick Henry to William Grayson, March 31, 1789, *V.M.H.B.,* 14 (1907–8), pp. 202–4; Patrick Henry to Mrs. Annie Christian, October 20, 1786, Henry, *Henry,* 3:380. For a full discussion of the authorship of *Decius's Letters* and the validity of the charges see Boyd, *Jefferson Papers,* 16:139–45. Boyd thinks the

author of the letters was John Nicholas, Jr. (1758–1835).

31. Report of Thomas Nelson on claim of Samuel Waterman, December 1, 1803, P.R.O., T. 79/73.

32. Ibid., P.R.O., T 79/73; J. Hay Colligan, "Note on Sale of Nelson House," *Transactions of the Cumberland & Westmoreland Antiquarian & Archaeological Society,* new ser. 9(1910):331–32; John Taylor to Nathaniel Burwell, August 25, 1789, MS, Duke University.

33. Thomas Nelson to General Horatio Gates, February 19, 1786, Emmett Collection, New York Public Library.

34. *Virginia Gazette or the American Advertizer,* August 16, 1786; Chancery Suit of Thomas Nelson against Carter Braxton, York County Loose Papers; York County, Deeds, no. 6(1777–91), pp. 147–48.

35. "General Nelson's Heirs," item 20; Thomas Nelson to Edmund Berkeley, May 15, 1787, Berkeley Papers.

36. Thomas Nelson to [Nathaniel Burwell?], July 30, 1785, Signers of the Declaration of Independence Collection, Wisconsin State Historical Society, Madison; almost certainly this letter was to Burwell. See "General Nelson's Heirs," item 13; Petition of Philip Nelson, December 7, 1839, *Journal of Delegates,* 1839–40, pp. 24, 31, 58, 61; *Virginia Gazette or the American Advertizer,* September 13, 1783.

37. Thomas Nelson to [Nathaniel Burwell?] July 30, 1785, Signers of Declaration of Independence Collection; Robert Wormeley, Jr., to [?], March 23, 1784, Wormeley Letter Book, U.V. Evidently Nelson still hoped the state was going to repay him for the February 1780 loan drive and he planned to use the money to make up part of the Burwell loss resulting from his having put their funds into the state treasury. He told Burwell that he would make the payment

"when the Country shall determine what is to be done with loans made to the public. . . ." See also Report of Thomas Nelson on Claim of Wakelin Welch, December 1, 1803, P.R.O., T. 79/73. It was reported in 1803 that Nathaniel Burwell had died leaving virtually nothing.

38. Henry Tucker to St. George Tucker, June 15, 1786, Tucker-Coleman Papers, College of William and Mary; Will of Nathaniel Nelson, March 18, 1786, York County, Wills and Inventories, no. 23(1783–1811), pp. 129–31.

39. James Madison to Thomas Jefferson, May 12, 1786, Boyd, *Jefferson Papers,* 9:517–22; Madison to James Monroe, June 4, 1786, Madison to R. H. Lee, July 7, 1785, *Letters and Writings of Madison,* 1:238–39, 158–59; Petition of Inhabitants of Norfolk, Vote on Petition of Brunswick County, *Virginia Gazette or the American Advertizer,* October 15, 1785, November 22, 1786; *Virginia Independent Chronicle,* October 18, 1786; *Journal of Delegates,* 1781–85, October 1785 session, pp. 45–46, 1786–90, October 1786 session, pp. 10, 11, 15.

40. *Journal of Delegates,* 1786–90, October 1786 session, p. 9; Hening, *Statutes,* 12:243–52, 283–87, 289–90, 290–91; James Madison to Thomas Jefferson, January 22, 1786, December 4, 1786, Boyd, *Jefferson Papers,* 9:194–204, 10:574–77.

41. James Madison to Jefferson, December 4, 1786, March 19, 1787, April 23, 1787, Edward Carrington to Jefferson, April 24, 1787, William Fleming to Jefferson, May 2, 1787, Boyd, *Jefferson Papers,* 10:574–77, 11:219–23, 307–10, 310–12, 330–31; *Journal of Delegates,* 1786–90, October 1786 session, p. 21; McIlwaine, *Journals of Council of State,* 4:42, 55, 62.

42. Thomas Nelson to Thomas Nelson, Jr., August 12, 1787, MS, V.H.S.

43. George Washington to General Nelson, September 24, 1787, Washington Papers, Library of Congress. The same letter was also sent to Patrick Henry and Benjamin Harrison.

44. James Madison to Jefferson, October 24, 1787, Boyd, *Jefferson Papers,* 12:270–84.

45. Madison to Jefferson, December 9, 1787, Jefferson to William Carmichael, December 15, 1787, Boyd, *Jefferson Papers,* 12:408–12, 423–25.

46. David J. Mays, *Edmund Pendleton 1721–1803, A Biography,* 2 vols. (Cambridge, Mass., 1952), 2:221, 391.

47. George Washington to Thomas Nelson, August 3, 1788, John C. Fitzpatrick, ed., *Writings of George Washington,* 39 vols. (Washington, 1931–44), 30:33–34.

48. Thomas Nelson to Benjamin Waller, June 13, 1788, MS, Massachusetts Historical Society; Page, "A Colonial and Revolutionary Family"; Prince William County, Personal Property Book, 1787, 1788; York County, Wills and Inventories, no. 23 (1783–1811), pp. 661–63. It was reported in July 1789 that Nelson's creditors "had just presented their claims, which, it seems amount to the enormous sum of £35,000." See David Stuart to George Washington, July 14, 1789, Jared Sparks, ed., *Correspondence of the American Revolution Being the Letters of Eminent Men to George Washington,* 4 vols. (Boston, 1853), 4:267. The court records show a debt of £13,323.1.1½. But if you add to this sum the £6,000 he paid Virginia creditors, as a result of court action prior to his death, and the unknown amount of British debts and the loans he guaranteed as a result of the February 1780 loan drive, a total indebtedness during the 1780s of £35,000 does not appear unreasonable.

49. Nelson's debts were eventually

paid in March 1791, but not exactly by the means he intended. A large part of the slaves were sold, plus lands in York, Hanover, and Frederick counties. Will of Thomas Nelson, December 26, 1788, Money Charged Against Estate, 1789–91, York County, Wills and Inventories, no. 23 (1783–1811), pp. 171–75, 661–63.

50. *Virginia Gazette or the Weekly Advertizer,* January 15, 1789.

51. Augustine Smith to Reverend William Bennett, October 17, 1790, Augustine Smith Letter Book, C.W.

52. *Virginia Independent Chronicle,* January 14, 1789; *Virginia Gazette or the Weekly Advertiser,* January 15, 1789.

Epilogue

1. *Dictionary of American Biography,* s. v. "Nelson, Thomas" (by Maude H. Woodfin); Virginus Dabney, *Virginia: The New Dominion,* (New York, 1971), p. 151. See also John Sanderson, *Biography of the Signers of the Declaration of Independence,* 9 vols. (Philadelphia, 1823–27), 7:289–91; B. J. Lossing, *Pictorial Field Book of the Revolution,* 2 vols. (New York, 1851), 2:315; William Meade, *Old Churches and Families of Virginia,* 2 vols. (Philadelphia, 1857), 1:211; R. A. Brock, *Virginia and Virginians,* 2 vols. (Richmond, 1888), 1:80; Matthew Page Andrews, *Virginia, The Old Dominion* (Garden City, 1937), p. 348; Dorothy Horton McGee, *Famous Signers of the Declaration* (New York, 1956), pp. 228–29.

2. William Allason to Henry Ritchie, December 22, 1784, Allason Letter Book, V.S.L.

3. Thomas Jefferson to Elizabeth Page, December 8, 1821, Paul L. Ford, ed., *The Works of Thomas Jefferson,* 12 vols. (New York, 1905), 12:211–12.

4. James Madison to Francis Page,

November 7, 1833, *Letters and Other Writings of James Madison,* Congressional Edition, 4 vols. (New York, 1884), 4:323–24.

5. Samuel Smith to Francis Page, September 18, 1837, MS, Massachusetts Historical Society.

6. Anthony F. Upton, "The Road to Power in Virginia in the Early Nineteenth Century," *V.M.H.B.* 62 (1954):271–72.

7. Hugh Nelson to St. George Tucker, December 28, 1820, Tucker-Coleman Papers, College of William and Mary. Tucker had completed a short biography of Thomas Nelson in 1817 which he had sent to Joseph Delaplaine, editor of *The Repository,* a journal published in Philadelphia. Delaplaine had not published the manuscript and Tucker allowed John Sanderson to use it in preparing the biography of Nelson he planned to include in his *Signers of the Declaration of Independence.* The original manuscript has not been found so it is not known how much of Tucker's biography Sanderson used. See Tucker to Nelson, January 5, 1821, Nelson to Tucker, January 20, March 10, 1821, ibid.

8. See Appendix.

9. For a further development of this theme see Emory G. Evans, "The Rise and Decline of the Virginia Aristocracy in the Eighteenth Century: The Nelsons," in Darrett Rutman, ed., *The Old Dominion: Essays For Thomas Perkins Abernethy* (Charlottesville, 1964), pp. 62–78.

10. See ibid., and Jackson T. Main, "The One Hundred," *W.M.Q.,* 3rd ser. 11 (1954):354–84.

Appendix

1. Dr. Augustine Smith to Reverend William Bennett, October 17, 1790, Augustine Smith Letter Book, C.W.

2. *Journal of the House of Delegates of the Commonwealth of Virginia* . . . , session of December 1821 (Richmond, 1821), pp. 60, 68, 170, 202.

3. Ibid., p. 202.

4. "General Nelson's Heirs," *Journal of Delegates,* 1831–32, document 9.

5. *Journal of Delegates,* 1830–31, March 1831 session, p. 267.

6. Ibid., 1831–1832, January 1832 session, p. 120; "General Nelson's Heirs."

7. H. R. McIlwaine et al., eds., *Journals of Council of the State of Virginia, 1776–1781,* 4 vols. to date (Richmond, 1931–),2:144, 165, 181, 191; Treasurer's Cash Book, 1777–79, pp. 115, 143, Treasurer's Receipt Book, 1778–80, pp. 11, 109, Treasurer's Journal, 1774–80, p. 210, all in V.S.L.; Richard Henry Lee to George Washington, June 24, 1778, James C. Ballagh, *Letters of Richard Henry Lee,* 2 vols. (New York, 1911), 1:419–20.

8. "General Nelson's Heirs," item 9.

9. Ibid., item 3.

10. James Madison to Francis Page, November 7, 1833, *Letters and Other Writings of James Madison,* Congressional Edition, 4 vols. (New York, 1884), 4:323–24.

11. *Journal of the House of Representatives of the United States* (Philadelphia and Washington, 1789–), 1st session, 23rd Congress, pp. 41, 200, 1st session, 24th Congress, p. 1188; *Register of Debates in Congress, 1825–1837* (Washington 1825–37), 10:2375–76; *House of Representatives Reports,* 3 vols. (Washington, 1836), 1st session, 24th Congress, vol. 3, Report 847; *Journal of the House of Delegates of Virginia,* session of 1839–40 (Richmond, 1839), pp. 24, 31, 58, 61.

Index

Index

Acts of Trade and Navigation, 4, 30-31
Adams, John, 52, 53, 58
Adams, Samuel, 58
Adams, Thomas, 66
American army, 54, 61-62, 73-75, 75-77, 118. *See also* Virginia: Military
American Revolution: burden of, on states, 84; causes inflation, 78; effects of, 139; effect of, on Virginia, 64; support for, in Virginia, 3-4
Andrews, Reverend Robert, 67, 116, 121
Archer, Thomas, 27
Armistead family, 9
Armistead, Lucy, 9
Arnold, Benedict, 54, 92-94, 96, 97, 99, 177-78
Articles of Confederation, 58, 60, 62
Association of 1769, 32-33
Athawes, Edward, 18
Athawes, Samuel: as Nelson traveling companion, 18; Nelson's advice to, 23; Nelson seeks aid of, 41; Nelson's letter to, 51; Nelson's letter on British oppression to, 40; Nelson's letter on tobacco to, 28
Atkinson, Roger, 61-62

Bank of England, 24
Barbour, Colonel James, 117-18
Barron, Commodore James, 90
Beaufort, duke of, 34
Benjamin Harrison and Company, 126
Berkeley, Edmund, 8, 121
Berkeley family, 8, 9
Beverley, Robert, 17, 18
Blair, John, 11, 12, 66, 135, 136
Bland, Richard, 48, 49
Board of Trade, 10
Boston, 34-35, 37, 41
Boston port bill, 35, 37, 38, 40
Boston Tea Party, 34
Botetourt, Lord, 12, 32
Braxton, Carter, 38, 59-60, 125, 133

British army: advances, 92-94; arrives in Chesapeake Bay, 66; combined force of, in Virginia, 98-99; evacuates posts outside of Yorktown, 119; fortunes of, 62-63; freedom of movement of, 105; in Virginia, 81, 89, 90; reaches Williamsburg, 106
British fleet, 89, 90-91
British mercantile community: and Parliament, 43; Virginia legislation affects debts to, 71-72; Virginia's attitude toward, 39. *See also* Samuel Athawes, William Carr, Robert Cary and Co., Edward Hunt and Son, Thomas and Rowland Hunt, John Norton, James Russell
Bruton Parish Church, 21
Burwell, Elizabeth. *See* Nelson, Mrs. William (Elizabeth Burwell)
Burwell family, 8-9
Burwell, Lucy, 8
Burwell, Nathaniel, 91, 133-34
Burwell, Robert Carter, 133-34, 175
Burwell, Robert, 8-9
Byrd, Mary Willing, 177-78
Byrd I, William, 16
Byrd II, William, 10, 14

Carey, Bernard, 50
Carr, William, 37, 42-43
Carrington, Paul, 38
Carter, Landon, 39
Chastellux, Major General, 124-25
Christ College, Cambridge, 17-18
Clinton, Sir Henry, 90, 111
Closen, Baron Ludwig von, 125
Coercive Acts, 42
College of William and Mary, 21, 61
Committee of Correspondence, 11, 34
Committees of Correspondence, 35
Congress, 148
Constitution of the United States, 131, 136-37
Continental Congress (First), 35, 40, 41-42, 44

195